All Rise

The Remarkable Journey of Alan Page

BILL McGRANE

TRIUMPH
BOOKS

The author is grateful to National Football League Films for making available the use of several comments from its film Black Star Risen: The Alan Page Story, *and to the Page family for use of photos from their collection. The author also acknowledges use of several photos by the* Minneapolis Star-Tribune. *Thanks also to Roberta Rubin, Betsy Lane, and Roger Williams.*

Library of Congress Cataloging-in-Publication Data
McGrane, Bill.
   All rise : the remarkable journey of Alan Page / Bill McGrane.
      p. cm.
   ISBN 978-1-60078-504-7 (alk. paper)
   1. Page, Alan, 1945- 2. Football players—United States—Biography. 3. African American football players—Biography. 4. Judges—Minnesota—Biography. 5. African American judges—Minnesota—Biography. I. Title.
   CT275.P178M34 2010
   977.6′053092—dc22
   [B]
                              2010016020

This book is available in quantity at special discounts for your group or organization. For further information, contact:
Triumph Books
542 South Dearborn Street, Suite 750
Chicago, Illinois 60605
(312) 939-3330 | Fax (312) 663-3557
www.triumphbooks.com

Printed in U.S.A.
ISBN: 978-1-60078-504-7
Design, editorial production, and layout by Prologue Publishing Services, LLC
Photos courtesy of Alan Page

"He is a gentle man, but he's no pushover. Babies love him because of that gentleness."
—Georgi Page, daughter

"Alan is a fire-breathing dragon when it comes to protecting the rights of our children to have an education."
—Mona Harristhal, former administrative director,
Page Education Foundation

Contents

Foreword

Iknew of Alan Page long before I met him. I knew of his athletic excellence at the University of Notre Dame and with the Minnesota Vikings and the Chicago Bears. I loved the exploits of the "Purple People Eaters" as they led that devastating Vikings defense. I saw Alan Page as an All-Pro defensive tackle, as a man of enormous strength and power, someone who thrived on the mayhem that every snap of the ball would bring.

Alan Page did thrive on that mayhem…he told me once that he loved everything about playing the game.

Then I met him. My goodness…he wasn't a "Purple People Eater" at all! He is tall and slender and soft-spoken. Alan Page is more than a gentleman…he is a gentle man. His hair is white now, and cut close; so is his beard. I first met Alan and his wife, Diane, almost 20 years ago at a luncheon in Minneapolis. Diane is a lovely, lively woman. Together, they make a great team. I knew of their love of running, so I had a member of my staff arrange a run with them that afternoon along the Mississippi River. That's a great thing about running…once we started, we were just three relaxed friends…"running buddies."

We have become good friends. I call the Pages whenever I'm in the Twin Cities. I attended a Page Education Foundation reception, and they have attended a number of my appearances on visits there. We even got in another run, around Como Lake in St. Paul. Alan and Diane visited Hillary and me in the White House when I was president, and I was pleased to praise the work of the Page Education Foundation in my book, *Giving*.

I am delighted that Alan Page's story is being told in this book. It's high time. And I am pleased to have been asked to share my thoughts about him and his enduring efforts to help others help themselves.

Alan has many outstanding qualities, but when I think of him, the first word that pops into my head is *education*. Alan was blessed with parents who recognized the importance of education, especially for African American children. Howard and Georgiana Page demanded the best of their children and made their own sacrifices to give them the best education they could. This focus on education—a love of learning, really—energized Alan to earn his law degree while playing for the Vikings. And it gave birth to the Page Education Foundation, which has, over the past two decades, led more than 4,000 Minnesota children of color to strive for the same dreams that inspired Alan Page.

Alan's law career, private and public, was a stepping-stone toward a career where he *knew* he belonged: as a jurist on the high court of the State of Minnesota. His decision to follow that dream was not without its challenges. Some dismissed his bid as merely a former athlete trading on his name. He proved them wrong. Some questioned his right to challenge state authority. He did that, too. And the people of Minnesota admired him for his dedication and courage. They elected Alan Page to the appellate court by the greatest margin of victory in any Minnesota election. Alan became the first African American ever to hold a major office in Minnesota.

Now in his 18th year on the Minnesota Supreme Court bench, Alan is its deeply respected senior member. He has been a vigilant defender of the rights and opportunities not only of minorities, but of all Minnesotans. He searches for the right decision on an issue, and once that decision is in hand, Justice Page stands his ground. Not all of his opinions have been well-received, but they have been the very best he had to offer.

The Page Education Foundation is just as dedicated and hard-nosed as its founder's approach to football and the court. Students don't "take the money and run." As Page Scholars, they are required to return to their communities and mentor younger children on the importance of continuing their educations. Alan Page doesn't just want to help people; he wants to empower them to help themselves.

An amazing athlete, a man of great compassion, a man with a lively sense of humor, a passionate seeker of truth, in the law and in life. Alan has found his own dignity and challenges others to do the same, for as

Diane and Alan running with President Clinton.

long as they live. At 64, Alan runs about five miles every morning. Every morning. And don't forget, he lives in Minnesota. A marathoner...not many football players can match that.

A husband, still head over heels in love with the lady he married 37 years ago. A father who doesn't cut his four kids a lot of slack, but who says he is "button-busting proud" of all of them. When they call with an issue, he is famous for saying, "Well, what do you think?" A grandpa to Otis and Theo, he delights in that role.

Along with Alan's story, this book tells us about many "All-Risers" who have reached out and helped others. They're here in these pages, telling their stories, because Alan Page didn't want some typical tribute book written just about him. Of course, there's not much about Alan Page that is typical.

In his modest, quiet way, this very rare man has led a memorable life, helping thousands of people, most of whom he doesn't even know.

When the judge enters his courtroom, the call "All Rise!" is one of respect. On behalf of all of us who know Alan Page, who know who he is, who know what he has done and what he stands for, I echo that call. "All Rise!"

—President Bill Clinton

Quarterbacks hate pass-rushers.
*They don't like cat-quick defensive ends, but they can
  deal with them...*
*buy that crucial extra second or two if there are no
  other problems.*
But what they really don't like
—freaks them out, actually—
*is pressure up the middle from a runaway defensive
  tackle.*
*Against the Vikings, a quarterback had two choices,
  both poor:*
*He could step back, and into the grasp of ends Eller
  or Marshall,*
or he could step up,
*into the loud, wild, shockingly quick and totally
  scary charge of Alan Page.*
No wonder quarterbacks are so well paid.

Introduction

What I had in mind when I approached Alan Page about doing a book was an informal telling of his intense story.

Alan is quiet now, but don't let the smile and the white hair and beard fool you; he's still intense, and much more. When I think of Alan, the word *probity* often pops into my head. So I looked it up, just to be sure I was on the right track. I was. *Probity* has 25 classifications of what can be boiled down to *doing the right thing*. I wanted this story to trace Alan's life. I didn't want to miss the challenges and pain and accomplishments, but I didn't want to get lost in them, either. Happily, as the late Howard Cosell once pointed out to me, "If you work weekends long enough, you're going to meet a lot of interesting people." Well, Alan worked a lot of weekends, and he met a lot of interesting people. It is my pleasure to bring many of those people into Alan's story and to add their rich brush strokes to his portrait.

I called the book *All Rise*, the warning the bailiff shouts out to awaken the dozers when a judge enters a courtroom. I thought "All Rise" would be a nice salute for Page's achievement-filled career. I thought the title suited him: legendary athlete, champion for education, distinguished jurist, trailblazer for Minnesotans (and others) of color who sought the opportunity to reach for the high rungs, just as he had.

Alan frowned when I laid my cards out. "I don't...," he hesitated, frowned, and then shrugged. "I don't want a story that is just about me," he said. Then he went back to frowning. His wife, Diane, chose her words carefully. "We have talked about what a book could be," she said. "What we don't want is just a feel-good story that prompts a reader to say, 'Well, that was nice,' then set the book aside and forget about it."

Progress. We knew what we didn't want. Now, to figure out what we did want. It took a while.

Diane later referred to this period as my epiphany. I thought it felt more like barking my shins in a darkened room before finally finding the light switch. What if the *All Rise* title went beyond the courtesy afforded a judge in his courtroom? What if *All Rise* went beyond Alan's life of benefiting others—actually a life of *leading* others to a place from which they might benefit themselves? Alan was an All-Riser—someone who has given of himself and grown as a result of giving.

What if we recognized the potential in all of us to be All-Risers? We all have it, probably just rusty or mislaid, covered up by a lot of *self*. ("I'd love to help, when I get some free time; life is so busy; I'll send a check…great to hear from you…blah, blah.") What if I didn't just tell Alan Page's story, but told the stories of other All-Risers as well? What if a reader might begin to believe that all of us can be All-Risers? Wouldn't that be something?

In fact, Alan Page doesn't know most of the people I identify as All-Risers at the beginning of each chapter of the book. This is fine—they haven't been involved in their various endeavors because of him. All-Risers help others, thereby helping themselves, which is probably about as fine as you can cut it. They don't do their thing for Justice Page, nor—and this is just my theory—do they really do it for those they help (though the help they provide is a very worthwhile by-product). They are All-Risers for themselves. Not in some sense of self-aggrandizement—far from it, in fact—but for their own growth. Because they know we either grow, or we wither. We don't stand still. Ask an All-Riser; they will tell you they get a lot more out of helping than the recipient does.

Thinking over my hypothetical question, Alan didn't answer right away, but when he did, he spoke softly. "When you said that, about all of us being All-Risers, I got a chill down my back," he said.

Not a "yes" yet, but a good sign. A month later, Alan called. "I guess we should take a shot at this," he said. A little lame as far as ringing endorsements go, but that's okay—we're taking the shot.

However! We have yet to mention the key that opened the doors—the doors to the law, the court, the fantastic wife and remarkable family, the gracious home in the smart Kenwood neighborhood of Minneapolis...to the good life. Alan Page wasn't always a distinguished jurist or a compelling leader of just causes. No, indeed. Before that, he was a football player, a big, scary, impossibly quick, incredibly gifted, hard, nasty-as-the-situation-called-for football player. One of the best ever.

So before the "All Rise" there was a lot of "All Down"—the down and dirty part of Alan's story. Alan Page says football is all but invisible in his rearview mirror today, and I'm sure it is. But it's there, and there it will remain. It has to—it's part of him, and it spirited him away from the mean futures afforded young black men in Canton, Ohio, in the '60s. A lot of us still see him, No. 88 jersey sagging, hands on his hips, standing a little stooped, one foot atop the other, his breath fogging his face in the old Met Stadium chill.

Football came first. And football remained.

All Rise

Snapshots

Canton Central Catholic High School

"We were playing Akron St. Vincent's. They were our big rivals. They had these two little Italian guys [who] played halfback. They were both tough, and they could run like hell." Bob Belden crossed his feet on the corner of his big old desk. You knew he was enjoying telling this story. "We had them penned up way back in their own end when they ran a sweep away from Alan's side of the line. One of those halfbacks popped into the clear. I can still see him running—he had his head back, his arms were pumping. He was flying.

"But then you were aware that he was being followed—this long, dark shadow, legs just eating up the ground. The St. Vincent kid was still going for all he was worth, but Alan caught him. Alan ran him down after 90 yards, right near our goal line. You ask people from around here who saw that game," Belden said, "and they'll always tell you about the play Alan Page made."

Notre Dame

Was Alan Page the best defensive lineman you ever coached?

"That's hard, singling out one player," Coach Ara Parseghian said. "Apples and oranges. I don't know how to do that. But that defensive line—Page, [Pete] Duranko, [Kevin] Hardy, and [Tom] Rhoads—was the best I ever had."

"I kept Alan out of his real position," Kevin Hardy said. "I was bigger, so they put me at tackle and put Alan out at end. The ends played real wide in our system, which was okay because Alan was so fast. Most offenses are right-handed; most of their plays go to their right. We were

1

on the offense's left side, so they ran away from us a lot of the time. It didn't matter; Alan could run anybody down."

Minnesota Vikings

"Alan Page was the best defensive player I ever saw," Bud Grant said. Grant was the Minnesota coach and, like Page, a Hall of Famer (twice, actually, in Grant's case—the United States and Canada, where he coached the Winnipeg Blue Bombers). "He was a great competitor," Grant said of Page. "As much as he protested so many things about football, when the game was on, he couldn't overcome that great competitive desire to play, and to play his best."

Jim Klobuchar, long the sports bard of Minnesota, smiled at the memory. "I think the officials called him offside on three straight plays," he said. "He was so incredibly quick when the ball was snapped, it was hard to tell. Well, Page was furious over the penalty calls. The Vikings were playing the Lions, and he took his fury out on that poor Detroit offense. I think he tackled the ball-carrier for a loss on two consecutive running plays. Then he sacked Greg Landry, the quarterback, on a pass play. Then he blocked a punt. He was all over the field, uncontainable. When they reviewed the film after that game, I believe it showed that Page wasn't offside."

Chicago Bears

Alan Page's 15th and final pro season was 1981, as a Chicago Bear. It was Steve McMichael's first season with the Bears. They were, at a glance, dissimilar—Page was reserved and McMichael was rowdy—but they shared a love for playing the game, and both were bright and perceptive. Asked to talk about Page, McMichael—the Bear his teammates called "Mongo"—was practically poetic.

"He was this hard, leathery old man. He'd been in every situation there was. He was able to visualize what he did before he did it, and you weren't about to stop him from doing it," he said.

"His last game [was against] Denver, at home. We were out of it, but they were after a playoff spot. It was like God reached down and touched Alan's shoulder that day and said, 'You, my friend, will have a special day." He sure did. I think Alan had three sacks [three and a half], and he just raised hell with that Denver offense. I doubt he weighed 225 pounds, and there he was, playin' by-God defensive tackle in the by-God NF of L! It was like Babe Ruth hittin' three home runs in his last game."

He Reminded Me

It was late, and I wondered when Barack Obama was going to get to Grant Park in Chicago to publicly share his huge joy at having won the 2008 presidential election.

What a remarkable night. Over the previous two years I had heard him ridiculed, scoffed at: "What business does he have running for president...he just got to Washington! Where's his experience? Does he think we're going to turn this country over to some Muslim who could be a terrorist, for all we know? For God's sake, his middle name is Hussein!" I heard people say we needed John McCain's courage and experience and leadership to get us through the tough times. Well, the tough times are here, and you can take that to the bank, provided you know of one you trust.

But on November 4, 2008, something happened that this country has witnessed just a few times in its relatively brief history.

Something magical.

A great wave of energy and excitement sped across the land, east to west. It swept up women and men of every color, creed, political bent, and bank balance; young people and old people, gay and straight, rockers and religious, bartenders and baby-sitters; cabbies and college professors, bosses and shipping clerks. It swept up people who live in Beverly Hills and people who live in Bed-Stuy. It swept up circumspect Iowa farmers and despairing miners who live on back roads and poor credit in the hills of West Virginia. A wealthy, lifetime Republican friend called and said, "I voted for him! I am so proud. I'm proud of him, and I'm proud of me." By the time the wave of energy crashed against the shore of the Pacific Ocean, Americans had, in overwhelming number, chosen to place their future in the hands of a tall, trim, handsome, young (as presidents go) biracial man—his mother was white, his father was black—who was raised in Hawaii and Indonesia.

I must have looked away from the television for a moment because suddenly, there he was, walking across a huge stage with the cheers of hundreds of thousands detonating in the fall night. He did not look joyful; he looked serious. He didn't hold his hands over his head like a winning boxer, didn't prance, didn't jump, didn't shout, and didn't pump his fist. He walked to the lectern waving politely—almost a shy wave, reserved—and smiling, although there was reservation in the smile, too. He looked like a man who understood the gravity of the task before him.

I wish I had called Alan Page on election night, although I have an image of how he would have looked. If he was at home, and I hope he was, he was sitting in a comfortable chair, wearing old sweats and slippers, smiling. Not hollering or grinning widely, just smiling with that soft gleam in his eyes.

I remember a video of Alan walking onto the field at the Metrodome in Minneapolis, where his old team, the Minnesota Vikings, play their games. Page and some former teammates were being honored 40 years after they played. It was a packed stadium. Thousands of people, many of whom had never even seen him play, roared their approval as Alan walked onto the field. I'm sure they cheered as much for who he is as for who he was. He wore his old 88 jersey, high-waisted, tucked into his suit pants. When his name was called, the sound poured over him like a wave. It was hard to recall that the Vikings fired him 30-some years ago. The Vikings may have fired him, but the fans never did. This was Loud Love. Page smiled. His head was bowed a little, as if he was maintaining that little privacy shield that always seems to surround him in public. He waved a shy wave. Watching Obama on election night reminded me of Page in that video.

Why link them? Because Barack Obama has walked a path Alan Page helped clear.

If you look up an old photo of the 1962 Canton Central Catholic High School football team, you will see one black face among the players; if you come across a picture of the 1966 Notre Dame team, you'll see the same thing: one black player.

Page was chided when he ran for the Minnesota Supreme Court: "He's a football player; he's never been a judge. He just wants to get by on his name. He has no experience!"

Alan Page was the first African American elected to major public office in Minnesota. He is the state Supreme Court's senior justice, now in his 18th year on the bench. When he ran for a second term, his margin of victory was the largest in state history—in any contested election. He is running for reelection in Fall 2010.

Paul Anderson, a fellow justice on the court, tried to talk Alan out of seeking election to the state's highest court. Anderson, who followed Page onto the bench, was a judicial aide to Minnesota governor Arne Carlson at the time. Anderson tried to point Page toward a district court where, Anderson said, Alan stood a very good chance of being named. Page said he wasn't interested in the district court. Anderson thought Page was being uppity. Years later, Anderson said, "Alan was right, of course, and I was wrong; he understood that his skills were more toward writing and the scholarly side of the law, toward the appellate court. The rest of us couldn't see that, but he could.

"Alan understands how much of a role model he is for African Americans and all people of color in Minnesota. He definitely is a groundbreaker, a pioneer in public life in our state and, I think, beyond it. He knew he was going to be judged harshly when he came on the court. He knew he would be criticized—he wasn't going to be given any easy shots."

From day one, Justice Page has paid close attention to researching and writing his opinions. "Nothing in a Page opinion is inadvertent," Anderson said. "He knows it's in there."

His siblings said he has been this way since he was a boy. "He was quiet-tough," his brother, Howard Jr., said. Alan has kept his own counsel. He will listen to others, but not be used by them. He accepts victory and defeat with equanimity. I think I saw some of Alan Page when I watched Barack Obama walk across that stage in Grant Park on a thoroughly magical November night.

A lady in the publishing business told me, "You've got to tell Alan Page's backstory, not just the part everyone can see." After two years of listening, looking, and sorting out, I believe he is an expert at recognizing and seizing opportunities as they present themselves. Early on, by his own admission, Alan realized that he "seemed to have some aptitude for playing football." That's really what he said—he keeps the brake down pretty tight when it comes to talking about himself.

Football carried Alan through college, to the pros, and to his future. Pro football would permit him, eventually, to examine interests that didn't require his wearing a helmet. He became a star as a player, a brilliant opportunist who pounced upon his opponent's tiniest mistake. If you played against Alan Page and showed hesitation or doubt, you were finished. Back in the day, he earned a handsome living from football—about $160,000 at his peak—far more than a young black man growing up in Canton, Ohio, in the 1960s had reason to expect. But more important, football let him step up to the next rung on the ladder, where he could reach the foundation of the rest of his life: the law.

I came across an aging letter in a box of Page memorabilia. It bore no date, but was written after Alan finished law school and after the Vikings had decided his football worth no longer met their standards. In part, the letter said: "Belated congratulations on your law school graduation. Bravo! Also, today I noticed your Viking football services seem to be no longer needed…so you, too, have gone from Gladiator to Litigator. *Salud!*" It was signed by Joe Kapp.

Now *there* was a guy—Joe Kapp. *Sports Illustrated*, on a cover, identified him as "The Toughest Chicano." He was a ridiculously hard-nosed quarterback. A *quarterback*, of all things! Quarterbacks were supposed to be stylish; Joe was as stylish as a punch in the nose, one that begs further description. At a Sunday night team gathering after a tough loss, Joe and middle linebacker Lonnie Warwick got into a discussion over which side of the team, offense or defense, was responsible for the loss. When the kitchen became too small to contain their discussion, they moved to the backyard. Joe showed up Monday morning with a black eye, a split lip, and a puffy cheek. Lonnie's nose needed redirection.

Joe Kapp and Alan Page were Vikings teammates from 1967 through 1969. Both, through their off-field efforts, would have significant impact on the lot of future players. Both were fan favorites, both played huge roles in the young Viking club's growth, and both, eventually, were shown the door—Page for getting too skinny and for other annoyances, Kapp for wanting a contract he thought was reasonable but the Vikings didn't.

Joe became a free agent when the Vikings refused to re-sign him. He signed instead with the then-Boston Patriots for a lot more than he had asked of the Vikings. However, after a year the NFL realized Kapp had signed a letter of agreement, not the accepted contract. The league said Kapp couldn't play unless he signed the standard player contract. Kapp didn't sign, didn't play, and in time sued the league over the validity of the contract, claiming it was in restraint of trade. Joe won the suit, but was awarded no damages. Interestingly, some of the complaints in Kapp's suit seem to have since been incorporated into the standard player contract.

After football, Kapp had a modest television and movie career with supporting roles in the movies *Semi-Tough*, *The Longest Yard*, and *Breakheart Pass*, a Charles Bronson suspense film in which Joe played a villainous railroad porter with a bad hat.

Kapp coached, too. It was his Cal-Berkeley team that pulled off "The Play" against archrival Stanford, a madcap, game-ending kickoff return featuring five laterals, with the eventual scorer dashing through the non-conformist Stanford band to reach the end zone, victory, and enduring glory.

Kapp was driving to San Francisco when he talked about Alan Page.

"Hey, I'm a Cal guy, I played and coached at Berkeley," he growled. "I know about intellectuals. Alan was an intellectual when he played, and I'm sure he still is. He was quiet—always on a mission. He had his goals, and I think most of them had nothing to do with football. When we played together I got credit for saying '40 for 60'—it just meant all 40 guys on the team playing as hard as they could for 60 minutes. Now, when I talk about Alan as a player—and he was an amazing player—I remember '40 for 60.' Alan knew he had Jim [Marshall] and Moose [Carl Eller] outside of him and [Gary] Larsen next to him. He knew Jim and Carl would get upfield, and he knew Lars would plug against a run—or Dix [Paul Dickson] would, if Larsen wasn't there. That left

Alan free to do his thing. What I mean is, he had help. We all did. We were a team. Teammates let you be better than you can be without them."

After his football days were over, Alan seized the opportunity to turn his intellectual prowess toward another goal: a career in law. Alan fought his way into the legal profession. The first time he tried law school, more or less on a whim, he failed promptly. By his own admission, he had no business being there. He made it his business the next time. He was ready, he buckled down, and he fought to get it. After graduating from law school, Page had to fight to pass the bar exam, failing on his first try. He took it again and passed the challenging exam on his second try.

Page said he didn't really value education until his second try at law school. That was when he learned how to learn, and then learned to cherish the exhilaration that came with learning. Although his parents had not gone beyond high school, both valued learning. Now Alan did, also. He wanted to give others the opportunity to experience the joy of learning. He wanted to reach young people whose circumstances would discourage them from ever seeking higher education. He just wasn't sure how to do it. However, his opportunity was not long in coming.

Alan Page's Pro Football Hall of Fame enshrinement in 1988 offered a bully pulpit for him to speak out on the need for educating our children. The ceremony, which took place on a sweltering Canton summer day, provided him with a live audience of thousands, as well as a sizeable national television audience. It was not an impromptu speech. Alan and his "gang" of closest friends had crafted the idea for the Page Education Foundation, a launching pad enabling young Minnesotans of color to better their lives through learning. They thought they had a good idea, but they needed public awareness. That Hall of Fame speech provided it.

At the same time, Alan began his private law practice in Minneapolis. He liked being a lawyer in private practice, for a time. And he liked being on the Minnesota Attorney General's staff. But at his core, he knew where he really wanted to be and where he believed he was best suited to be. He knew how he could best help others and serve Minnesota: he wanted to be a judge, and not just any judge. This would be among the greatest opportunities of all.

The sitting governor appoints many of the Minnesota Supreme Court justices. It is possible, however, if a seat is open for election, to file as a candidate and take your case to the electorate. In the 1990s the governor was Rudy Perpich. Attorney Page wanted to be on the judicial ballot. Page did the paperwork for filing in St. Paul. Before he had left that building, however, sitting justice Glenn Kelley announced his resignation; Perpich promptly appointed a replacement, then removed the election from the ballot. Those who know Alan Page know that he is not easily discouraged. In 1992 Arne Carlson, who had replaced Perpich as governor, moved to keep a senior justice, Lawrence Yetka, on the court despite being within 18 months of mandatory retirement age, a move that would again thwart Page. Court term is six years. Page and his counsel, Tom Kayser (a basketball stalwart at Lawrence College), contended that the primary purpose for Yetka's continued presence on the court would be to improve his pension position. They didn't think that was right.

Jim Klobuchar—a writer and a keen student of the Minnesota condition—once said, "Alan will knock politely on your door. He will do it several times. But if you ignore his knock, and if you continue to ignore it, he will kick your door down."

Page sued the governor and the secretary of state for wrongfully blocking his effort to stand for the court. The sitting state supreme court recused itself with respect to hearing the case, and a special court was empanelled. The special court found for Page.

Many a legal eyebrow was raised in Hennepin and Ramsey counties. Football star, to be sure, but wasn't he overstepping? A lot of the fuss probably had to do with rocking the establishment boat. And some of it probably had to do with the color of the boat-rocker's skin, because a black man had never been elected to a major office in Minnesota.

Alan ran against an attorney named Kevin Johnson, whose base message seemed to be to remind voters that Alan Page, while a decent enough guy, was a football player with no real qualifications for the court. Page's message to the voters was to voice his goal that the court be the best it could be, and that each person who stood before it would be treated equally. He didn't talk about his football exploits. The voters didn't listen to Johnson; they listened to Page and elected him.

Only one opportunity was more meaningful than being elected to the bench, and it arose by sheer chance—way before the court and even lawyering. Alan Page, football player and entrepreneur, was leaving a meeting at General Mills in Minneapolis. Alan owned a snack-vending-machine business and had met with his suppliers. He forgot his briefcase after the meeting, leaving it at the lobby desk. Page realized his oversight when he got to his car. He went back to the lobby, where he found not only his briefcase, but Diane Sims, a beautiful and bright young marketing whiz who had just emerged from an elevator after her own meeting. Sims was a lukewarm football fan, but she recognized Page and suggested to her boss that they go over and say hello.

What we have here may be an echo of Jung's theory of synchronicity— "temporally coincident occurrences of acausal events"—an unexpectedly meaningful intersection of time, place, and opportunity. If Alan Page had not forgotten his briefcase, or if Diane Sims had emerged from the elevator a few minutes earlier or a few minutes later than she did...but he did, and she didn't, so...bang! Synchronicity.

That was two kids (actually, there are four Page kids, Nina and Georgi are from Alan's first marriage, Justin and Kamie are from his marriage to Diane) and two grandkids ago, and I challenge you to find a couple more in love than Diane and Alan Page. Diane arguably knows Alan better than anyone does, and her perspective rounds out the portrait of this remarkable man. But who is he?

He is not patient with mediocrity, although he masks much of what he's feeling unless he is close to you. Most see him as polite, sober, thoughtful—grave, even. The innermost circle sees him as an irrepressible cut-up. His confidence is remarkable, but not a vanity; it is a gift seeded by his mother but brought to fruition by Alan himself. He thrives on work, exercise, and a vile green drink that he blends each morning using whatever he finds in the fridge that is green, although Granny Smith apples and kale are requisite ingredients. I don't think Alan likes it, he just drinks it. He's like that. When his back began to trouble him, a therapist gave him a set of exercises to strengthen the muscles around the tender area. They take an hour to do and they hurt like hell. He does them every morning. "I'm to the point where I get some kind of perverse enjoyment from them," he said.

He enjoys nature, music, and running—and he's pretty fond of pie, too. I think the many people in his past who want to "stay close" puzzle him, as that isn't his way. He travels light—his wife, his kids, a good car, and his love for the law—he doesn't seem to need much more. That doesn't mean he doesn't care for the people from his past, but he recognizes that they are just that, part of his past. He's neither back there nor up ahead. He's here and now. He's been beaten up some for traveling so light, but he respects others' right to an opinion.

He will talk about football, but it's clearly also in his past. I think he feels he gained by it, but gave, too. Some people will tell you he hated football. I think he loved playing football, being in the game, competing. But I think he railed against a lot of the trappings and limitations that those who ran the game wanted to put upon him.

As a player, Page became immersed in player union activities. The union and the owners scuffled regularly. The players sought more freedom—any freedom, essentially, since they had none. They were well paid by '60s and '70s standards, but far from rich. And if you signed a contact with the Vikings or the Rams or the Steelers or the Packers, then that's who and what you were and where you would remain. Your club had rights to your services for as long as they wanted them. Didn't want to play for the Eagles anymore? Fine—go to Canada or get a job. Or sign at our price. Some players fought against this and other issues that they saw as servile; Alan Page was in the forefront of their ranks. A lot of players—especially the African Americans—supported the union; others did not. A lot of players were content with the situation, or at least content enough to go along. Page wasn't, and he wasn't quiet about it. Some Minnesota teammates didn't want him carrying any flag for them. "Don't make waves," they said. It was a message wasted on Alan Page.

His voice is soft and can be very caring. It can also scorch a lawyer's backside for an indifferent presentation. Alan Page believes every man should be equal before the law and before his fellow man, as well. He behaved similarly as an official of the NFL Players Union, speaking for what he believed was right.

Page needs to exercise his mind and his body and is happiest being with people who have like needs. His family runs. Many of his friendships grew out of running. Alan has run seven marathons, including a 62-mile ultramarathon with his soul-buddy, the late Steve Boros, and an "ultimate runner" event, which Page says includes runs of 100 meters, 400 meters, one-mile, 10 kilometers, and 26.2 miles (marathon). Indeed, running would imprint his football career. He still runs, with Diane when she's able to join him. Alan will circle Lake of the Isles in that distinctive, high-stepping gait of his, sometimes twice. Sometimes he'll run Isles and neighboring Calhoun. Tim Baylor, former football player, friend, and running buddy, offered this tongue-in-cheek comment: "If you were in Minneapolis and you didn't know what time it was, and if you could find your way to Lake of the Isles and saw Alan running, you'd know it was 6:00 in the morning."

His kids are reflections of him, and family discussions can become impassioned. "When they play Scrabble," Diane said, "it's kind of scary—intense."

He is awed by nature. I would say he is more spiritual than religious. He believes that he is here to serve a purpose. To date, that purpose has included loving his wife, caring for his family, and serving the law and young people who want to achieve an education. He's also pretty serious about the future of our planet. My sense is that something else will come along one day, and Alan will add a new purpose.

He does not look back. Is he at peace? "Some days," he says. Some will accept him under the terms of his life, some will not. I think he's good with that.

Forward from the Spring Porch

A lan Page sat in a metal chair that was too small for him, perched forward slightly, although still relaxed. Page stands 6′4″ and weighs 230 pounds, so he fills most chairs. His hands, very large, dark, and scarred, were quiet in his lap, even the left pinkie, which takes a permanent, outward, 90-degree turn at the first knuckle. (Page says this is not a bad thing. Neighborhood kids, when first confronted with the misshapen digit, usually say, "Gross!" But when Alan points out that it's a handy left-turn indicator when he's riding his bike, they think it's cool.) We were in south Minneapolis, sitting on the Page's bright spring porch with promising garden views on two sides.

Just to be on the porch with Alan, talking about Alan, cannot be dismissed lightly. It's un-Alan. Moving forward from the spring porch was the challenge.

I met Alan some 40 years ago when we both worked for the Minnesota Vikings. I was a former sportswriter and a fairly new PR man. Alan was an emerging star and an old hand at keeping to himself. One year in the Vikings' training camp, a touring columnist from out east wanted to talk to Alan on a Sunday morning. Nobody did interviews on Sunday morning unless it was Ralph Reeve, who covered so well for the *St. Paul Pioneer-Press and Dispatch* and enjoyed pestering Paul "the Growler" Dickson at any hour.

Alan had a van at camp and was in it that Sunday morning. I approached the vehicle with less than ringing enthusiasm; Alan had never evidenced much interest in me or what I did. Throw in the fact that many of us in the carpet section fidgeted under his gaze, and you'll understand my hesitancy. A Page stare felt heavier than a suitcase full of encyclopedias.

Was he scary? Well, that's a silly thing to say, isn't it? I mean, we were all adults, working together, right? Of course he was scary. He was big and ominous-looking in a detached sort of way, like a storm forming up that left you feeling uneasy, especially because you knew there wasn't much you could do about it.

I knocked on the side door of the RV. Nothing. Maybe he wasn't there. Maybe I wouldn't find him. Maybe I could go to the dining hall and have breakfast. I turned to leave, but then I heard the door roll open. I remember the vehicle was carpeted all over inside—ceiling, walls, floor. Yellow or orange, as I recall. Alan looked out at me but didn't speak. He had a lot of hair then and a fierce gun-fighter moustache. The hair and the moustache did nothing to lighten that suitcase stare. But he asked me in. I think I squatted while Alan sat cross-legged. I told him about the columnist wanting an interview. Actually, the columnist had left a note on my dorm door after I went to bed, asking me to wake him up when I had Page in tow. In tow…right.

Alan sat in the fuzzy RV, quietly considering my request. His eyes held mine while he thought. I'm not sure what I said; I probably talked about the importance of cooperating with the press. I have less trouble remembering what Alan said: "No." Happily, the columnist had a hang-over more acute than his desire for an interview.

I do recall how being around Alan after that seemed more relaxed, even when we had some trying times. We got along. We were together a while longer in Minnesota, then later with the Chicago Bears, and here and there in between. I like to think we advanced from putting up with each other's company to enjoying it, albeit gingerly.

Alan's reluctance to talk about himself in a book may seem at odds in a man of such public accomplishments. He has more major athletic, civic, and humanitarian awards, more honors and honorary degrees, than you can shake a stick at. He has a street named after him back in Canton; sadly, it's a favorite haunt of drug dealers now.

"Alan was quick and agile as an athlete," Diane said, "but he is very methodical in his personal decisions. He postpones making them, [sometimes] until they are made for him." Which spoke to the book-project reluctance. People who heard about the project wanted to see

Alan do it. The Pages had dinner in Hawaii with their friends, Susie and Ernie Collins. The possibility of a book about Alan came up. Susie and Ernie offered to help beat Alan up if he said he wouldn't do it.

Why is that?

I think it's because he is admired and respected, and those who cherish him want to share him with a wider audience, not just Minnesota. Diane said, "I have never met a person of greater character than Alan. He has had it since the day I met him. If you wanted me to describe him in one word, I would say 'character.'" Speaking to an audience of lawyers once, Alan said he believed character "is who you are at your core."

As jurists go, Alan Page is imposing, a little scary-looking, actually. He towers over his fellows on the bench and most entreatants who come before him. His short hair and short beard are gray now, nearly white. He enters the courtroom with that same rumble-of-thunder look he brought to the football field. He still calls it his game-face, and rightly so; the decisions demanded of this court are weighty. "It needs to be apparent that we take seriously every issue that comes before us," he said.

There's more, however, to Alan Page than judicial robes and football honors. He is a tuba player of limited resource but dogged resolve. When a local marathon streams past his street corner each fall, Alan hauls out the tuba, stands on the corner, and plays "Whistle While You Work" (the only song in his tuba repertoire) as entrants pass. He receives many sweaty high-fives. He loves music, cars, gadgets, and the humbling resonance of the law. He dotes on his kids and is crazy about his wife. His newest passions are his grandsons, Otis and Theo.

An older passion is cars. When they were dating and even when they were first married, Diane Sims-Page spent many a hot, oil-smelly evening at a drag strip, watching her man jam his purple car down those short, shiny, slick straightaways. To know Diane is to know how far she is removed from drag strips, but she is one remarkable and adjustable lady. Diane says Alan is still a gearhead, and the three or four vehicles in their garage seem to support the claim. That's in addition to the 1906 Buick Diane's father restored for them.

Alan is a private public figure. We had dinner after sitting on the spring porch and visiting Justice Page's chambers at the courts building in St. Paul. We went to Lucia's, a fresh little place not far from their home. I asked if they went there often. "We don't eat out often," Alan said, "but when we do, this place is one of our favorites." That's a vintage Page answer: careful clarification. Diane said they both like to cook and enjoy preparing meals at home. Alan is an improving cook. His kids tease him, remembering the old days when chicken and rice dominated the menu and improvement was hard to detect.

Diane and Alan are a team. When I asked Alan about him being black and Diane being white, he fixed me with a look that was both gentle and intense. "There is something you need to understand," he said. He looked at his wife. She looked at him. You could have walked across the strength of that shared look. "We are a team," Alan said. Diane didn't say anything and didn't have to.

Finally, we talked about Alan's passions: education, character, racial equality, and taking action. That's Alan in a nutshell. To Alan, passions are full time; you have to hold to them even when you *don't* feel like it, not just when you do. They're not always convenient or comfortable. They can pinch.

We talked about how "All Rise" asked each of us to identify our own passions, and then act on them and make a difference. Preachy? Alan Page doesn't preach; he acts. He went on strike once when he thought management's negotiations with the football players union were unfair. Not his team—just him. Ed Garvey, who ran the union, called, frantic: "Jesus Christ, Alan! You can't go on strike by yourself! Get some of your teammates to go with you." Page said that was for his teammates to decide.

During his lunch hour, he helps a third-grader with her reading lessons. Is he influencing educational needs by reading with a child? Some might say no, but that's not the way Alan thinks. Helping one child is how it begins, and that third-grader he helps lights up Page's face when he talks about her. He says she helps him a lot more than he helps her.

I think Alan Page wants the rest of us to find our stories and our passions. A week after I first sat on the Pages' spring porch, I was in a little café in Freeport, Illinois. I talked to a lady named Georgia. She was saying how she just works a short shift at the café now because she's doing a little teaching and then she started volunteering at the retirement home. Georgia's 81 years old. I asked her how she finds time to do all she does. She said she doesn't care much for television.

So, who "gets it?" Who sees the big picture and their place in it? Jurists. They see the single issue before them, but within the whole cloth of the law. Some athletes, the good ones, get it—they see their own assignment, but always within the greater scheme of the team's goal. I think Alan and Diane Page get it. And, God knows, Georgia out in Freeport gets it. That's a start, right?

"I am from Black Rock, Arkansas. My daddy was a sharecropper. I am the 13th of 14 children and the first to go to college [Philander Smith]. I finished high school when I was 16. I didn't want to stay on the farm. One has to learn how to survive, to control your own destiny. You can't let it control you. If you do, there is no hope, and there is hope."
                                    —Willarene Beasley, educator

Canton

"Back in the day, this was a nice neighborhood. It didn't have the boarded-up houses you see now. I'm probably one of the oldest neighbors here; [it] must be 40 years I've been here. Most people now are in and out, in and out. But I'm comfortable here in my comfortable house, and here is where I'll probably stay." —Gwen Singleterry, cousin

Bezaleel Wells, a surveyor who laid out the town, named it out of respect for Captain John O'Donnell, an Irish trader who imported goods from Canton, China. That was in 1805. President William McKinley's Library and Museum are located there, as are the Canton Crocodiles, a lesser baseball team. A building demolished not long ago in the downtown area housed, at one point, the Ralph Hays Hupmobile Agency, where representatives of 12 professional football teams met in 1920 to form the American Professional Football Association. Later, the APFA became the National Football League. The representatives sat on automobile running boards in the Hupmobile showroom. One of the men, George Halas, represented the Decatur Staleys, who would soon become the Chicago Bears. Halas owned and coached the Bears and pretty much molded and shaped the National Football League with his hard, knobby hands.

The Pro Football Hall of Fame is in Canton, and stands on George Halas Drive. Alan Page is enshrined at the Hall, the first Canton native (Dan Dierdorf followed him) to be so honored. Halas is there, too, as a charter member. When Alan played his final professional football game, it was as a Chicago Bear, and George Halas ignored the bitter December cold to lead a pregame ceremony honoring Page.

Try to imagine old Canton, not the new one skirted by proper suburbs and neat lawns, their care usually outsourced to teams of smiling young gardeners dressed in green twill. Not the shopping centers offering designer clothing, the wide world of Wal-Mart, and an almost endless procession of fast-food possibilities. Both north and south tug at Canton, so you might find Burger King rubbing elbows with Chick-fil-A.

That's today. The Canton of the 1940s and '50s was short on lawn services and smart ladies' clothing lines, to say nothing of burger or chicken sandwich stores that assemble a meal to your specifications in practically no time at all. Back then, you sewed, wore hand-me-downs, or bought ready-to-wear at Monkey (Montgomery) Wards or the dry goods store. If you ate out—which you didn't, at least not often—it was at a café or a supper club on those special occasions when the kids were left home with their grandmother or a sitter. Today's suburbs and Canton's old city center, like a lot of others, are a poor match.

But you can still get a breath of old Canton, although the old staples—the steel mills and the Hoover Company—are mostly gone. Most of the downtown retail businesses moved out to the suburbs or out of town, and plenty of today's urban Canton residents have their lawns tended, dress smartly, and eat out frequently. That's not it; it's more the little tug-in-the-gut feeling you get when you leave the freeway for downtown Canton. It looks tough. The first thing I saw was a grimy old auto repair shop. I stopped for directions. The guy had no smile, not many teeth, and grease smears over tattoos that looked like he'd gotten them in the Navy. But he pointed me in the right direction. Neighborhoods from the '50s and earlier hunker down around the city center. Old factory hulks lurk behind new bank buildings. Canton's not unique—I can show you the same neighborhoods in Minneapolis or Boston or Sioux City, Iowa. If not unfriendly, they seem at least wary and in need of a wash or a new roof, or both.

Canton was a mill town before the war and after. It's got the look— tough, hard, given more to function than form. Republic had a mill there. A black man had his best chance for employment at Republic, but Diebold and Timken were in Canton, too. Alan Page's cousin, Michael Umbles, worked one summer at Diebold; Michael's father worked there his whole life. "I considered it an honor to have that job," Michael said. "I was a janitor. I swept up scrap metal. I got cut up some, but it wasn't considered a dangerous job. I got paid a little over the minimum."

Howard Page Sr., Alan's father, was a black man but he was no mill worker. He was called "Baker Boy" because he was a baker's son and, as a boy, sold his father's breads and pies on the street. He remained a fair hand in the kitchen. "Baker Boy" was a fair hand at a lot of things, and he did all of them with flash. He had a record shop and distributed records to jukes around town. He was a promoter, bringing well-known entertainers—Dinah Washington and Sarah Vaughan among them—to southeast Canton. Black Canton. But Howard's main business was a bar he owned on Cherry Street called the Main Event. And the real interest at the bar was a back room that was a gambling parlor.

"Baker Boy" Page was always in style, a dapper fellow in sharp suits and hats. He loved good times and good cars; he always drove a Cadillac. (His sons would share that passion for cars: Howard Jr. is a Cadillac man; Alan had a much-loved Mini Cooper and currently drives a Mercedes SUV. Diane loves cars, as well: only recently did she give up an elderly Mercedes wagon and the same 1968 250SL BMW convertible she drove when she met Alan. They also enjoy a 1906 Buick touring car—a gift from Diane's father, Irving Sims. Alan and Diane enjoy driving the vintage Buick in sedate summer races.)

Howard Page, high stepper, married Georgiana Umbles, a religious and proper young woman, and a more unlikely pairing—surfacewise, anyway—you would be hard-pressed to find. But Georgiana loved her man, and he loved her. Besides, the focus in her busy life would come to be her children—Marvel, Twila, Howard Jr., and Alan. Georgiana had a variety of jobs, too, and a social life with her lady friends. When Alan returned to Canton to be inducted into the Pro Football Hall of Fame, his high school teammates held a luncheon in his honor at Brookside Country Club. During his remarks, Alan pointed out that his mother had worked at the club as the attendant in the women's locker room.

It wasn't that Howard Page ignored his kids, but he was gone a lot.

"He could be out late or out all night. And maybe all the next day and the next night, too," Alan said. "But I measure him by the time he was *with* us. When he was there, that was quality time. I think sometimes we can get hung up on quantity as opposed to quality."

"Dad might be gambling the whole weekend after they paid at the mills," Howard Jr. affirmed.

Sisters Marvel and Twila weren't even aware that their dad ran a saloon until much later, and even then, they weren't allowed anywhere near it.

"We girls weren't allowed in my dad's club," Marvel Page Jackson said. "In fact, we weren't even allowed on Cherry Street, unless it was to visit my grandmother. Mother said there was nothing down there for us to see."

I asked Howard Jr. for his memories of his parents.

"I didn't know it so much when we were growing up," he said, "but my dad was a gambler, that's how he made his living. He'd leave on Thursday night or whenever the steel mills paid, and we wouldn't see him again until Monday." He said both of his parents took care of them, but his mother was there more of the time. "She was the disciplinarian, too. She'd send you out to cut a switch. You knew you were in trouble then. My parents worked hard so that we could go to Central Catholic High School. My mother worked hard, so did my dad. They made sure we went there and stayed there."

The Page-Umbles clan was like one family. Gwen Umbles Singleterry was the older cousin, and her younger brother, Michael, was the tag-along. "We loved to go to Uncle Howard's house," Michael said. "They had the neatest stuff. They had a pool table and a jukebox down in the basement. The jukebox always had the latest hits. Uncle Howard was a gadget guy, so there was always something new and interesting."

Alan didn't fall far from the gadget tree. Nina, Alan's second daughter, describes her dad as "a gadget freak." She adds that he also "loves to take pictures and send them to everybody, regardless of how good or bad they are."

Alan and his siblings had nicknames; Howard Jr. was and still is called "Roy" or "Roy Boy." Alan was "Tootie," and Twila was "Honey." "I didn't know my real name until I started school," Twila said. Marvel says she didn't have a nickname.

The Pages lived in southeast Canton at the corner of Market and Housel when Alan was young. It was a black neighborhood then and remains one today. The house, which was modest, is long gone, but there's a little scrap of a neighborhood flower garden on the corner. Howard Sr.'s Main Event is just a memory, too, its ghost supporting an elevated highway as it spans Cherry Street. The Market-Housel corner is close to Skyline Terrace, a housing project where the main street is named Alan Page Drive. The neighborhood was safer in the '40s and '50s, but even then it was a concern for Howard and Georgiana with four young children. The Pages worried about the quality of education available to their children. "Baker Boy" Page might have logged more time at the gaming tables than he did at home, but he shared his wife's non-negotiable goal: that their children would have an education. Accordingly, the couple decided they would move their family away from troubled South Canton for better streets and better schools.

East Canton, a separate town, was nicer, but not overly warm to a new black family. "There was one other black family with kids in our school," Twila said. "Roy Boy and I were always getting kicked off the bus. I didn't take a lot of guff from people. We were called names every day."

Alan was asked if he was aware of racial bias growing up. He paused before answering, an Alan trademark. "If you were black, you knew your place," he said. "You knew which side of the tracks you belonged on. In Canton, that was the southeast side."

Alan was nine years old when the Pages moved to East Canton. They lived in a brick house. The kids said it was on a hill. Probably it was more of a modest rise, and from the sound of it, a fairly open and plain patch of land. Both house and hill are gone today, but at the time, they were awfully exciting to a young family leaving the mean streets of southeast Canton for a fresher, more open atmosphere.

The house on the hill in East Canton was large. There was a fireplace in the front room and a basement with a pool table and a jukebox.

There was a yard to play in and blackberry bushes at the foot of the lawn behind the house. The boys picked berries, and their mother or sisters baked pies—always at least two, maybe more. To this day, Alan places a high priority on pie—homemade, preferably, but he orders it in restaurants, as well. As we were leaving a Minneapolis restaurant one evening, having just enjoyed a slice of coconut cream pie for dessert, Alan signaled our waiter. "You better wrap up another piece of that pie," he said. "I might want some for breakfast."

There weren't many kids who lived out near the Pages in East Canton, although there were a few who surfaced dimly in that selective memory of Alan's. "I got beat up a couple of times," he said. "There were a couple of older kids—I guess they didn't like me. I remember being afraid to walk home from school because these guys might be waiting for me. The being scared part was worse than getting beat up; I don't remember that as clearly."

Other than the risky walk home, Alan liked school and his teachers. Math was a favorite subject. He doesn't remember his first grade teacher's name, but he remembers her favorably. "She encouraged me," he said. What else did he like about school? "I liked the fact that it was relatively easy, and that I got reinforcement from some of my teachers."

Alan's primary playmate growing up was his older brother, Roy Boy. "I'm closer now to Roy than I was when we were kids," Alan said. Roy, being the older brother, probably didn't get as much attention as did Alan, the youngest. "Roy needed someone to punch on," Alan said, "and I filled that need. I was the baby of the family, and I guess I did get a lot of my mother's attention."

"Alan was spoiled," cousin Gwen Singleterry agreed, adding that Georgiana babied Alan. "If he wanted something, he got it. But she was everybody's favorite aunt," Gwen said. "She looked after her kids. Their dad did, too, but he had that business that kept him out of the house. Georgi made sure those kids stayed together and got their education."

"My relationship with my mother was very special," Alan said. "Gentle, sensitive," he said, when asked to describe her. It was suggested that he has those traits. Page paused. "I don't think about it, but I guess I have more of her characteristics than my dad's. He was more outgoing than my mother, and he had this great awareness of everything. My dad saw more, did more than my mother. But he knew the difference between right and wrong.

"My parents only went through high school," Alan said, "but they were both very intelligent people. I believe they both would have been able to accomplish much more in their lives if they'd had college educations. That's why it was so important to them that we go to college."

Georgiana and Howard liked East Canton, but they weren't happy with the schools. Although not Catholic (she was Baptist, he was Christian Scientist), they decided to send the children to Central Catholic High School in Canton for a better education. It was about 15 miles from where they lived. The girls went first, then Howard, then Alan. The girls rode the bus until Roy started school, and then they often drove. It was a team effort. "I had a license," Twila said. "I knew the gears and I could steer, but I wasn't very good with the foot pedals. So I did the top part, and Roy worked the pedals. We got there."

Alan Page's football career dates from Central Catholic High School in Canton, but it began on the sloped backyard of the Page home in East Canton, where the brothers played football with a rolled-up newspaper as the ball. "I don't think either one of us understood much about the game, but we liked being active," Alan said. But football didn't make a serious impression early on; in those early days, both Page boys preferred building model cars.

Was the Page family rich? Poor? Somewhere in-between? Opinions vary. Some who knew Alan growing up said the family was poor. Georgiana worked as a locker room attendant at the country club and often worked preparing for and cleaning up after private parties at members' homes, and all the kids worked at the club at some time, in some capacity. Alan worked in the kitchen alongside his mother. "Alan liked it," Marvel said. "He got to eat a lot."

Marvel remembered that when the children were young, they enjoyed a monthly shopping trip to Cleveland. They would eat dinner in the Forum. "We weren't allowed to have watermelon," she said. Who said? "Mother," Marvel replied.

You don't get a sense of poverty from the Page siblings, and when you talk to relatives, you learn that the Page children were well-dressed, that most family gatherings were held at their home on the hill in East Canton, and that the kids had lots of games and gadgets. "They were always nicely dressed," said Gwen Singleterry. "We usually went there for holidays," Gwen's bother, Michael Umbles, recalled. "There would be turkey and ham and all the trimmings. And a lot of desserts. It was a festive house."

Rich, poor, or middle-class, the Pages seemed comfortable. And, in reflecting on the family's economic status, Marvel stressed the greater gift all of them enjoyed, that of family.

Over time, Georgiana Page's full life and schedule—family, work, and friends—took a toll. She was frail. "Our mother was very proud," Roy said. "She never seemed to slow down. I'm sure she worked too hard. Mostly, I remember her working hard and being sick. She was proud of all of us, proud of what she and my dad had been able to accomplish. But she was frail." And she had a bad heart, although the children didn't know that.

"Mother went into the hospital for tests," Alan said. "It was in the spring of 1959. The doctor said she would only be there overnight, but she never came home."

Georgiana Page was dead at 42. Alan was only 13, Roy was 15, Twila was 16, and Marvel was 18. "It was a trauma for all of us," Michael Umbles said of his Aunt Georgiana's passing. "We all felt so close to her, Pages and Umbles alike. We were really one family, and we had lost our star."

There was brief talk of breaking the kids up after their mother's death, but the idea was quickly tabled. Twila was four weeks from graduating high school. Alan spent the summer with relatives. "That's when he started to get big," Marvel said. But they came back together as summer ended. Cousin Gwen, although considerably older, stayed close and eventually lived in the Page home, a surrogate mother.

I asked Alan what it was like, losing his mother. I asked the question 49 years after he lost her.

"I was devastated," he said. "Lost."

Were you a long time getting over losing her?

"If ever," Alan replied. "The getting over is more an evolution than anything I did. Diane will tell you, I've got my blinders; I can put them on so I don't have to look at something. And I put things in my 'denial box' and move on. I suppose that also is part of not living life looking in the rearview mirror. But it hurt. There isn't a day I don't think about my mother. I still feel the hurt of losing her."

Did his dad help him in a time of need?

"He did. He supported me; he took interest in what I was doing, especially in my getting an education. I didn't know much about my dad having a bar and being a gambler; I knew him away from that life. It was a time when I needed someone to love me, and he did."

Absent their leader, the Page family wasn't breaking up, it was just moving on. Marvel left for Merrimack College, Twila would attend Kent State, though neither girl especially liked college. Roy was still at Central Catholic, and Alan was headed there.

And how was young Alan Page remembered as he headed for the next level, high school?

"I think, even back then, he was pretty much the way he is now. He was steadfast," said Gwen. "Whatever he felt in his mind and in his heart was right, well, that was what he was going to do, even at that young age. If he thought kids were playing a silly game and he didn't want to be part of the silliness, then he wasn't part of it. He always had that serious side to him. I guess I've always looked at him as a gentle giant."

"Honest, truthful, stubborn," Marvel declared, "and I don't think of him as some big deal. He ended up being a football star and a judge, but he was just my little brother. I changed his diapers, and I've told him that. I say, 'To me, you're just Toots.'"

Roy had said Marvel was the closest of the siblings to Alan. Were they alike? Roy laughed, tickled by looking back at that memory. "Not really," he said. "Mar spent her life getting out of work, and Alan spent his getting into it." I suggested that he might not have made that statement so readily if Marvel had been there to hear him. "You got that right," he said.

"Alan and Marvel were close, however. When we moved to East Canton, other kids called us names. I probably didn't handle it very well, and neither did Twi. I think Alan and Marvel just kind of ignored it. Twi and I fought it. We probably didn't make things any better for ourselves. Alan was the calm one," Roy said. "A lot rolled off his back." Sometimes. "He had a temper," Twila pointed out. Marvel said it was a "hot temper." Jim Marshall, the gallant old Minnesota Viking who was probably closer to Alan than any man he played with, offered his assessment. "Alan was calm or volatile, depending on what the situation called for. He's calm now; he doesn't have call for getting volatile anymore. But he's passionate in his work."

Alan frowned when asked if he keeps contact with his siblings. "Not really," he said. "Not like I should." He chuckled. "Of course that's a two-way street. It isn't that we don't get along; we just don't seem to be very good about checking in with each other. I know we'd be there for each other if we were needed, so it's not that." Alan thought for a moment. "We used to have conference calls, a four-way telephone hookup. That was fun. We'd get caught up, we'd laugh, talk politics...whatever. Everybody got his or her say. We should start that again."

But for now, here is Alan Page, 14, newly bereft of a mother he was extremely close to, still scared by thunder and lightning. When he was younger, he had a fear of being left alone. Now, he was going back to Canton to an essentially all-white school where he would study under demanding men who represented a religion that was foreign to him. He would take the initial steps—not always with enthusiasm—on a road that would lead to an acclaim he still is not all that comfortable with.

Pat Grant died of Parkinson's disease. What a loss! She was Bud Grant's wife and just a great gal. Pat was fun; she was the pepper on Bud's boiled eggs. Bud buffaloed a lot of people, but Pat wasn't one of them. The Grants had six children. It might sound like a zinger to say Pat raised them, but it might also be pretty near the mark, too. At her funeral, Bud spoke about how Pat never missed one of the kid's events or activities. When one of the boys played football at UM-Duluth, Pat made the drive from Minneapolis to Duluth and sat in the rain or cold for every home game. When the Grant kids were grown and out of the nest, Pat took in foreign students and supported them in their activities. They say that Bud, ever the stoic, broke down and cried when he spoke at Pat's funeral. Asked once why he wasn't emotional, Grant said, "I am emotional—I've got six kids!" And a wife he loved.

Central Catholic High School

"Alan delivered the commencement address at our school in 1990. A lot of times, graduation speakers talk a lot. Alan had very few points; he spoke to the kids and their parents in a way they could hear. Everything he said made total sense. The man was talking basically off the cuff, but everything he believed in was in that talk. The big thing was not stopping here, but to continue on. To set goals and meet them. The kids were very attentive." —Father Bob Kaylor, Canton Central Catholic High School

Canton is in northeastern Ohio, within an industrial-agricultural area that pushes up to Cleveland on the south shore of Lake Erie. Northeastern Ohioans are strong people, taking the best licks Lake Erie and the economy can offer—and those are some substantial licks. Over the years, these Ohioans have earned their way—talking here about the rank and file—with sweat and muscle, whether in the field or the factory or the mill, more comfortable with lunch buckets than business lunches. They hold tight to family, community, and their values.

High school football is just one of those values. Indeed, Paul Brown, "P.B.," the messiah of high school football, grew up and later coached in Massillon, just west of Canton. The messiah of football, period, some say. Brown's 1940 Massillon Washington squad outscored the opposition 477–6 for the season—that's not a typo: a high school team, 477–6!

I knew Paul Brown, but he didn't really know me, other than to nod politely and offer that trim, shy little smile of his. I was on Pete Rozelle's staff for a while at the National Football League office in New York. By then—it was the early '70s—Paul Brown was in Act IV, Scene II of his dazzling football trajectory, having earlier lent his excellence to high school, service teams, and the college game. Moving on to the pro game, he led the Cleveland Browns to a level of success other teams weren't familiar with, and later founded, owned, built, managed, and coached the Cincinnati Bengals.

In another show of what a small world the NFL is, near the end of World War II the man who coached Alan Page to pro stardom played for Paul Brown at Great Lakes Naval Training Center. Brown liked Bud Grant's athletic ability, but he liked his intelligence, discipline, and confidence even more. Years later Grant, as coach of the Minnesota Vikings, would prize those same qualities in Alan Page—for a while, at least.

But back to Canton and its fierce love for high school football. McKinley, North Canton, Alliance, Barberton, Massillon Washington, Akron, St. Vincent's, Central Catholic, and others all had active teams supported fiercely by their communities.

Canton Central Catholic High School has a handsome campus; it looks like a small college with its grand lawns and stately trees. The old main building is made of stone, tall and turreted; newer wings came later. There are side buildings, residences, and tennis courts to be seen from the driveway. You have to go down a wooded path from the main campus to reach the football stadium. A brick ring wall is all that remains of the stadium from those nights when "Page One and Page Two" (Howard Jr. and Alan) played there. The rest—the field, stands, and surrounds—is new.

We talked to a man who was there during the '60s. "[We had] zero discipline problems," John McVay said. "The girls were on one side of the building—the nuns taught them—and the boys were on the other. The brothers taught the boys."

McVay is a pleasant Californian with a long and distinguished football history. John started in humble high school circumstances and ended up as general manager of the San Francisco 49ers during their glory run with Bill Walsh and Joe Montana. He lives, in his words, on the right side of Folsom Lake, as opposed to the other side, where

Johnny Cash made Folsom prison famous in song. McVay taught biology and typing at Central Catholic in the early '60s. He also coached the football team, the Crusaders.

"Alan's brother, Howard, was a year ahead of him," McVay said. "Howard was a very good player. He was more sturdily built than Alan, and not as quick—a big, tough lineman." McVay laughed. "For one road game, Howard forgot his uniform. The crazy part of it was the school we played had the same colors we did—green and white. Their coach loaned Howard a uniform. We won, and after the game I told that coach he was a truly Christian man. I told him I wasn't sure I would have done the same thing for one of his players."

"When Alan started school, his dad came over to see me," McVay said. "He asked me if I thought I could handle those two sons of his. I told him that if I couldn't, I knew who could: the brothers." McVay laughed.

That was a different time for boys in high school; the Jesuits excelled at maintaining order. McVay said, "If a kid thought about getting out of line, he had one of the brothers to deal with, and the brothers were tough guys."

Alan Page arrived at Central Catholic in the fall of 1959, within months of his mother's death. He was a long way from being a football player; in fact, he didn't have any football plans when he showed up.

"I just wanted to keep my head down," Alan said. "I wasn't much for meeting new people and putting myself into situations that were new to me. I figured I had enough going on, just getting started in my classes." The scar of losing their mother was still fresh for all of the Page children, perhaps most of all for Alan, the youngest. Going into high school, he planned only to study and play tuba in the school band. Any new school at all was a new experience, let alone a Catholic high school where there were very few students of color. The Pages went to mass every school morning, just like the Catholic kids, although Alan has little memory of doing so.

Awkward and gangly as a youngster, Alan was usually one of the last chosen for what few neighborhood games there were in East Canton. He knew he hated baseball. "Why anybody would want to stand up with a stick and let somebody throw a ball at them—a ball that was hard—was beyond me. I tried basketball in grammar school," he said, "but I wasn't very good."

That left football, or so he thought. Alan knew Howard went out for football and enjoyed it, so he thought about it. That's what Alan does— he thinks a thing through. Years later, Alan would be a Hall of Fame classmate of Mike Ditka. Asked to describe Ditka, a fellow once said, "Ready, fire, aim." Alan could be described this way: "Ready...now are you sure you're ready? Are you *prepared*? Okay, aim...be patient, don't hurry your shot. Everything good? Okay...fire." Alan decided he wanted something as an outlet besides band. The only other activity available was football, so he decided to try out.

He remembers his first day. "I didn't have a clue about equipment," Alan said. "When I showed up the first day, I was supposed to have an athletic supporter. I didn't know what an athletic supporter was, so needless to say, I didn't have one." You may wonder, as did I, why older brother Howard didn't tell Alan he'd need a jockstrap. However, after getting to know the Pages, I'm not all that surprised. I think it's pretty Page-like. They don't communicate a lot. Even more important, they don't horn in. I have this mental image of one of them falling down stairs in the dark while a sib, who knew the step was wobbly but hadn't said so because he or she didn't want to appear take-charge-ish, asks in real concern: "Are you okay?"

"I really didn't know very much about football," Alan said. "I was a big, uncoordinated kid. The first year, I learned how to stand and started to learn how to run. I didn't really learn; I started to learn. That was about it." Another thing he learned was that football players were expected to go out for track in the spring.

"They told me I was a shot-putter," Alan said. "I can see why; I was pretty big and I was awkward, so they knew I wouldn't be much of a runner. Of course, I had absolutely no aptitude for the shot-put, either. I tried, but with my long arms, I couldn't get the right kind of leverage (remember that word, *leverage*, because we'll hear it again) to make that iron ball go anywhere. The shot-putter needs short, explosive lift, and for that he needs explosive arms. But just because I couldn't put the shot, that didn't mean my time on the track team was over. They told us we all had to run, too."

"It's pretty interesting, with all the running I have done [as an adult]," he said, "but after that first year on the track team, I didn't want to ever run again. They made us run varying distances. There's a huge difference between *having* to run [and] *wanting* to run. This was 'have to' running.

"The spring of my freshman year, they made us run the 400 meters," Page said. "And I'm the shot-putter, right? I sure wasn't much of a shot-putter, but that's what I was. And I definitely wasn't a quarter-miler. That's a long race that you run pretty much full out. It was a hideous race. I had never done anything even close to that."

Alan will never forget running the 400 meters. "When the monkey jumped on my back on the backstretch, it was like, 'Hey! I'm dying here—dying. Does anybody see me?' My body went numb; I couldn't feel anything. My legs were like mush. When I finally got to the third turn, I still had 100 meters to go. I thought my lungs were going to explode. People talk about feeling like they have a piano on their back; that's what I felt like. I came off the curve and I had lost all form; all I could do was put one foot in front of the other. The coaches were standing along the side of the track, and they're screaming, 'Faster! Go faster!' I'll never forget it."

Alan had a classroom problem early on in high school: it was too easy. "I could coast and do pretty well," he said. "The downside of that came when reality set in, when school wasn't easy. I didn't really learn how to study. It would have been easier to learn from the beginning, to learn how to learn as opposed to just using your innate ability. I would have been a lot better off if I had struggled earlier. You learn from struggle. In the context of education, going through that learning process is easier earlier than it is later."

He learned on the football field early on, although it wasn't dramatic. Alan played, but he wasn't noticed much until he was a junior. In vintage Alan Page minimalese, he said, "I discovered I liked it and that I had some aptitude for it."

"He kept improving steadily and rapidly as a junior, and then as a senior," McVay said. "I wasn't there Alan's senior season, but I saw a lot of his games and his films. He was an awesome physical specimen. He really developed before his senior season. He was very fast and quick. There's a difference between fast and quick, and he was both. He was naturally strong." (Years later Buddy Ryan, one of his pro coaches would say, "He had the kind of muscles every guy wanted, that washboard belly, but I don't think he ever lifted a weight.") "I think what set him apart on the football field was his intelligence and his ability to focus," said McVay.

Jim Osborne was a teammate of Page's when he played at Chicago. "I hated playing in cold weather," Osborne said. "I was from Florida, and I hated the cold. I'd see Alan dress for a game in terrible weather. He'd wear this little half T-shirt, his shoulder pads, his jersey and his pants, stockings, and shoes. That was it. The cold didn't seem to bother Alan during a game. Finally, I asked him how he did it. He said, 'Just focus on the game, don't think about the cold. It's going to be cold; you can't do anything about that. Focus on the game and what you have to do. Ignore the cold.' It sounds crazy, but it worked. For the first time, I wasn't dying from the cold out on the field."

Alan's education extended beyond the core curriculum and the football field. "One day in my biology class," John McVay said, "I asked if any of the boys knew how to type; I was the typing teacher, too. Nobody held up a hand, but I told them that if they ate their lunch really fast, they could come up to the typing lab and I'd give them 30 minutes of typing. We had those old upright, manual typewriters. I remember Alan's hands were so big even then that when he'd hit a key, two or three keys would come up. He spent a lot of his time untangling keys."

Asked years later for his memories of Coach McVay, Alan smiled and said, "He taught me to type! That may have been the most valuable class I took away from high school."

McVay left Central Catholic before Page's senior year to become an assistant coach at Michigan State. "Alan about got me fired my first year at State," he said. "One of the first things [Michigan State Spartans head coach] Duffy Daugherty said to me was, 'You'd better get that Page kid from Canton.'"

Roy, Alan's older brother, had gone on to Tennessee A&I on a football scholarship. Was Roy a good college player? "I thought so," Roy said, another Page-ism. He remembered coming home spring weekends when Alan was a senior at Central Catholic. "There were usually letters on the table from different schools wanting to recruit him," he said.

Bob Belden was a sophomore quarterback at Central Catholic when Alan was a senior. Today, he runs Belden Brick. If you spend much time looking around Canton and environs, you'll see the Belden name on developments, shopping centers, schools, you name it. And if you look at Notre Dame Stadium in South Bend, you'll see a lot more Belden brick. Bob was a quarterback there, too. He is a tall, trim, comfortable man in a big, cluttered, and not-at-all fancy office. The office is sturdy, just like the rest of the brick-company building.

"When Alan was being inducted into the Hall of Fame, a bunch of us who played with him held a luncheon in his honor at Brookside Country Club. I called him that morning and asked if he wanted a ride to the lunch. He said, no, he'd get there on his own. I was the emcee," Belden said, "and it was getting close to noon, the starting time. No Alan. I was nervous and so were the others. Still no Alan. Then it was noon, straight up, and here came Alan, wearing that little bow tie, strolling around the corner, relaxed as he could be. Right on time. I had worried for nothing.

"Alan kept developing as a player and as a man," Belden said. "A lot of guys who excel in sports have a hard time letting go of that part of their lives. You could see Alan grow at every level. He advanced from high school to college. He advanced from college to pro. And then he advanced to what I think was really important to him: the rest of his life.

"He has a code," Belden said. "If Alan believes he's right—and he doesn't decide that quickly—he'll stand his ground. A lot of people don't have it in them to take a stand, to make unpopular decisions. Alan does. I think that is one of the great lessons he brings to those kids he is always working to reach."

Belden went to Notre Dame after Page and still has a sharp memory of his first day on the practice field against the varsity team. He was a freshman quarterback. "I took the snap," he said. "I moved two, maybe three steps to my left, on the option, when this gold helmet hit me dead-center in the chest. It was Alan. I was flopping around like a fish; I'd had my wind knocked out. Alan stood over me for a second, looking down. He didn't look mad, he didn't look glad to see me, he didn't look anything. He just studied me, then he was gone."

"He dominated," Coach McVay said. "He got bigger, he got a lot stronger, and he got quicker. He turned games around. He had this incredible leverage (long, strong arms worked in football); he could just move people out of his way, like he was rearranging them, sorting them out."

As his graduation from Central Catholic approached, Alan was thinking seriously about going to Purdue. Michigan State, with McVay on the case, made a strong push for him. So did Ohio State. And he had heard from Notre Dame.

In Evanston, Illinois, Northwestern's bright young coach, Ara Parseghian, worked on his recruiting map after the 1962 season. Two young men at the top of Ara's board were Jim Lynch, a linebacker from Lima, Ohio, and Alan Page. Parseghian had played and coached in Ohio. Both of the players he wanted were strong students who could meet Northwestern's tough academic requirements. But Parseghian knew he wouldn't get either one of them. "Notre Dame wanted them," he said. "I knew I wasn't going to beat Notre Dame on somebody they really wanted. The rest of us recruited—Notre Dame selected."

Alan visited the Notre Dame campus in South Bend after his senior season at Central Catholic. Norm Nicola, another Central Catholic man, had gone to Notre Dame. He was two years ahead of Alan and played center and linebacker. Nicola took Page out for pizza during his South Bend visit.

Evidently Page liked what he heard and what he saw on campus and on the field. In the spring of 1963, Alan Page committed to Notre Dame.

John McVay didn't get fired by Michigan State as threatened, but we may assume his ebullient boss, Duffy Daugherty—a man who used to invite sportswriters to his home for dinner the night before games, for heaven's sake—was not pleased.

And in Evanston, Illinois, Ara Parseghian accepted with equanimity not being able to sign the prized Ohioans, Lynch and Page, and went about his business—for the moment.

"I don't think my father knows it, but there have been certain ideas of his that have been very influential on me. Here is a small thing, but it's a big thing, too: just be kind to your neighbors. I try to do that every day, to smile at the people in my building or ask them how they're doing. You never know; it might mean a lot to a person to have somebody care."

—Georgi Page, daughter

Notre Dame

*"He was a very determined young man. His focus was on being successful. He was never a problem to coach. He was very serious about everything—academics, football, and his future." —*Ara Parseghian, Notre Dame coach, on Alan Page

Why Notre Dame? Why not Michigan State—strong school, great football program? State had black players, a much larger black presence on campus, and no religious issue. To top it off, John McVay, Alan's old high school coach, was there. Why not Purdue or Ohio State or Northwestern, for that matter?

Because of the rear-view mirror. Remember? Does Alan Page look in the rear-view mirror? Not often.

Football was his "now," and, hopefully, there would be more football in the future. Football was the key to the future, but not the future; football might be the train, but it wasn't the destination. But whatever there might be "out there" beyond football did nothing to lessen the harsh change for a tall, shy, black youngster, so far from home, family, and other people of color.

But no matter: this is Notre Dame, with its sun-splashed, spectacular Touchdown Jesus mural on the Hesburgh Library, visible from the stadium, with arms upraised over the end zone in a portent of good things to come on the field below. The library stands on hallowed ground: the site of old, green-fenced Cartier Field, where Rockne's teams played and Leahy's lads practiced. There's the stadium, filled with excited thousands; the marching band; the Leprechaun mascot dancing a mad jig as the blue-jerseyed (ever since Ara) Irish spill out of the tunnel onto the bright green turf. Adoring fans squeeze onto the cramped tiers of bench seating, where knowing old-timers never stand to watch a big play, lest they lose an inch of precious fanny space. Shake down the thunder! Notre Dame football! A big deal? A monster deal!

That's in the fall. We see fewer pictures from South Bend and the Notre Dame campus as winter settles in like some thoughtless relative who comes to visit early and stays well past his welcome. Bare black tree limbs, grim-visaged old brick buildings looking grumpy among newer structures with far less personality. Students and faculty schlepping to classes, bundled against the cold. South Bend is up near the top of Indiana, pressing against the Michigan border. It's close to Lake Michigan in the area Chicagoans refer to as "the bottom of the lake." Winter storms love the southern rim of Lake Michigan and those towns and folks huddled beneath it. When it's clear in Chicago's Loop, or in Kalamazoo, you might be up to your knees in snow in South Bend, with a wind that is anything but Christian probing you and your garments.

How many African American students were at Notre Dame when Page got there in 1963?

"Twenty-five or thirty," he said.

Out of how many students?

"Six thousand, I think."

His freshman dorm room had its own bathroom. "That was gold," Alan said. "I have no idea how it happened. That dorm was probably built in the 1940s. The others were turn of the century, all wood. If you walked around barefoot, you'd get splinters in your feet."

Did he have African American teammates?

"Three, I think, over the course of my four years. None when I was a senior." He had one black teammate as a senior at Central Catholic.

Although an assistant, Hugh Devore recruited Page to Notre Dame. Joe Kuharich was the head coach. Joe certainly looked the part, with a face like a map of Ireland—rugged but jolly. Joe coached college and pro football with decent success (101–108–3 overall). He was colorful, too, and football's resident master of the malaprop until Bill Peterson showed up in Houston, where he fractured the syntax and prepared the way for A.O. "Bum" Phillips, another fellow who talked funny. It must be something in the water down there. Jess Thompson, a celebrated old pro scout from Oklahoma, once described a college prospect's personality as follows: "This boy is friendlier 'n a two-petered pup." Bum Phillips, asked to critique a team his Oilers had beaten soundly, said, "I believe them boys have got their plow stuck in some hard ground." However, just to prove that northerners knew how to turn a phrase, Kuharich, commenting on how a planned game strategy might turn out differently than expected, told a reporter, "Well, that would be a brown horse of an entirely different color."

Joe coached at Notre Dame for four years. As bad luck would have it, the leanest of his coaching years came at South Bend. Kuharich is the only coach in the school's history to have a losing career record—17–23. The Irish went 5–5 in 1962, and Joe resigned the following spring. Devore was named interim coach. His interim effort produced two wins and seven losses, but Irish fans would learn that their bleak years were coming to an end, and promptly.

That was a year, 1963. President Jack Kennedy shot from ambush in Dallas, dealing the nation and the Notre Dame campus a sore blow. On campus, the new library opened, affording Touchdown Jesus his first look down into Notre Dame stadium. He would like what he saw. And Alan Cedric Page of Canton, Ohio, was a freshman.

One football team that had beaten the Irish with embarrassing regularity (four times without a loss in recent years) was Northwestern, that Ivy League–like exception to much of what Big Ten football programs hold dear—get them in school, then wrestle with the classroom challenges.

Northwestern, in 1963, was coached by the young Ara Parseghian, who made his bones at Miami of Ohio, first as an assistant under the legendary Woody Hayes, then as head coach. Following that '63 season, Parseghian was going through a rough patch of his own with Northwestern athletics director Stu Holcomb. Vexed, he called Father Edmund P. Joyce, who was in charge of Notre Dame athletics. Parseghian asked if Devore was still an interim coach, as opposed to the head coach. Joyce said he was. Parseghian promptly applied for and then landed the Irish job.

Above: Alan (top row, third from left) in East Canton Grammar School, and one of the few times he didn't wear a bow tie.

Below left: Alan (left) and older brother Howard Jr. spar for the camera.

Below right: Alan in his band uniform in eighth grade. He played the tuba.

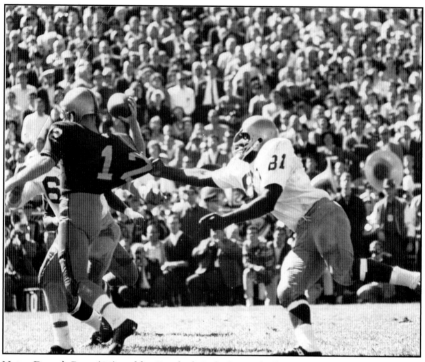

Notre Dame's Page (81) tackles Purdue's Bob Griese (12).

Page began working on that "rumble of thunder" look at Notre Dame.

"Old friends" meet again—Viking Page (88) rushes Miami passer Griese (12).

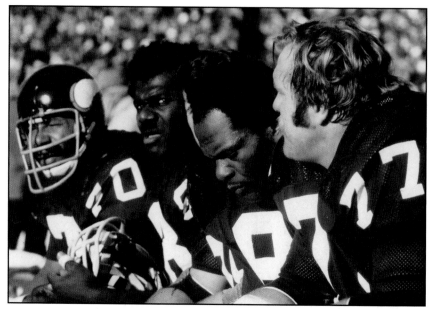

The "Purple People Eaters" of Minnesota: (left to right) Jim Marshall, Alan Page, Carl Eller, and Gary Larsen.

An exception to the rule. Non-drinker Page sips champagne after being named NFL MVP. Coaches Jocko Nelson (left) and Neill Armstrong and teammate Jim Marshall look on.

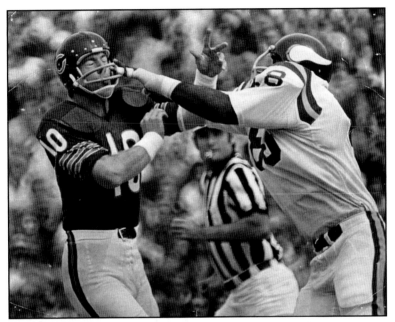

Viking Page (right) greets Bears quarterback Bobby Douglass (10).

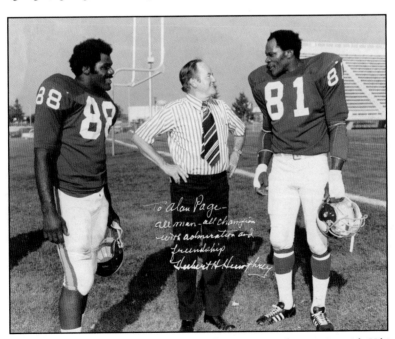

Three "Happy Warriors"—Vice President Hubert H. Humphrey visits with Vikings Page (88) and Carl Eller (81).

Bride Diane serves wedding cake to groom Alan after their whirlwind Las Vegas wedding.

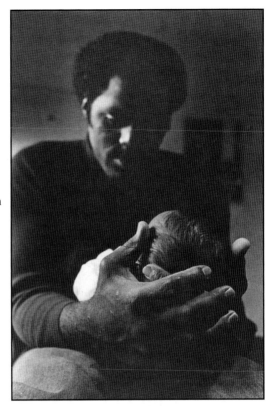

Safe in those big hands...Alan
with son Justin.

Both of them open
wide...Alan feeds Justin.

A "moving" holiday greeting: (from left) Justin, Nina, Alan, Diane, Georgi, and Kamie.

The Pages growing up: (clockwise from left) Nina, Alan, Justin, Diane, Georgi, and Kamie.

French-Armenian, intense, fiery, and charismatic, Ara Raoul Parseghian was the first non–Notre Dame graduate to coach the Irish. To raise eyebrows even higher, he was not Catholic. (Neither was Rockne.) What he was, was a winner—and that made everything good. Parseghian's first Notre Dame team went 9–1–0, narrowly missing a perfect season. In all, he would be at Notre Dame 11 years, posting a 95–17–4 record, the best among modern-era Irish coaches. It was truly the "Era of Ara." The records for Alan Page's three seasons under Parseghian were 9–1–0, 7–2–1, and 9–0–1. That last team, the 1966 squad, won the national championship. Notre Dame was back.

A sweet irony for Parseghian came upon arriving in South Bend, where he found Canton's Alan Page and Lima's Jim Lynch—the two talented Ohioans he had wooed and lost to Notre Dame while still recruiting at Northwestern—waiting for him. "I stumbled onto two great players," Parseghian said.

Ara made a lasting impression on young Page. "I think it was his first meeting with the team," Alan said. "He drew a football field on the blackboard, then told us the game was really pretty simple; it was about position and possession. That was it." Field position dictates what you can do on offense or defense. Ball possession determines how much luck you'll have at getting into the other team's end zone. Fumble; throw an interception; miss a key catch, block, or tackle; or draw a crucial penalty, and you wreck field position and, probably, possession—and you're not apt to win. "I had never stopped to think about a plan for football before," Page said. "I just played. Now, here was a coach, and he was making so much sense with this simple, basic theory. He turned a light on for me."

When Ara heard this, he shrugged. "We taught unity," he said. "Every player had to hold up his end. It was always about the team, not the individual."

When Parseghian talked about Alan Page, he spoke first of Page the person, not the athlete.

"He was one of a very few black students on campus."

Do you think that was a problem for him?

"Absolutely. The Catholic factor, the lack of social involvement with his peers…all of these things created a burden for a young black student.

I'm sure it was tough as hell for him. Katie, my wife, said she remembers Alan as being homesick. She said she heard it from a nun."

"It was tough to be a black student on campus when Alan was here," said Father Edwin "Monk" Molloy, president emeritus of Notre Dame. "South Bend was largely Polish and Hungarian, although there was an African American neighborhood. I think the social attitude reflected the fact that people here didn't know very much about African American culture. Most of them had had very little exposure to African Americans. All of that was part of the discomfort of being a black student at Notre Dame."

When asked for his early impressions of Alan as a player, Parseghian commented on Alan's "tremendous potential. You could see that it was all there—speed, quickness, intelligence, strength, leverage. Alan was very serious, anything but boisterous. I think he enjoyed being part of the team, but he was a determined young man; his focus was on being successful. He was never a problem to coach. He was very serious about everything—academics, football, and his future."

The further Alan goes in life, the less football seems a part of it. Parseghian is not surprised by this. "Alan always had his sights on his whole life, not just football," he said. "He had things in perspective. I think his expectations of himself were always high. So were my expectations for him. I'm proud of him. I'm pleased, but I'm not surprised. The essentials for all that has happened in Alan's life were there when he was 18 or 20 years old, if you cared to look."

Do you have a favorite memory of Alan Page?

"I was in New York when Alan and John Huarte [a Notre Dame Heisman Trophy winner] went into the College Football Hall of Fame. Notre Dame put on a nice dinner for the two men and their families. Being at that dinner, seeing those wonderful families, exactly as you would want them to be—they were All-American families."

Page, Hardy, Rhoads, and Duranko, with Lynch, et al., behind them, made for a stout defensive bunch. Hardy played professionally, but briefly, for San Francisco, Green Bay, and San Diego. He has nine knee surgeries and three back operations to show for his time on the field. He can still play golf, however, and works in an investment management firm in Northern California. Surgical record notwithstanding, Hardy loved the game. He roomed with Page on some road trips and lived in the same dorm with people Alan knew. "We played a lot of cards," Hardy said. "Not Alan, other guys in the hall. But he'd poke his head in to check on us."

Hardy's description of Alan Page?

"Steadfast. He always worked hard. It didn't matter if it was on the field or in class, if we were ahead or behind. I can't speak for the other years, but at the time we were playing, Alan was the best there was."

Kevin Hardy is an All-Riser, himself—he enjoys working with and actively supporting the NFL Alumni's program to help kids in dire need.

Hardy told me to talk to Tom Rhoads. John Heisler, who has followed so ably in Roger Valdiserri's footsteps as Notre Dame's sports information director, had already given me his number. But the best way to come to know Tom Rhoads is not to talk, but to listen.

"I've sold [things] most of my life, everything from caskets to property at Hilton Head," Rhoads said. "We're moving to Raleigh to open a kennel. It's my daughter Laura's idea; she lived in Los Angeles and ran an animal shelter. She left that to come back here. Our other daughter decided she'd come, too. Laura will be in charge. I'll be the chief pooper-scooper. I feel like Colonel Sanders; he started selling chicken when he was in his sixties. I'm in my sixties and just getting started at pooper-scooping.

"I like Alan Page, and I miss him. We lived across the hall from each other for two years; my old room's a girl's john now. Alan and I roomed together on the road some. When we got to our rooms, we went straight to bed; we were always tired. Alan was very quiet. He was friendly, but I didn't see a lot of him away from football. He studied a lot in his room. A bunch of us played bridge. Alan would come in to say hello, but he didn't play. Our other favorite activity was drinking beer, and he didn't drink, so he wasn't part of a lot of really important stuff like playing cards and drinking beer. He had to make do with the boring stuff like going to class. I'm sure it was difficult, being one of a few black students on campus. Notre Dame was working hard then to get more minority students, but there weren't many. I think Alan helped with the minority students who visited campus.

"I have a picture of Alan and me almost blocking a field goal in that 10–10 tie with Michigan State when we were seniors," Rhoads said. "We just missed it." (Over the course of his football career, Page successfully blocked 28 kicks.) "Alan was the only black player on our team in 1966," said Rhoads. "Michigan State had a lot of them, and great players— George Webster, Clint Jones, Bubba Smith, Gene Washington. Duffy Daugherty got a bunch of black players forwarded to him from his coaching friends in the South who couldn't get them into their schools."

Daugherty wasn't the only northern coach to benefit by such racially inspired largesse in the 1960s. Murray Warmath, who coached at Minnesota, had Bobby Bell and Carl Eller virtually dropped into his lap by Jim Tatum, a Warmath pal who coached at North Carolina. "I can't recruit them, and I damned sure don't want them playing against me," was the way Tatum's reasoning went. Eller eventually joined Page as one of the Vikings' famed Purple People Eaters. Bell, who played for the Kansas City Chiefs, may be the best pure athlete ever to play football. He played tackle in college and linebacker as a pro. I believe he could have played any position on the field. He could block, tackle, run, catch, throw, punt, and kick off. He could throw a football 70 yards—accurately—standing flat-footed, and 80 when he took a wind-up. Bell wasn't on the Minnesota track team, but took his shoes off one day at indoor practice and high-jumped more than six feet several times in street clothes. He was a reserve on the varsity basketball team and a fearsome rebounder. He had friends on the Gophers hockey team and sometimes he'd lace 'em up, grab a stick, and skate through practice wearing blue jeans. Like Page, both Bell and Eller are in the collegiate and professional halls of fame, but neither man ever got to play college or pro football in their native North Carolina.

"We had this huge freshman tackle," Notre Damer Rhoads recalled. "He must have stood 6'6″ and weighed 300 pounds. He had to practice against us. He went against Pete [Duranko] first. He blinked, and Pete was past him. Went against A.P. [Page] next. Alan gave him a gash on his chin. I gave him a forearm to the throat. He called his high school coach that night and asked, 'Why did you send me here? These guys are trying to kill me.'

"Our defense would get upset if you made a first down against us, and we'd really get pissed if you scored," said Rhoads. "Our goal was to hold opponents to negative yardage. I looked up the old stats; we held half of our '66 opponents to negative yardage.

"Alan blocked a kick and ran it in for a touchdown. He was so quick, so cool. He did it his way," Rhoads said. "I think football was different for Alan than it was for the rest of us; for us, it was like going to war. We formed a bond, and it lasted. I see pictures of those old guys who fought together so long ago, and I can identify with them. I don't think it was like that for Alan." (Rhoads was right. Page has said that football was a challenge, but rarely personal. Opponents were problems to be solved.)

Rhoads continued, "I'd like to have a conversation with him. I'd ask him what happened. We weren't strangers. For whatever reason, he cut his ties to us as Notre Dame guys. We had 40 guys in Johnstown, Pennsylvania, last spring at a benefit for Duranko, who has Lou Gehrig's Disease. We also had a lot of the guys in South Bend for the unveiling of the statue of Ara. I missed Alan at those things."

Summing up, Rhoads shared a final thought on Alan Page: "He had a plan, and he stuck with it." To Rhoads' question, what "happened" to Page, there is a simple answer: nothing, with respect to football. Life happened; it went on.

Rhoads was drafted by Buffalo and then traded to Cincinnati. "I was at Cincinnati one game, and they suggested retirement as an option," he said. "I was a small defensive end in college. The pros said I was a linebacker, but I wasn't." His pro career was about as brief as that of Kevin Hardy who, like Page, was a first-round draft choice before injuries took away his future.

Page and Duranko were the stars of the defensive line. "Duranko was just an incredible athlete," Rhoads said. "We called him 'The Diesel.' You'd be walking down the sidewalk with him, talking one minute, then you'd look and you'd be talking to his shoes—he'd be walking on his hands." Duranko, from Johnstown, Pennsylvania, played football, ran track, and put the shot at Bishop McCort High School. Duranko outrushed opposing high school teams by himself. When he left Notre Dame, he played for the Denver Broncos.

Rhoads, too, is an All-Riser. "My greatest blessing is family. What have I done? I helped build three churches," he said. "I've been married 39 years and I'm still married, which sure is more of an accomplishment for my wife than it is for me. I've tried a lot of things, made money, and lost money. Our daughter got married in our little church when we were in Ludlow, Kentucky. I redid the church to where it was really beautiful."

Parseghian was the master organizer, strategist, and motivator, but he had help. John Ray coached the Notre Dame defense. Ray was tough and tyrannical. He had a hoarse, harsh voice and could use it to undress you out there on a cold, windswept practice field.

Joe Yonto, Ray's lieutenant, coached the defensive line. Yonto stood 5'7", maybe 5'8", and he was feisty. His first coaching job was at Michigan's Port Huron High School. He was hired to coach football, basketball, baseball, and track, as well as teach a class or two. Ed Senyczko, the sports editor of the local *Times-Herald*, asked Yonto how he intended to coach all of those sports by himself. "I told him I didn't intend to," Yonto said. "Then I congratulated him and told him he was the new backfield coach and the track coach. We never had any bad press.

"I'm short and I had a handicap in connecting with those big defensive linemen at Notre Dame," Yonto said. "I was always looking up at them. But I figured out a way to get their attention. I'd have them run gassers [short sprints], then I'd tell them to take a knee. When they were kneeling down, I was taller than they were! I'd grab their face masks and give them a good shake. 'How's that helmet?' I'd ask. 'That a good fit for you?' Then I'd shake it some more."

I told Yonto that Page had said Coach Ray was the meanest white guy alive. Yonto laughed. "He told me the same thing," he said. "I told Alan not to feel bad, John yells at everybody. He'd ream out some player, then he'd point over at me and tell the guy, 'You listen to that little Italian!'"

Told of Yonto's comments, Justice Page smiled mournfully. "The inference here might be that they used a good cop–bad cop routine." Alan shook his head. "Oh, no." He laughed again. "They were both bad, very bad."

At Notre Dame, Alan Page was far from home, without many friends, struggling under tough coaches. Norm Nicola, another Canton Central Catholic man to play at Notre Dame, shared his perspective on Alan's experience as a player and the challenges of getting from Canton to South Bend. "As a player," he said, "I think of Page's speed and mobility. But I think his biggest attribute was mental. He anticipated so well. It wasn't a hunch; it was the result of paying attention in practice and films and meetings. Alan really worked hard at preparation.

"Neither one of us had much money," Nicola said. "Alan asked me how I got back and forth to Canton. I told him I hitchhiked and showed him my sign; one side said 'Cleveland' for when I was going east, the other said 'Chicago' for going west. So Alan made himself a sign and starting hitching. He got a few rides, but he told me it was tough going. I took his arm and hauled him over in front of the mirror in my room and I said, 'Alan, look at you…who's going to give you a ride?'"

Told of Nicola's story, Page laughed. "I don't remember," he said, "but I sure don't doubt it. Standing out on that cold, windy highway, and when you think back to the times, the chances of a big black guy getting a ride weren't real great. That's like when I tried my hand at selling cars in Minneapolis, new or used. My success was modest." He grinned. "Would you buy a used car from this man?" he asked. "Don't worry, you're not alone; nobody else wanted to, either."

"I'm sure Notre Dame wasn't an easy place for a black kid," Nicola said. "There were very few black students and there was the Catholic thing. Then throw in that people in South Bend weren't especially fond of Notre Dame students; I mean, they looked at us and saw rich kids going to an exclusive school, a school that was out of the reach for most of them. Then, if you were a *black* Notre Dame student…well, I doubt that made things easier."

Page has not attended reunions of Notre Dame players, but he has made numerous trips back to South Bend, received honors, and been a commencement speaker. Nicola expressed understanding for Alan's not being at reunions, and his trait of looking ahead rather than in the rearview mirror. "Take a still picture of society back then," he said. "There was pain that went with being an African American student at a school that was mostly Catholic and practically all white. If you broke your leg, you'd remember how it hurt, and I believe Notre Dame was a challenging time for Alan."

Joe Yonto, Page's position coach at Notre Dame, said Alan was ready to go home at one point. "We had moved him from first team to last in practice to get him fired up," Yonto said. "Somebody told me he'd packed his bags and was about to head for the bus depot." Yonto and defensive coordinator John Ray found Alan and convinced him to stay. "We told him he'd feel better, and the best thing to do was to come back and kick the hell out of somebody. Which he did."

Alan said he doesn't remember wanting to quit or being convinced to stay. Or of kicking the hell out of somebody, for that matter. Perhaps this is simply selective memory.

So, once again: why Notre Dame? "I believe I sold myself on the idea that Notre Dame would be better for me than those other schools," Alan said. "I came to understand that when I left school, the Notre Dame family would present more opportunities. It's a pretty amazing place, when you think about it, the way the alums stay connected. Looking toward the future, I was pretty sure that being a graduate of Notre Dame would be a good thing. It's more than prestige." He laughed. "I lived in Chicago for three years. It seemed like everybody in Chicago was from Notre Dame. Most of them weren't, of course, but that didn't stop them from being total Notre Dame people in their minds and in their hearts. And, let me tell you, those people have some strong feelings.

"Maybe part of it is that Notre Dame spirit—the mystique," Alan said. "But the connection between people goes beyond spirit, so that 20 or 30 or 50 years down the road—when you run into another Notre Dame grad—it's not like running into another..." he smiled and gave me and my Hawkeye roots a little shot, "...University of Iowa grad." Page shrugged. "I can't really say why, but it isn't the same thing. There's something about Notre Dame. There's a magic to it. They look out for each other. I think a young person graduating from Notre Dame today has a better chance of finding a good job than other graduates. Harvard...I know, Harvard is Harvard. You have the institution, the name behind you. But at Notre Dame it's people; real people in real jobs that help you. It's pretty powerful."

What was it like, coming to South Bend and Notre Dame?

"Bad timing in one sense," Alan said. "The Studebaker automobile plant had just closed, which meant a huge hit on the South Bend economy. Here's Notre Dame, all of this wealth, a beautiful campus. My sense was there was very little interaction between the town and the school. It wasn't hostile, but I can't imagine living in a poor place like that, next to all that wealth."

Doesn't sound fair, does it? It wasn't—but unfair treatment was something the Pages had all experienced at times, since way back in Canton. And of course their experiences were not unique—racism was the accepted norm then, in more places than not. For example, one day in 1970 Howard Sr., Roy, and Twila went to a Canton café for breakfast. Twila's order came out wrong, and she sent it back...once. She had asked for firm eggs, and the eggs were runny. The order came out wrong again. The waitress serving them had become agitated, Roy said, and when he attempted to pay the bill, the woman broke into tears. Unknown to the Pages, a call had already been made to the police, saying the Pages were causing an incident. When officers entered the café, the waitress told them the Pages had refused to pay their bill. Twila became angry, and a policeman grabbed her, Roy said. Then Howard Sr. jumped in. "When they took us out of the café," Roy said, "the street was full of police cars." The Pages were arrested and jailed. Long hours later, Howard Sr. was allowed to call the mayor of Canton, who sent a representative to the jail to have them released. Charges had been filed but were eventually dropped.

When Marvel and Alan heard about the incident, they were first incredulous and then furious. Alan didn't go back to Canton until his induction into the Pro Football Hall of Fame, save for one stormy visit when striking NFL players picketed a Hall of Fame game played by "replacement" teams. Alan was a player union leader.

A year later, in 1971, Alan was named Athlete of the Year by Stark County, the seat of Canton and the Hall of Fame. Alan, in a polite letter, refused the honor, saying he felt it would be hypocritical, considering the treatment members of his family and other blacks had received in Canton.

Perhaps this type of treatment is one reason Alan Page has spent most of his professional life standing up to interests that treat others unfairly. Tom Rhoads called Alan Page out, however mildly, for turning away from his old Fighting Irish teammates. From many of those old mates' standpoint, you bond for life. If you ever had to dig in down there on the 2-yard line in the fourth quarter with a hostile road crowd roaring, and you ignored the pain and the exhaustion and the fact that your rear ends were hanging over your own goal line, you summoned some final bit of resolve you didn't even know you had and turned your opponent back, stopped them from scoring…stuffed them! You took their best shot, you turned them back, and you won. The closeness of those moments endures. Rhoads and many of his old mates surely savor those memories. Alan Page does, too; he appreciates them, but he seems to have moved on.

It all comes back to that rearview mirror. It's not that Alan Page doesn't care about the men he played with at Notre Dame. Indeed, I'll bet that any of them who walked back into his life today would be greeted with warmth. Of course, they'd probably have to do the walking. When Notre Dame football ended for Alan, he turned the page (no pun) and moved on. I don't think Notre Dame or the people he knew there and played with are unimportant to him. Similarly, the fact that he was a star and an All-American on a national championship team while he was there is probably less important to Page than most. I'm sure he appreciates the recognition, and what he did has some satisfaction for him, but to dwell on singular honors? You'd probably have to remind him of them.

Bob Belden talked about people who need to hang on to their athletic memories, who take their identity from them, while others live those times, then move on. Page falls into the latter group.

Alan Page is no stranger to Notre Dame. He has been called back twice for the conferral of honorary doctorates. He has helped out whenever he was asked. He has delivered a commencement address and many other speeches. Charlie Weis asked him to speak to his Irish team the night before a game. Page did and got a standing ovation from the players when he finished.

Page's football days didn't end at Notre Dame, but we may take a measure of his feelings for that sport and for his life from a lecture he delivered at Mount Union College. "If I could choose a way to be remembered, it wouldn't be by association with football," Page said. "Football is in the past. It was a good past, but I would want to be remembered with children—my children and other children."

Going back to that rumps-over-your-own-goal-line image, no player fought with more resolve to turn back the foe than Alan Page. Much like today. We, as a nation, have our rumps over the goal line of our future, faced with staving off the advance of danger and inequity (unfairness, if you will), and of not caring. Do we fight against the bleak prospect of many of our young people falling to the side, disenchanted, knowing the world of meaningful jobs and lives has little place for them? Or are we indifferent? Nobody fights with greater resolve to stave off that fearsome enemy, indifference toward future generations, with more resolve than Alan Page.

"Alan is a fire-breathing dragon when it comes to fighting for our children's right to an education," said Mona Harristhal, former director of the Page Education Foundation. Toward that goal and toward his future, graduate Page received a bachelor's degree in political science from Notre Dame in the spring of 1967. And what a future awaited him!

"I grew up in northeast Minneapolis in a neighbor-hood where none of the parents had gone to college. My dad only went through eighth grade. Other than not being a person of color, I think I was kind of in the same boat as a lot of the kids in the Page Education Foundation. I spent my summers in our park when I was growing up; the parks hired college kids to do stuff with us. They would talk about college. That was when I decided I wanted to go to college. I told my parents; I know they didn't believe me. Our coun-selors at Edison [High School] did a great job of get-ting us to graduate, but they didn't think we were going to college. I went. I worked my tail off, but I went and I made it. Summers, I worked two jobs. My parents let me live at home; that was their contribu-tion, and it was huge. I got my degree and a wonder-ful education. I understand about little kids getting the word about college from college students. When I read about PEF, I said, 'That's like my life.'"

—Mona Harristhal,
former PEF administrative director

Siblings and Cousins

"Alan was a quiet little kid who was pretty much of a loner."
—Twila Page, sister

"Alan was stubborn, but I think all of us can be unmovable."
—Howard Page Jr. (Roy), brother

"Alan's good qualities? He's honest and [laughter] stubborn."
—Marvel Page, sister

"I'll be driving a Cadillac."

Howard Page Jr. had offered to pick me up, so I called to say I was waiting curbside at Reagan National airport.

It was a warm summer morning, and it wasn't but a few minutes until Howard Jr., or Roy, as he is known within the family, arrived. He looked comfortable and well settled on the car's rich leather seat. He was wearing a big, flowing leisure shirt and looked like a Page. The Pages don't really look alike, but I see similarities in Twila, Roy, and Alan. Marvel, to my eye, looks a little different from the others. Maybe it's just her very short hair, which is stylish, or her manner, which is crisp.

Roy is tall and heavy-shouldered, every bit the old defensive line-man (Tennessee A&I). Football's gift to Roy was bad knees, but he looked relaxed, with a good, solid smile. He retired from the Air Force after 20 years and now has a business remodeling kitchens and bathrooms. He lives in a pleasant home on a quiet Maryland road with woods and a stream alongside the property. The home shows the fine touches of Roy's late wife, Rosalind. Rosalind Page died recently, while this book was in preparation. Her illness was brief, and her death a blow to all who knew her. I barely knew her, but I miss her. She was a tall, slender, graceful woman. She seemed a little grave at first, but that was nothing permanent. Rosalind grew up in South Carolina near the shore. She dragged a cotton sack in the picking fields as a youngster and dug clams along the beach to put food on the table when money was short. She worked for the Federal Communications Commission at the time of her death. "There were more than 20 people from the FCC at her funeral," Alan Page said. Rosalind Page, another All-Riser.

Marvel—the eldest Page sibling—had told me she'd drive over to Roy's place at some given time we'd arranged in advance. Roy laughed when he heard me say that—a rich, James Earl Jones sort of a laugh. "Well, you better get comfortable, then," he said, "because bein' on time is not one of Mar's specialties."

While we waited, I asked Roy where the athletic ability came from in the family.

"Clayton Umbles, our cousin, was a Little All-America running back at Toledo," he said. Georgiana Page, their mother, was an Umbles. "The Umbles men did some boxing, too," Roy said. Roy said his dad was not athletic. "He liked to go to car shows. He always had a Cadillac, and sometimes a motorcycle," Roy said.

Did Roy see his younger brother coming as a great athlete?

"I can't really say I did. He was lanky, and he had some speed and strength, but I guess it was still just developing in him. I don't think Alan got a lot of attention until his senior year in high school. I was gone by then."

In fact, Roy said neither boy played much football before high school. "We'd box some; we weren't any good, but we liked rough and tumble. We played a little for-fun football with a rolled up newspaper. Football's hard to explain—it was just something you did when you got to high school."

So Roy and I visited. Rosalind served coffee and cake, as I recall, and all three of us wondered where Marvel was. While we waited, Roy talked about the times he and his dad watched Alan play for Notre Dame.

"We watched that big game with Michigan State when he was a senior," he said. That was a huge game, hype-wise, and a controversial game. They were the two top college teams in 1966, and Notre Dame played for a tie at the end. Like a lot of things, it's not as cut-and-dried as it sounds. The game was at Michigan State, and the Irish fell behind 10–0 early. They lost two starters to injury as they rallied back to tie the score 10–10. Late in the game, Notre Dame coach Ara Parseghian elected to settle for the tie, rather than have a turnover result in a loss after the mighty effort his team had made to draw even. (When asked if the players agreed with Ara, Alan said, "I don't know about the others, but I did. There was too much to lose. I think Ara did the right thing." Turned out he did; Notre Dame was named national champion that year.)

"We weren't at the game, we saw it at a theater in Cleveland," said Roy. "But we did drive up to South Bend for other home games." He smiled. "Once Dad picked me up in Cleveland and we set out driving. It was a Friday, the day before the game. There was a big card game that night in Toledo, so my dad stopped. He played all night. We barely made it to South Bend in time for the game, but he cleaned them out."

When Marvel showed up, she brushed off Roy's teasing about being late as easily as she might have brushed crumbs off her lap. We all chatted about weather and traffic and the usual starters. Then Marvel turned her attention to the family. "Alan was different," Marvel said. "He wasn't a rough-house type like a lot of young men, but he was tough-minded. He did his own thing. I don't remember that he looked for a lot of help from the rest of us."

Marvel talked about reading as an influence on the Page children. "We read together on Saturday mornings," she said. "Our parents read to us when we were young, but then we read on our own. My brothers would have to walk a mile on Saturday and Sunday mornings to get the [Cleveland] *Plain-Dealer*. We'd take turns reading it. We all read books;

I think we still do. When I was little, there was this streetlight outside our house. When everybody was sleeping, I'd go sit on the steps and read my book by the light of the streetlight. I'd read real late, then I couldn't get up in the morning. We were all bookworms."

She talked about young Alan. "Twila babied him," Marvel said. "He was her baby brother, and Twi was always the motherly type." (Twila later agreed with this, saying, "I remember the day he came home from the hospital. I loved babies. He'd cry, and I'd say, 'Mommy, baby's crying.' But I wasn't allowed to pick him up.")

What would make Alan angry? "Playing cards with Roy was one thing," Marvel said. Roy gave a brotherly snort. "They'd play after school, and they'd always end up in a big argument. Alan was quiet, but he did have a temper, a very hot temper."

Later I asked Twila what she liked about Alan. "First of all, he's my baby brother," she said. "He is uncompromising. If he can see the mountain, and you can't go over the mountain or around it or through it, he will still find a way to get past that mountain." Twila cares for children in Toledo. She started college at Kent State but didn't finish. "Marvel was an inspiration to me because she went to college," she said. "I wanted to be a doctor, a pediatrician, but I didn't like school. When I went away to Kent State, nobody knew me, [which] was hard for me." Since then, however, Twila has been a working inspiration to a lot of youngsters, her own and others, who have come under her care in Toledo.

Michael Umbles, a cousin, is a near-sib, like his sister Gwen. The Page-Umbles families were essentially a single unit. Georgiana Page was an Umbles. Michael spent a lot of his young life at the Page home in East Canton. He lives in Toledo, Ohio, now and works in sales. "Those guys were so big," Michael said, recalling the Roy and Alan of his youth. "I remember one time my mom cooked a big buffet for the two families. It was Thanksgiving, I believe. Roy and Alan took so much food they both needed two plates to hold everything. Then they ate at the piano, because it was big enough to hold four plates. I found a picture of me with the two of them; I was like their little mascot, although they liked to terrorize me."

Michael told me what he liked about his cousin. "Dignity is what I think of," he said. "Alan has carried himself with dignity through a time when athletes and other public figures can easily get swayed into bad situations." He was also focused on family. "In 1995 Alan visited Notre Dame to be part of a law review," Michael said. "He invited me and my son to go there for the weekend and see the football game. I wanted to impress my son, to show him some of the success that surrounded Alan. Alan had box seats—the president of the university gave them to him. I knew Alan wasn't going to the game, but he wanted my son to see what it was like there on game day. I had never sat in seats like that before, and my son was thrilled. Alan? He was on his way home."

Gwen Umbles Singleterry, Michael Umbles' older sister, was with her cousins the Page kids a lot, especially after their mother died. "They called me Auntie," she said. Gwen's brother Clayton was another source of strength for the Page children after their mother died. "[Gwen] was like our mentor," Marvel said.

Gwen has kept tabs on the Page kids. I spoke with her later, in her kitchen back in Canton. "What do I admire about Alan? He's steady. He always had that serious side to him also, but I look at him as a gentle giant." She smiled, then continued. "He'd sit right here at this table. One time, he brought Bobby Bryant and Bob Lurtsema and Charlie West [Vikings teammates]. I cooked pork chops, and they ate a bunch of them." She smiled. "We don't get to see him too often now—he has so many commitments. But every once in a while he'll call."

The Vikings played in four Super Bowls during Alan Page's tenure—and lost all of them. "Those Super Bowls were like family reunions," Gwen said. "We didn't win, but we sure had a lot of fun." (Twila later commented, laughing, that "Alan sometimes has selective memory, like those Super Bowls. He hardly remembers them—but we do.")

Gwen told about attending a Vikings game in Detroit. "Some of us drove over, and we didn't get there until pretty late at night," she said. "The hotel wasn't going to give us any rooms, although Alan had reserved some for us. The front desk finally called Coach Grant, because they couldn't put calls through to the players' rooms that late.

Coach Grant came down and said we were to have the rooms. He was very nice about it, seeing as how we woke him up."

Then Gwen spoke of Alan's longstanding devotion to young people, and to helping them earn the opportunity to help themselves. "I'm sure that in his heart Alan feels for these kids. He will do whatever he can to encourage them. There are so many kids now who need a push, need someone behind them to let them know there are people who care about them. It's these kids who make him the happiest. Who would have thought that his spot in life would have made him be so caring of others, and that other people would see the gentleness in him?"

Gwen's Canton neighborhood is not an easy place, but it has a number of the residents like Gwen who work at keeping themselves and their places up. They're mostly the older ones, now. It's probably harder for the younger residents, who see a longer road, and perhaps less hope, ahead. There's still spirit in the neighborhood, but spirit takes effort, and effort isn't easy when the world, rolling past on the nearby expressway, is so far away.

"We had three young white teachers who lived in the neighborhood," Gwen recalled. "We found out the activities they had been putting on for the kids after school was with money out of their own pockets. We neighbors got up some funds that let them do things for the kids without it being on their money. Those teachers left three years ago, and we haven't been able to get the people to come back together on activities at the school. But we do keep up our neighborhood garden." The garden is just across the street from Gwen's house, and it was a brave patch of reds and pinks. "The garden's sort of a symbol, it says we do have a neighborhood and we're proud of it."

When I first met Alan some 40 years ago, he was far less chatty than he is today. But he's still pretty economical with his words. His siblings were polite and pleasant, but, like their brother, none of them burdened me with conversation beyond what I might have asked. Roy Boy can fold his large hands across his belly in comfortable silence, much like his brother. Their exposure to me was brief, and they would not have met with me at all but for the email each received from Alan that went as follows: "Bill McGrane and I are working on a project, and your cooperation is appreciated." That's Page-speak. I would love to be a fly on the wall when the four of them get together and laugh and carry on as I am sure they can. Then I'd have some real Page-speak, as opposed to the carefully measured variety.

"My father was a member of the group President Truman formed to establish a national health care program. That was 60 years ago. I am working with AARP to realize that goal. It is a pledge I made to myself and to my dad. That's time enough, 60 years—let's get going."

—Hubert H. "Skip" Humphrey III, friend

Graduate School

"I believe Alan played on the right defensive side, which would have put him up against Bob Skoronski, our left tackle. Bob was such a smart guy...he just never made mistakes. He's made it big in business, which is no surprise to me. Bart [Starr, Packers quarterback] used to say Bob was the most underrated guy on our team. Forrest Gregg played right tackle; he got a lot of recognition and earned it, but Skoronski was one hell of a player." —Paul Hornung, Green Bay Packers running back

Forty years ago and more, football's midsummer night's dream was a game played at gloomy old Soldier Field in Chicago between the reigning champion pro team and a team of graduating college seniors called the All-Stars. The game was the brainchild of Arch Ward, sports editor of the *Chicago Tribune*. The game prospered. In its early years, it was a boon to the pros, who lagged far behind the college game in public acceptance. Lagged, that is, until Pete Rozelle replaced Bert Bell as commissioner of the National Football League. Bert was old-school. Pete was about as old-school as the Gucci loafers he favored for casual outings.

While the pro game rocketed in popularity and television exposure, Rozelle and the owners (particularly the old-liners like Halas in Chicago, the Rooneys in Pittsburgh, Billy Bidwill in St. Louis, and Well Mara of the New York Giants) maintained their loyalty to Ward's clambake out in Chicago. A lot of the pro teams didn't like having to play in the game; it made a longer preseason and thus more exposure to injury, there were ticket-pricing issues, and so on. But they played. It is safe to assume that the late Vince Lombardi may have done some grumbling when his Green Bay Packers had to break their routine and bus down to Chicago's lakefront to take on the 1967 College All-Stars.

Alan Page, All-American, late of Notre Dame, was an All-Star defensive starter. Alan sighs a lot when you remind him of that game. Sighs, when he isn't chuckling.

"[When] you're a young guy," he said, "you make it in college by running over people, by outmuscling them, or by running around them every once in a while. I had quickness, I was pretty strong, and I wasn't ever too intimidated by reputations." He groaned gently. "But, oh my. I sure got a lesson that night. You talk about frustrating."

Alan would have been up against Bob Skoronski and sometimes Forrest Gregg, the Packers' offensive tackles. Page isn't sure which one. "I don't think it mattered," he said. "The results would have been the same, whichever one it was."

He laughed. "So I started out by trying to run over my man. Then I tried to run around him. He didn't care; he just wanted to impede my progress. Want to run over them? That was fine, because when you're trying to run over them the play's already gone downfield. They were masters at getting in the way."

They weren't especially big hitters. "They'd hit you, but not all that hard." Page sighed. "They just kept getting in the way. Every blessed play, one of them would be in my path to the ball. It was so effective, and it was really a good lesson to learn early on. It wasn't all about muscle, wanting to overpower some guy. It took me a long time to figure what it was about, but it didn't take long at all to figure out what it wasn't about," he said. "Here were all these young college players, grunting and groaning and sweating. And then you had the Packers. It was like they were saying to us, 'When you're done, when you've had enough, then we'll go home.'"

"At the end of the evening," Page said, "I'm sure those men went away confident that their livelihoods were secure. And all because of that one little rule: they stayed between me and the ball."

In the years ahead, Gregg, Skoronski, and a lot of other offensive tackles would find the rule harder and harder to enforce against Alan Page until, finally, they couldn't enforce it at all.

The morning after the 1967 All-Star Game, sleepy and stiff, Alan was picked up at the Orrington Hotel in Evanston, Illinois, and put on a flight to Minneapolis. Then he was put into a waiting car and driven to Mankato, a quiet little college town about 85 miles southwest of the Twin Cities. His future was there, awaiting him—and he hadn't even had breakfast.

"I operate Mixed Blood, a theater for the performing arts in Minneapolis. We opened 32 years ago. Alan was with the law firm then. He helped with fundraising by sending letters to donors. He told me I could have some of his stuff from their basement for an auction to help the theater. I went there. It's a great home, filled with African American art. Down in the basement, he's got all these football awards and treasures piled up and kind of forgotten. We named our auditorium for him, the Alan Page Auditorium. I get asked if it's because he made some big donation. I kind of resent hearing that; I felt the honor was ours, not Alan's. Alan stands for social justice, which is at the core of our beliefs. I am on the state's board for racial fairness in the court system. Our charge is to guard against or identify racial disparity. I like to think our lives run kind of parallel; my vehicle is theater, and Alan's is the court. We both want to make the world a place that is fair for all."

—Jack Reuler, friend

Mankato

"Training camp was intense. So much of it was football and discipline that the players would come up with diversions for their free time. One year, the offensive players made a rocket ship out of tape cans. Clint Jones was the project engineer. 'Astro-Frog' rode the rocket. The rocket went as high as the third floor of Gage Hall, but then it flamed out, turned over, and crashed on the parking lot. [Jim] Vellone gave Astro-Frog mouth-to-mouth, but to no avail." —Ralph Reeve, all-pro beat-man, St. Paul Pioneer Press & Dispatch

It is farming country, attractive and rolling. You see a lot of German and Scandinavian names on the mailboxes. Take Highway 169 southwest from Minneapolis, past Le Sueur, where they used to have "Korn on the Kerb" weekend and still may. The Jolly Green Giant stands over Le Sueur, smiling down on his Green Valley. St. Peter is the biggest town along your route, home of Gustavus Adolphus College and decades of law officers who have pursued speeding Minnesota Vikings. South and west of St. Peter is New Ulm, the home of Sauerkraut Days. Ten miles south of St. Peter, you leave the divided highway at Mankato, a pleasant town nestled alongside the Minnesota River.

Take a few turns and follow—back in the '60s, anyway—the old, hump-backed red brick streets attended by tall, stately oaks and maples. Then go up the hill with its curve to spill out onto what was then a largely bald plateau, the site of the Mankato State University campus, its dorms and athletic facilities. The Minnesota Vikings have held summer training camp there since 1966.

It has been a very long time since Alan Page and I spent summers in Mankato, and I am sure that much has changed. For instance, I doubt that the Century Club is still there, down by the river, a lively spot where Gummy Carr, the defensive backfield coach, performed outrageous improv dances. It was also at the Century Club where the late Norm Van Brocklin, the Vikings' first head coach, gallantly asked an outspoken feminist who was giving him a definite earful if she would mind removing her ample bosoms from his change, which was on the bar, so that he might go back up the hill to camp and his dorm room. I doubt Alan ever saw the inside of the Century Club.

Alan Page arrived in Mankato in early August of 1967, tired, rumpled, and looking out of sorts. He remembers that he was hungry, too. He went through the noon chow line silently, turning heads as he did, then was joined at a table by Bob Hollway, the defensive line coach. Bob was a Michigan man, tall and handsome, as you would expect a Michigan man to be—he even had perfect Stewart Granger flashes of white in his dark sideburns. He went over some basic defensive sets and charges with Alan after lunch, and then told him he would be starting in that night's intrasquad scrimmage. Hollway didn't tell Alan he would be playing the entire scrimmage since several veteran defensive linemen were feeling puny, as veteran defensive linemen will do in training camp.

Playing a football game can leave a defensive lineman feeling, the next day, like he's been thrown off the back of a speeding truck—and that's without getting up early, skipping breakfast for a flight, and a car ride to some place he'd never heard of. Then, to learn that he would play a game-length scrimmage that same night with and against professionals he didn't know in a system he was unfamiliar with…well, it could make a man look peevish.

Alan Page was a member of a turn-around draft for the Vikings. He was that draft's linchpin, in fact. Between their first season in 1961 and 1966, the Vikings had caromed up and down the NFL development scale—amazing one Sunday, abysmal the next. But the '67 draft, orchestrated by Jim Finks, would begin to change things. Finks was the team's canny general manager, but he spent that course-changing draft in a suburban Minneapolis hospital, making a grouchy recovery from gall bladder surgery. (Finks pulled off another huge draft score in 1975—featuring Walter Payton—while running the Chicago Bears. He toughed out two draft days that year, swabbing his sore teeth with a numbing solution. Once the draft was over, Jim underwent four root-canal procedures. Pain seemed to bring out the best in him.)

The Vikings had three first-round draft choices in 1967. First came Clint Jones, the aforementioned Astro-Frog project engineer and a running back from Michigan State. Finks got Jones by honoring quarterback Fran Tarkenton's request for a trade, sending the Scrambler to the New York Giants. Over time, the Tarkenton trade would provide four starters—Jones, receiver Bob Grim, Hall of Fame tackle Ron Yary, and All-Pro guard Ed White. Finks then selected Gene Washington, an antelope-gaited receiver, also from Michigan State, on the Vikings' first-round pick. With just a minute or two remaining before the draft's 15th selection, Finks obtained the choice by trading veterans Tommy Mason and Hal Bedsole to the Los Angeles Rams. He drafted Alan Page.

Scout Frank Gilliam had described Page as "intelligent, consistent, gets the most out of his initial drive...great at slipping blocks...if he goes down, he is up again in the blink of an eye."

The '67 draft also included defensive back Bobby Bryant, who would become a lifelong friend of Alan Page's. Tight end John Beasley was drafted, too. Beasley played well enough for a couple of years, but then got the sobering call to go see Coach Grant in his office. "I walked in, and he was sitting at his desk, holding a shotgun," Beasley said. "I didn't know if he was going to cut me or shoot me." Grant just cut him; he was cleaning the gun to go duck hunting.

There was a final rookie in the class of '67: Grant himself. The new coach would do much of that turning around.

They played the intrasquad game the night of Page's arrival in Mankato, and a stadium full of southern Minnesotans applauded politely when the announcer introduced rookie Alan Page. "I played the whole game," Alan said. "I don't remember a lot about it. I was kind of in a trance." It was a trance Page would perfect over the years when it came to training camp. "I mean nothing against Mankato and the people there," he said. "I've been back there a number of times since I played, and I've enjoyed the people and my time there. I just hated training camp." Advised of Page's comment many years later, Grant laughed and said, "I hated it, too, but it was part of the package."

"It's one thing when you're first there," Alan said. "You're 22 or 23 years old, and everything is new. It's another when you're 30 and you have a family. It was especially hard in our time—no cell phones, no computers. We didn't have phones in our dorm rooms; we had to use the pay phones in the lobby. If you wanted to call home, you got in line in the lobby. We were told when to go to bed and when to get up, what to eat and when to eat it, when to meet, when to practice, when we had time off."

The camp regimen was difficult enough for the stoic rookie from Ohio, but then tradition got in the way. Tradition dictated that the rookies go out with the vets to a selected field one night and drink beer until they got sick. It isn't real sophisticated; there's keg beer, pitchers to drink from, and garbage cans to throw up in. Jim Marshall, the leader of the Vikings' players, noticed that the rookie Page wasn't drinking and that the other vets were beginning to take notice. Marshall took Page aside.

"Drink some beer," Captain Jim told him.

"I don't drink," Page said.

"Just drink one pitcher."

"No."

"Just drink a little, that's all you have to do. One drink and it's over."

"I don't drink."

"You won't drink any beer? All the other rooks are doing it."

"No, I won't."

Marshall walked away, shaking his head. But he wasn't gone long; he returned with a pitcher of Coke.

Page tasted it, and then shook his head.

"You don't drink Coke, either?" Marshall demanded.

"I don't drink warm pop," Page said.

"At that point," Marshall recalled some 40 years later, "I told him he'd better get the hell out of there."

"I did," Page recalled. "The next morning, I was expecting to get a lot of grief." Nothing like Page's refusal to drink had ever happened. "I went to the locker room the next morning expecting the worst," Alan said, "but nobody mentioned it." Page went 11 times to Mankato for summer training camp. Actually, he should have gone 12, but Grant excused him from the Mankato portion of preseason one year when he was in law school. That special treatment (and by Grant's standards, it was extremely special) didn't sweeten Alan's memories of training camp. "We made the best of what was really an awful situation," he said. "We made fun of being there; we built rockets, and we had a bocce ball tournament every year." (Grant and Hall of Fame safety Paul Krause were annual winners.)

The year Page missed camp, Grant greeted him with special treatment when practice resumed at Midway Stadium in St. Paul, the club's regular-season practice site. "I knew Alan would be in great shape—he always was," Grant said. "But I also knew the players would be jealous of him for getting to skip camp while they were sweating it out in Mankato. I used to warm the players up with up-downs: a player runs in place, I blow my whistle, he flops on his belly, then bounces back up and starts running again. Do a few of those, and you're nice and loose. Well, when Alan came back for his first practice, I called him out for his own special up-downs.

"I don't care how well-conditioned the athlete is," Grant said. "He can't win. I can blow my whistle longer than he can keep getting up. But I'll say this: I never saw a player do up-downs like Alan did that day. He just flew. The energy he put into them, his attitude…they were just furious. Players were razzing him when he started, but not for long. They saw how hard he was working. Finally, Alan got to where he couldn't get up; he didn't have anything left. The players were all around him then, patting him on the back, praising his effort."

Page roomed with Bryant, a wiry white cornerback from South Carolina. "We met at the East-West game," Bobby said. "We just hit it off. When we got to Mankato, it just seemed to follow that we'd be roomies."

In those years when he was at training camp, Alan, like his teammates, was ready to haul back to the Twin Cities once camp ended. It was almost a parade, leaving Mankato—a parade accompanied by another ritual: police cars along the way, patrolmen with ticket books at the ready. "I think they got word the minute we left camp," Page said. Marshall would lead, with players' cars strung out behind him. When they hit the divided highway, they lined up in the pass lane. "One year," Alan said, "I was behind Jim in my Dodge van; we were probably going 80. We got on the other side of St. Peter, and a trooper on the southbound side of the divided highway spotted us. It wasn't too hard—there must have been 15 or 20 of us. I guess it took him a while to turn around. I had slowed down some by then, and the others kept going, so he got to me first. He pulled me over and asked me if I knew how fast I was going. I told him I was just keeping up with traffic. He obviously hadn't clocked us. He gave me a lecture and let me go."

Alan recalled another time and another training camp road. "I was going back to camp on a Sunday night," he said. "I had this wonderful little Ferrari; it was silver and black, just a sweet car. I took the back road out of St. Peter because I wanted to see what it could do. I got up to 60 in first gear. I went over a hill at 8,000 rpm. I shifted around a curve, and here was a trooper coming from the other direction. I was probably going 70 when I saw him and I was gearing down by then. If he had been 30 seconds farther down the road, he would have had me at 95 or 100 miles an hour. No warning that time—just a ticket."

In his chambers, judicial robes hanging in the corner, Justice Page smiled. "I'd love to drive a track fast once," he said, "but my reflexes aren't what they used to be." Like Indianapolis? He beamed. "That would be awesome," he said.

Training camp '67, Page's first as a pro, ended with many of the Vikings wary of, or at least curious about, their new coach and his new ways. The veterans had played for Grant's predecessor, "Dutch" Van Brocklin, who smoked Camels, drank beer, and frequently addressed front-office types, game officials, newsmen, and players in a parlance that could have removed paint from lawn furniture. Grant didn't swear, didn't smoke, and didn't raise his voice. He preferred ice cream to alcohol—he didn't even drink coffee, for God's sake, and the NFL *runs* on coffee!

After the last practice before the first preseason game, Grant called the players together and explained that they were going to conduct national anthem practice. A few snorts and whistles could be heard from the ranks. Bud ignored them. He explained, patiently, that showing respect for the flag and the anthem was not only a duty, but a privilege, as well. He then called defensive end Carl Eller out of ranks. "Moose" Eller was 6'6", lanky, and amiable—as defensive ends go. He smiled and stepped forward. Grant nodded his approval. "Moose," Grant said, "is going to show us how to stand during the playing of the national anthem."

Years later Eller explained—with a distinct note of pride still evident in his voice—"Bud chose me to demonstrate because he knew I was in the National Guard, and I'd had some training." Before long, demonstrator Eller was standing with his heels together, back straight, head up, eyes to the front, helmet held facing up and forward on his left forearm, the fingers of his right hand touching the seam of his pants. He stood rock solid as a portable phonograph provided a faint and tinny version of the anthem.

They practiced for almost an hour that first day. Over time, and with improvement, the Vikings' pregame attention to the playing of the national anthem became the talk of the league. Other teams called it the "Grant Formation" and complained because it made their players and coaches look bad. The usual NFL anthem formation involved gum chewing, scratching, working out neck kinks, and checking the stands for pretty girls. Grant changed that. Other teams eventually followed suit, but none looked as good as the Vikings. Minnesota played the Eagles at Tulsa in their first preseason outing. I don't remember who won, but they looked good, standing at attention for the anthem. It seems to me that there is less attention paid the anthem on the sideline these days despite the chancy times. Of course, Grant's gone.

It may be my imagination, but I suspect Alan Page would have handled introducing the anthem formation to the team in the same way Bud Grant did—quietly, patiently, and thoroughly. Time would tell that they had a lot of shared traits.

My friend Mike B. knows a young woman who lost her driver's license, so he drove her to work every morning for more than a year. They're just friends, but if it weren't for Mike, she probably would have lost her job. Several evenings a week, Mike takes dinner to Scotty, who's a shut-in. He takes Scotty to the doctor and looks after, orders, and picks up Scotty's meds, which are several, and unscrews the paperwork when Scotty screws it up, which is often. Mike doesn't need "attaboys," and he'll probably skin me alive when he sees I've mentioned him here.

Diane

"Strong, savvy, independent, lively, determined, very progressive. Great mom." —Kamie Page Friesen, daughter

While Alan Page was becoming a football star at Central Catholic High School in Canton—his best efforts to remain anonymous notwithstanding—Diane Sims was doing everything she could to avoid remaining anonymous at Robbinsdale High School in north suburban Minneapolis.

"I was the total leader of the school," Diane said. Now, if you or I said that, it would come off sounding hokey. But not Diane. I have no doubt she was the leader, just as I have no doubt she would not have settled for less than leading. She's a lady you not only can enjoy, but also feel obliged to respect.

"I was the first girl chosen to be president of the student council," she said. "I was co-editor of the school newspaper. I organized students to canvass the community to get people to vote for a new stadium for our high school. We went door to door. It passed; we got the stadium. The high school was torn down years ago, and my stadium got torn down, too. That was probably my first political adventure. I loved Robbinsdale because I was so involved."

Diane's parents, Irving and Bernice Sims, spent most of their lives in the same rambler. Irving expanded by adding bedrooms as the kids came along. Irving and Bernice are in their nineties now. He was a woodworker, and a fine one; she was a homemaker. Bernice still drives. Irving has Parkinson's but still likes to tinker with vintage cars. Diane has two sisters, Patty and Karen, and a brother, Jerry.

"I was a leader and organizer in high school," Diane said. "When I got to the University of Minnesota, I discovered men. I was in a sorority and I loved the social life, the parties." Her parents paid the tuition and her Pi Phi house bill, but spending money was up to Diane, so summers she worked at Pillsbury's corporate headquarters, pushing the taste-test cart around. She majored in political science with a sociology minor. Things kept cooking at Pillsbury. Diane was promoted off the taste-test cart, and several jobs later, while still at the university, she got a real job at Pillsbury, doing research as a project administrator. "I've worked in market research ever since," she said.

She reports never having a steady boyfriend, but adds, "I dated a lot. I don't know what it was, but I was never in a relationship where someone said, 'Let's think about marriage.' I was independent. Maybe I was independent enough that I scared off some guys. Besides, I had money, I had a job, I had my nice little sports car, and I lived in a great apartment tower downtown. I wasn't in any hurry to get married."

Pro football players had off-season jobs in those days because they didn't make anywhere near what today's players make. Jim Finks, then the Vikings' general manager and himself a prudent fellow, reminded every player who would listen that football was a means to an end, not the end. This was solid advice, although it wasn't always heeded. Of course, it fit nicely with Finks' knack for keeping the Vikings' salary structure lean.

Alan Page, true to Finks' counsel, was trying his hand in a variety of areas besides football. The first thing Alan did was decide to go to law school. He had wanted to be a lawyer, although his initial attraction for the field seemed a bit flimsy. "I probably watched too many *Perry Mason* shows," he said. "It seemed like a good way to have a nice life without working too hard." Alan entered law school—night school. He needed just one week to learn that he was in hopelessly over his head. It took three more weeks for him to get out of law school and to try something else. After an unprofitable stint as a car salesman, he became an entrepreneur, launching Alan Page Enterprises, a vending-machine company. Alan got his machines into office buildings and sold snacks purchased through a subsidiary of General Mills in Minneapolis.

As noted earlier, a business meeting at General Mills brought Alan in chance contact with the woman who would eventually become his wife of these last 37 years. Memories are fuzzy, but Diane thinks they met in 1971.

"I was interested in meeting him, so my boss and I walked over and said hello," Diane recalled. "I remember I told him I volunteered one night a week at the Boys Club on Blaisdell Avenue. I said that if he could go there some night and hang out with the kids, they would freak out, which was the truth. He said he might be interested in doing that. I gave him my card, or he gave me his, I'm not sure which. Somebody called somebody, and he did come to the club. Of course, everything went wrong. I just wanted him to hang out with the kids and shoot baskets or play pool, but the man who ran the club saw it as a great opportunity for him to spend time with Alan and take him on a grand tour. It wasn't at all what I wanted, and I'm sure it wasn't what Alan was expecting. Actually, it was a disaster, except that we saw each other."

No whirlwind courtship, this; scarcely enough of a breeze, in fact, to stir the leaves on the trees.

"It was weeks before he called and invited me to lunch," Diane said. "Then more weeks would go by, and then we'd have lunch again. I think we met for lunch three or four times, and it was three or four weeks between lunches. But then he started dropping by my office. We'd just chat. I don't know what we talked about—probably politics, because we both were into politics. But we talked about ourselves, too. What we did was get to know each other. I don't know how long that went on, but one day when Alan stopped by to visit, he asked if I liked to dance. I love to dance, and I told him so. We went to a place called Louie's—it was the hot spot at that time. We'd been talking and becoming friends, but now he was asking me out on a date; that was taking things to a different level."

It was a different pain level, too. What Diane didn't know on their date was that earlier in the day, while Alan was moving a vending machine, a pulley slipped and the machine fell on his big toe. Being Alan—some family members call him "Mr. Taciturn"—he didn't say anything about it. (Stoicism in the face of pain is not unique to Alan

Page; it's part of the pro football package, to varying degrees. Years later, while playing for the Chicago Bears, Alan had hemorrhoid surgery on a Friday before a Sunday game at Oakland. He arranged for the procedure himself, flew to Oakland with the team, played the game, and then flew home. He didn't mention anything to Fred Caito, the team trainer, until after the game.)

Back to the date: Alan's toe was swollen and inflamed, even beyond NFL discomfort. "He should have told me about it, but he wasn't going to cancel for anything," Diane said. "I think we danced one or two dances, and I could see he was in agony. He reluctantly told me what had happened. I told him we were leaving so he could get off his feet. We laughed about that in later years, but it wasn't funny that night."

When asked if she had been nervous about dating a black man, Diane answered, "I wasn't. I really liked him. But I think I was pretty naïve. It was fine for me, but I'm not sure the community was ready for it. I lived at the Towers apartment building in downtown Minneapolis. At that time, it was *the* place to live. I had a good job, and all the stuff that went with it. Then, here comes Alan Page into my life, driving a racecar. He had a big purple Dodge with "Freedom" written on it in gold letters. That was the car he came to pick me up in. It was the car he drove in races, too. So here he comes, down to the Towers in this purple car that no one could miss, this big guy in a leisure suit that was either lime green or purple, with a shoulder bag and a big Afro. I'm sure my neighbors were hanging out the windows." You can bet on it. This was back before Minneapolis had become so avant-garde, a time when Garrison Keillor was still in Lake Wobegon. Why show up wearing a purple or lime green leisure suit in a purple car with "Freedom" written on it in gold lettering? Shock value? Not likely. More like Alan Page value. Probably nothing more than who he was and where he was, just like he's who he is and where he is today. That kind of directness is still unsettling to some, even without the leisure suit. Alan will point out, quietly, that he can't control to what degree others are comfortable with him. He hopes they can be who they are, as long as he can be who he is. And be assured that he will be.

"No one ever said it to me, but I know some people thought my dating Alan was scandalous," Diane said. "But when you're falling in love, you know, you don't notice stuff like that."

Right from the start, back to those infrequent drop-by chats in Diane's office, they just seemed to click. There were bumps—some of them spectacular—but they still clicked.

We were sitting on the spring porch of their home on Knox Avenue, just south of downtown Minneapolis. She had a bandage on one foot to accommodate a running injury. She is still dark-haired with lively eyes and what used to be called a "peaches and cream" complexion. Diane smiled, enjoying the memories.

"I think when we first met, we didn't have a lot of shared interests, but we also didn't have any trouble talking for two hours about a little bit of everything. We were very comfortable with each other right away. We bonded, and then we just kind of evolved together," Diane said. "I think we were lucky because in any relationship one person can take a left turn and, for whatever reason, become interested in something else, and the other partner doesn't want to go there. The relationship breaks down just because somebody goes left and the other person doesn't. When one of us takes a left turn, the other one does, too."

"We didn't have any trouble communicating," she said, and then she laughed. "We definitely got along, most of the time, anyway, which is interesting because we probably don't seem compatible on the surface. Alan's more of an introvert, and I'm more of an extrovert. I used to feel like I intimidated guys before I met Alan because I was so independent. But I don't think he was ever intimidated by me," Diane said. "Alan is never about trying to change you. He sees your strengths and your weaknesses, but he's not about trying to change you. That is so huge in a relationship. If I had married someone who saw my strengths and my warts and decided he was going to take away my warts and change me, it would never have lasted. I'm me—warts, too! I don't want to be changed. I think that would create so much tension in a relationship."

Diane added, "I think Alan and I were serious from the start." But the pace was a little too measured for her. "It was two years until we got married," she said. "It seemed like an eternity to me because I was in love with Alan and I wanted to be married to him. I had never had a serious relationship; I'd never been in love." She shook her head. "I broke up with him once because our relationship had dragged on so long. I didn't trust that he wanted to get married. He said he loved me, and that we would be together forever, but why did we really need to get married?"

She continued, "I didn't want to hear that. This is my true love. I'm 29 years old, for God's sake, which was ancient for a woman back then. I've got this wonderful guy, we're totally compatible, but it seemed like we were stuck. We had some hassles in those years. I sort of broke up with him. I left on vacation to Acapulco by myself to get over Alan. I was miserable. He was back in Minneapolis and he was miserable, too. When I got home and walked into my apartment, the phone was ringing. He'd been calling every day. I went to answer the phone and must have tripped on the cord, because we got a disconnect. Alan was devastated. He thought, after all that time, I finally answered his call and then hung up on him."

Diane and Alan took a trip to Europe in the spring of 1973. Europe was nice, but the return flight was a calamity. "I broke down on the flight home," she said. "I cried…he was never going to marry me, blah, blah, blah. We'd had this wonderful trip, but now we were flying back to the same old deal. It was an eight-hour flight. Here's Alan…I'm in tears and there's no place for him to go. So he writes this beautiful proposal letter. I wish I knew what happened to it. Poor Alan, he came up to me after I'd read the letter, and I said, 'I don't believe you!' Then I started to cry all over again. He was miserable—he has this sobbing woman on this long flight, he proposes to her, and she doesn't believe him."

The trip, the tears, the proposal letter, the rejection, and then more tears—it all added up to Alan telling Diane that they would be married during a June trip to Las Vegas for a NFL Players Association convention.

Diane still had her doubts. Once they were in Las Vegas, she asked Alan about his pledge to get married before they left the city. She told him they should get the license. Alan mildly tried to procrastinate, which was not what the lady wanted to hear. "I put my foot down,"

Diane said. "We got the license, but I still didn't know when we were going to be married."

The last night of the convention, at a cocktail party, Ed Garvey, director of the Players Association, asked Alan if he and Diane had plans for dinner. Alan said they couldn't go. Garvey asked why. Alan said because they were going to get married. "Within minutes, word spread around that cocktail party," Diane said. "I think some of the guys kind of rolled their eyes and smiled and said, 'How long do you think this is going to last?' I'm sure some of them probably thought the whole thing was kind of a novelty."

One of the player reps in attendance, Dallas guard John Wilbur, looked back on the Pages' thrown-together wedding. "I got married in church in a big ceremony," he said. "Diane and Alan got married in a Las Vegas wedding chapel. They're still married, but I'm not; I guess there's something to say for those Vegas weddings."

Ed and Betty Garvey didn't give the groom a chance to waver. While Diane called the Chapel of the Bells, Garvey called down to the front desk and ordered a suite for the reception, a wedding cake, and punch. Diane had her wedding dress with her, just in case: a pink, floor-length dress. The groom wore a white tux. Players began piling into cabs to head for the ceremony. The bride's flowers came from a vending machine at the chapel. Betty Garvey got rice from the hotel kitchen. The Garveys served as best man and maid of honor.

"I loved our wedding," Diane said. "Those were our friends—the players from the convention who were close to Alan, and the Garveys. We lived in different parts of the country, but when we got together, there was real bonding."

At first, the marriage was hard for Diane's parents to accept. "They grew up in a time when mixed-race marriages just weren't something that they knew," Diane said. "I think my folks were fearful for us. [My parents and I] were apart for several years. My brother and my sisters were great, and I think they worked behind the scenes with my parents to eventually get all of us together. It was so crazy—here's Alan, the greatest guy in the world. I think it was just the times. Now my folks love Alan."

How did it go when Diane met Alan's family? "It went really well. Maybe not as well as if his mother had still been living, but well. Alan's dad was very accepting of me. He was nice, a good-looking guy. When he was in his seventies, he was dating young women. He loved women, and he was very proud of his kids." She smiled and cringed a little, remembering one visit. "I went to a family reunion. Everyone was great, we were getting along, and I loved everyone. When they put out the buffet meal, I went through the line and got some food, and sat down. Alan's sister Marvel came over and asked if I was going to get Alan's plate. I didn't know that was the custom, that you got a plate for your husband first. I felt terrible. Here I was, trying to impress his family and show them that Alan had this nice person as a girlfriend, and I made this huge faux pas. But at the same time, knowing Alan, I knew he wouldn't want or expect me to get a plate for him. It all worked out."

Diane chose one word to describe her husband: *character.* "He had character when I met him; he has always had it. He's strong, he's very intelligent, he has great values, he is compassionate, and he is honest."

And Alan's description of his wife? "She is incredibly perceptive. She has the ability to pick up cues from people and understand people in a way that I haven't seen much of. She obviously is smart. She's tough. She's fun. She likes to laugh. She doesn't suffer fools lightly. She has her own mind. She's independent. One of the things that makes us a team is that we're both independent; I don't know just how that works, but it does. What drew me to her? All of those qualities, plus the fact that she was and continues to be drop-dead gorgeous."

As if that wasn't enough. "Diane is not going to be bullied, deterred, or intimidated, and she is not going to sell herself short," Alan said. "She has an incredible ability to work with people. I saw her focus groups with young people—sixth, seventh, and eighth graders. She wanted their view of the world. These were inner-city kids. They didn't know each other, they didn't know her, and they never talked to strangers. But they were comfortable. There were no tricks; she just warmed up this cold, austere room. It was the damnedest thing I'd ever seen."

The four Page kids are Nina, Georgi, Justin, and Kamie. Justin and Kamie are the children of Alan's marriage to Diane. Nina and Georgi are the children of Alan's first marriage, to their mother, Lorraine, which ended in divorce. The four Page kids are good friends.

"At one point, we had four kids at home, and I had a career," Diane said. "Alan was just getting started as a lawyer. It was a lot, but we shared the load. That way, neither one of us got the resentments. I think a lot of women end up resenting their husbands. I didn't. Alan did half of everything there was to do, and sometimes a lot more." She laughed. "I was gone a lot. When I was, Alan made dinner and helped with homework. I might be in Chicago, doing focus groups, then having dinner with clients in a lovely restaurant. Then I'd go back to my hotel room and fall asleep. It was great!"

"Mom had to travel a lot, or she had night meetings in town, so Dad would cook supper," daughter Nina said. "He cooked chicken almost every night. We sat at the kitchen table, eating chicken and watching *Wheel of Fortune* on this little TV. One night he cooked spaghetti; it was just this one big blob. But he got better; Dad's a good cook now. Of course, he can't match Mom's world famous Mississippi Mud cake. He likes to eat it, though; he's got a huge sweet tooth. When I learned to make cookies in high school, I'd make triple batches, not just double batches. He would come home from work and take a huge handful."

When they first married, the Page home was decorated with modern art and artifacts. Some years later, however, a visiting friend braced up Diane. "She told me I had four African American children and there wasn't one thing in our home to support that fact. So we changed. We got interested. We got out and looked and learned and found items that spoke of the life of the African Americans in this country." Much of it has not been a good life, and the Page collection demonstrates graphically what a hard life it has been. There are signs and placards directing and demeaning "Colored." There are chains and branding irons and any number of harsh reminders of white America's painful embrace of black America. Diane did most of the work, tracking down and gathering their extensive collection. It stuns you, regardless of color. "It's our history," Alan said. "It's who we are."

Diane crammed collecting in amidst a lot of other projects and activities. "I'm a little bit of a workaholic," she admitted. "My weekends were pretty intense. I'd be writing reports for focus groups, usually there would be some activity with the Page Education Foundation, work in the garden, running, and searching out memorabilia for our African American collection. It was a full plate."

Diane believes there are three main reasons the Page marriage has endured. "First, we each have our own money. I had a career before I met Alan and I've continued to work, so we both have our own money. That means we don't fight about money. I have my checking account, and he has his. We share the expenses of the household. Second, we're not about trying to change the other person. Third, we're a team in every sense. We're supportive of each other, we share the workload, and we're honest with each other."

As for retirement, Diane says that both she and Alan will likely continue working in some capacity. "I'm a little freaked out by it," she admitted. "Alan doesn't see his life as not working, and I don't, either. Work has defined our lives for so many years. There's talk that Alan would like to teach young students after he retires. We'll see about that. One of my dreams is to get a local college to dedicate a wing of a new building to house an Alan Page Library and African American Museum. We could contribute all of the sports memorabilia, the awards, Alan's legal papers, and our African American memorabilia collection. Setting that up should take three or four years."

The future? For Alan Page, another of those steps through life's mirror without looking back: "Nice to have been here; let's see what lies ahead." For both, more of their remarkable, self-refreshing closeness and excitement over life's possibilities. And the kids...there will always be kids who need a hand, and the Pages have sure hands.

"I was an open-door teacher. A lot of teachers aren't—they're in their offices the day they have a class. I wanted to be there whenever a student had a problem or needed to talk. Or when they needed someone to challenge them. I'd leave board meetings and say we had to trade the concept of the student for the reality of the student."

—Karen Boros, PEF pioneer and friend

He Changed the Game

"Alan Page changed defensive line play. There were other good defensive tackles, but I can't think of any before him who had his combination of power and speed. And he could be ferocious. He forced offensive coaches to change the way they thought about their blocking schemes." —Jim Klobuchar, writer

"We had to start a rookie against him because our starter was hurt. I talked to our kid early in the week. He asked me if I had any tips for him. Tips? For going against Page? I told him to put on two of everything, because it was going to be a long afternoon. It was." —Norm Van Brocklin, former coach of the Vikings and the Falcons

There were some fine defensive tackles in the league in the late 1960s: Bob Lilly, the "Purple Cloud," at Dallas; Henry Jordan at Green Bay; Merlin Olsen and Roger Brown out in Los Angeles; Jim Houston at Cleveland; and Fred Miller at Baltimore—to name a few. As defensive tackles, the Minnesota Vikings had Paul Dickson, a flinty, bad-tempered Texan, and Gary Larsen, a blond Scandinavian with shoulders as wide as a hay bale. The Vikings had been in the NFL for six seasons before Alan Page joined them in 1967. Drafting Page was so un-Viking-like—good scouting, to be sure, but more than that, amazing good luck. First-round draft choices are not always the hardiest bloom in the NFL garden, and more than a few die on the vine. To that point, the Vikings had never been long on luck...unless you count *bad* luck.

Historians say Minnesota's 1967 draft was a corner-turner. Running back Clint Jones and receiver Gene Washington were first-rounders, along with Page. Jones and Washington were fine college players, and both had serviceable pro careers, but neither realized the level of play their draft rank called for. Still, the '67 draft included dependable possession receiver Bob Grim, tight end John Beasley, and cornerback Bobby Bryant—the gem of the class as a seventh-rounder.

But the corner-turning was done by Alan Page of Notre Dame. The Vikings had fine defensive ends when Alan arrived—Jim Marshall and Carl Eller. Eller is in the Hall of Fame, and Marshall should be. They were pass-rushers, but they could play the run, too. There may not have been a better set of young defensive ends in the league.

Defensive tackles Dickson and Larsen were tough but slow. (A lot of defensive tackles in the 1960s were slow). It's a good thing to have slow tackles playing the run; they stay at home and beat hell out of anything that tries to come inside. It is less advantageous to have them rushing the passer. On passing downs, Marshall and Eller would get good pressure, coming from the outside, but the slow inside rush meant the quarterback could step up inside the rush of the ends, but still out of reach of the tackles, and gain a precious extra second or two to get a pass off.

Page changed that. At 6'4" and weighing close to 270 pounds, his reaction time was unmatched. (In fact, now and then an official didn't believe his eyes and penalized Alan for starting too soon. More often than not, the official had erred. But they don't give the five yards back.) "I've never seen a defensive tackle with that quickness," said Vikings teammate Eller. "He was moving as soon as the ball was moving. Jim and I were getting good outside pressure before Alan joined the team, but once we got Alan, the quarterback had no place to go." Now, quarterbacks stepping up to avoid Marshall and Eller were stepping squarely into Page's stunning charge.

"Alan was a different breed, but maybe most of us were," teammate Marshall said. "I know my antics qualified me for that title. I think when you're building a team, you want people who bring different things, different outlooks. I know this: Alan Page is one of the greatest football players I ever saw. Offense, defense…it doesn't matter."

There are teams within teams. The Vikings played a 4-3 defense—four defensive linemen up front, with three linebackers behind them. And four backs behind that front seven. Ideally, the line pressures the passer or strips the protection away from a running back, keeping the linebackers freed up to make tackles. The Vikings' front four had Marshall, Page, Larsen, and Eller. The linebackers were Wally Hilgenberg, Lonnie Warwick, and Roy Winston. In their prime—a three- or four-year window—those seven were the scourge of the NFL. They were called the Purple People Eaters. The nickname annoyed Alan. "I wasn't purple and I didn't eat people," he has said.

One end and the tackle next to him work as a team in most schemes. They might run a twist where the outside man (the end) loops down inside the tackle; or the tackle loops outside the end. The first is an "ET" twist. The opposite, when the tackle goes first, is a "TE" twist. That end and tackle and the linebacker behind them also work as a triangle. Marshall and Page had Wally Hilgenberg behind them in their trio.

Wally was a real kick in the teeth in those days. He played for the Detroit Lions before reaching Minnesota. One day at Detroit, Chicago Bears great Gale Sayers ran a little drag pattern over the middle on a pass play. Gale was looking back for the ball when Wally caught him with a linebacker's dream—a roundhouse forearm that took Sayers by the neck and cart-wheeled him. I don't think they let linebackers do that anymore—at least I hope they don't. In a rainy game between the Vikings and the Los Angeles Rams at old Met Stadium, Wally, by then a Viking, slid into the Rams' bench area on a tackle in the mud and slop. He jumped up and ran both gooey hands down the front of a white jacket worn by a stunned George Allen, the Rams' coach. (George switched to a deep blue jacket for the second half.)

Roy "Moonie" Winston, one of Paul Dietzel's old "Chinese Bandits" at LSU and the Vikings' strong-side linebacker, laughed recalling teammate Hilgenberg. "He sure could stir things up," Roy said. "We were playin' some team, and when their tight end flopped over to my side, he said, 'Man, I'm glad to get over here. What's wrong with that guy on the other side? He liked to take my head off!'" Just as it was a different game back then, it's a different world now, and a lesser one: Wally Hilgenberg died of ALS while this book was being written. He dealt with a devastating illness with characteristic courage, humor, and huge faith.

Bud Grant, the new coach, made sure the Vikings' approach changed. Prior to Bud's arrival, they were the dead-end kids of the NFL, killing themselves with mistakes. Grant despised mistakes. He was a tolerant man in many respects, but his tolerance ended well short of penalties, fumbles, interceptions, and other mental errors.

Getting used to Grant was a learning process for the players. Where Norm van Brocklin's Vikings had been swinging for the fences, Grant's were more conservative. As Alan Page had learned from Ara Parseghian at Notre Dame, Grant cared about few things more than "position and possession," although he was flexible on possession. Bud didn't get upset if the other team had the ball, so long as they were backed up deep in their own end. Indeed, he gave Joe Kapp, his fiery quarterback, a simple mandate: don't take risks. Move the ball as far as you can, then punt. Just don't put the defense in bad field position.

It worked. Kapp threw ungracious passes, and Dave Osborn and Bill Brown hammered away on the ground. (Brown once ran a goal-line plunge with such emphasis that he flew through the end zone and hit a goal post square on, denting his helmet like a ten-gallon hat. He returned to the game the next time the offense came out.) Then, when the offense left the field, the defense would come trooping out to make some quarterback's life miserable.

The 1967 Vikings finished 3–8–3. In 1968 they upped their mark to 8–6 and advanced to the playoffs, where the Baltimore Colts took them to school. Flying home from that game, Grant watched his somber players and said, "They don't know it now, but they'll be better because of that loss." They were: over the next eight seasons, the Vikings won 87, lost 24, and tied 1 regular-season game. They won eight playoff games. The 1969 defense allowed 133 points in 14 games, a 9.5 point-per-game average. During those eight seasons, they lost all four Super Bowl games they played in, a burden the franchise still carries. Ironically, Grant went 0–4 in Super Bowls after going 4–2 in Grey Cups, the Canadian championship.

The defense dominated. Alan wasn't a starter until the fourth game of his rookie season; thereafter, he started 160 games in a row. Jim Marshall was the defensive captain and played end next to Page on the right side. "Captain Jim" was less buttoned-up than Alan, to be sure, but no less remarkable. Jim Marshall played 19 seasons—270 games—at defensive end, out where the bullets are flying, not in some safe, behind-the-lines position like kicker. Marshall's NFL-record string of consecutive games played lasted until 2009, when it was broken by another guy who loves the game, Brett Favre. Marshall played through illnesses, concussions, sprains, strains, tears, fractures, and stitches. And to this day he would be annoyed if you asked him why he did it. He did it because it was his job. Marshall was a true pro, and that he is not in the Pro Football Hall of Fame is the game's failure. Pete Rozelle built today's NFL and gets deserved credit for doing so. He built it on the backs of men like Jim Marshall.

"My first year, I caught a finger in a face mask and it popped out of joint," Alan said. "It hurt so bad. I was in the huddle, all hunched over, my hand between my legs. I must have looked like some little kid, ready to bust out crying. Jim looked over at me and said, 'What the hell's the matter with you?' I held up my finger. He got this annoyed look. He grabbed my hand, yanked my finger back into place, and told me to line up for the next play."

Some say Marshall was the Good Shepherd to a young Alan Page. It took Alan a while to smile when he came to the Vikings; he was quiet and reserved. In the rowdy atmosphere of a locker room, that manner is an awkward fit and can be taken for aloofness. When he bridled against drinking beer in the traditional rookie hazing, the veterans knew they had a different sort on their hands. Jim Klobuchar put it nicely, as he usually did. "Alan came with an air about him. I don't think he was angry, I think he was just being Alan Page. He kept his own counsel, and that made it difficult for him to mix with a lot of other players. But his persona worked, and he kept it."

Marshall accepted Page. Marshall was someone all of the other players looked up to, so when they saw that Jim was accepting of the new man, that helped. "You could see his ability as a player right away," Jim said. "[He had] tenacity. He was so focused and so intelligent. Alan was a person who made the right decision. It wasn't luck, it was preparation; he made right decisions because he was prepared to make them. I suppose I've made a lot more snap decisions than Alan has. Actually, I wish I were a bit more like A.P. in that sense. Was I his good shepherd?" Marshall shrugged. "Alan was no different than any other new player coming in. He needed some molding. We all did."

"They all helped me," Page said. "Carl [Eller], Jim, Gary [Larsen], Dix [Paul Dickson]…I had a lot of shepherds." He smiled and nodded to himself. "But Jim is special." Page goes on. "I'm sure a lot of [my teammates] were wary of me. I think I was as comfortable as I was going to get the first time I walked through the locker-room door. I think it took them longer to get comfortable with me. I understand that; I'm sure I wasn't the typical new teammate. The beer thing was a difficult situation, and I'm sure it was rare for them to give me a pass," Alan said. "But we all do things by degree, we have our limits. I'm sure there were things I did that I didn't want to do, but I did them. Not every issue that comes up has to result in World War III. But there are issues; some you can compromise on, some you can't. We face those decisions all our lives. The difficult part is figuring out which fall on the compromise side of the line and which don't. I go through that regularly now. It takes an exercise in judgment; it's not easy, it's not always written down for you. Sorting out which side of the line the issue lies on—that's the challenge."

Doug Sutherland, a Vikings teammate, played offensive lineman briefly, but then was moved back to defense, where he had cut his teeth. "I didn't have to block Alan for very long," he said. "I was thankful when they put me back on defense. It was embarrassing, like he was invisible; you couldn't get your hands on him. Blocking Larsen or Dickson, you knew they were going to try to run over you, but when you tried to block Alan, you fell off of him. He was bulletproof. [He also had] unbelievable reaction time, great technique, and leverage. He was like a wrestler in that he was so quick to get away, to escape a block.

"Alan led most by example, but I can remember him speaking up. When things weren't going well for us, and the younger guys started to get down, Alan and Jim [Marshall] and Moose [Eller] wouldn't let them. 'Just wait, good things are going to happen,' they'd say. 'We're going to make them happen,' they'd say."

Watch a football game on Sunday, and it's exciting, colorful stuff. But watch a practice on Wednesday, and it is long, tedious, boring, and sometimes angry. And don't forget the weather, which went from God-awful hot to soaking wet to freezing cold. Nobody had practice domes in those days.

"You line up across from the same guy every day," Page said. "It's not game-fast, so it gets to be routine. We would scrimmage every day, for at least part of the practice. Everybody knew the tempo; it was close to what a game's like, but not really. But every now and then somebody or something would set me off."

He didn't fight. "Why fight a guy if you can beat him on the next play? You get in a fight on the field, and all you've got to show for it is skinned hands and maybe a busted finger. But if you beat somebody on the next play, they understand that. I would go off every now and then, and that would be the end of a drill. I don't know if they couldn't get their minds right and get back on tempo, or if I'd gotten so crazed they couldn't have blocked me with a bulldozer. So they'd run 10 plays at me, and I'd destroy every one of them. Or they would go the other direction, and I'd destroy those, too. Why would you fight? You can get mad, but why would you fight? 'Let's double-team him!' 'Good idea!' 'Well, that didn't work.' 'Can we triple-team him?' Why fight?"

Tedious as practice might be, Page had a knack for getting everyone's attention. I always thought it sounded like a loon's call, just louder. Kapp, the quarterback, said it reminded him of a coyote howling, then barking. "I don't know where he got that scream, but I've never heard anything like it," Carl Eller said. "Now and then, Alan would slip right up behind Coach Grant and make that cry. I'm surprised Bud didn't jump out of his shoes. The rest of us couldn't believe Alan would do that. We were all amazed."

Questioned today about his outrageous behavior, Justice Page fails at masking the twinkle in his eye.

"Practice," he says, "got boring."

"I had been cut by the Vikings. I got a call from my defensive coach, Bob Hollway, who said he had recommended me to the company that was building Winter Park, the new Vikings headquarters. The company wanted to mentor a player in the construction business, and Bob got the club to recommend me. I didn't like Hollway; I didn't think he played me enough. So I asked him why he recommended me. He said it was because he always saw me reading business magazines on charter flights while most of the other guys watched movies or played cards. I took the job because I wanted to learn construction appraisal, which I would need because I wanted to become a developer. Through the opportunity Coach Hollway got for me, I met some people in McDonald's. Eventually, I became a consultant in their real estate division, siting stores throughout the Midwest. Now I own three McDonald's franchises and I'm a development appraiser."

—Tim Baylor, friend and former Vikings player

Star

"Not many people appreciate their abilities. Most people take their talents for granted, they come to depend on them without ever thinking of trying to improve them. Alan put a lot of effort into working on his strengths as well as his weaknesses. He always wanted to improve. That extra effort made him a remarkable player." —Bud Grant, Vikings coach

Things got worse as Page got better. His first marriage was ending. His role in the NFL Players Association was growing rapidly, along with frustration at what he saw as management's disdainful attitude toward the players and their concerns. And, in locker-room-speak, despite brilliant play, he "wasn't getting no respect." At least none that he could put in the bank.

Alan was named the NFL's Most Valuable Player in 1971. It was astounding news within the football community. Defensive players—defensive linemen in particular—were not considered to be MVP timber. That honor went to offensive players, the headline-makers—quarterbacks, usually, or great running backs, maybe here and there a receiver.

"He deserved it, but I never thought it would happen," teammate Jim Marshall said. "A defensive lineman? MVP? Are you kidding me?"

Time magazine wanted to do a cover story. A *Time* cover on a defensive lineman! I think even Alan was impressed.

I was the Vikings' PR man then, and *Time* was working through my office. I set up the three nights' worth of interviews with Alan, plus sidebars with his family, Grant, and his teammates, and the photos. I also was the guy who went over to practice on a gloomy Thursday to tell Page his cover story had been scrubbed because of some big, unexpected story of international portent. "Breaking news" was the way *Time* explained it to me. They said they'd have a nice inside piece, which they did—about a column long, as I remember. I broke the news to Alan out on the cold, damp, raggedy sod of Midway Stadium in St. Paul, where the team practiced. He showed no reaction for a moment, although there may have been a little sigh. Then he raised his eyebrows and smiled. "Figures," he said, before turning to walk away.

Then—wouldn't you know it?—Fran Tarkenton came back to Minnesota.

An eventual Hall of Famer like Page, Tarkenton had been the Vikings' quarterback before Alan arrived. After the 1966 season, Francis said he'd had enough of playing for Norm Van Brocklin. In fact, he went on to say, he wouldn't be back in '67 if Norm were still the coach. Jim Finks, who never did take especially well to threats (despite any private feelings he had for Van Brocklin), solved Tarkenton's dilemma by trading him to the New York Giants for a clutch of high draft choices. Later, in his own time, Finks met with Van Brocklin and told him he thought all would benefit if Norm resigned. Van Brocklin sniffed back a tear or two, grinned, gave a huge sigh, and agreed. By leaving, Norm paved the way for Finks—an old Canada hand—to call home a legend: Bud Grant.

Grant was revered for his heroics at the University of Minnesota. He starred in three sports. More recently, his Winnipeg Blue Bombers had dominated Canadian football for a decade, winning four Grey Cups, the CFL equivalent of the Super Bowl.

As more proof that pro football is a small world, Finks traded to reacquire Tarkenton from New York before the 1972 season, just a year after Page won MVP honors. Both men had great pro careers. Tarkenton, who brought the term *scramble* to the NFL glossary, was a breezy Georgian, polished by five years in New York, and a fan favorite for his daring play. Page, a cautious and thoughtful speaker, was no loner, but was most comfortable setting his own course. He also was big, black, and intimidating-looking—important image considerations.

Comparing a very good quarterback to a great defensive tackle, team-wise, might be a push on the football field, but sizzle-wise, in the ad agencies, it was no contest. Marketeers welcomed Tarkenton back as the prodigal son. Indeed, agents of a savings and loan institution met Fran as he deplaned on his first trip back to Minnesota. They signed Tarkenton on as company spokesman and had commercials on the air before the weekend was out. Page, under agency noses all along, attracted no such attention. That was how it went. Tarkenton got the endorsements; Page got the "attaboys."

It had to be a pinch for Page, measuring his accomplishments against the fuss stirred up by Tarkenton's return. He didn't hold back when asked his opinion of the trade. "We're a long way from being in need of a savior," Alan said. "We've done fairly well the last few years, and I don't see where the addition of Tarkenton will add or detract from our team. We don't have a one-man show."

Finks, the man who had sent Tarkenton to New York and then reclaimed him, had a tart observation for Page's public assessment of the trade. "We have asked a good many things of Alan this year," Finks said, "but assistance in making trades was not one of them."

The facts, for 1972 at least, supported Page. The Vikings were coming off four straight Central Division titles, and their record over the past three seasons had been the best in football. In 1972, with Tarkenton, the club finished 7–7 and out of the playoffs.

It was a rough time for Page, and the stress showed up in unexpected ways. For example, teams are regularly asked to donate autographed footballs to assist benefits, cheer children who are ill, and so on. Balls were passed around the locker room on Mondays for players to sign. I remember getting a ball I had requested for some cause. I noticed Alan had signed his name "Al Pag." I thought maybe it was a mistake, so I asked our equipment man, "Stubby" Eason. Stubby shrugged and said that was the way Alan had been signing lately. When I mentioned the corrupting of his name to Alan while we were working on the book, he said, "I was not in a very good place then. That's one of those things you wish you had back."

Day to day, Page and Tarkenton coexisted as teammates. If they rubbed up against one another occasionally, that wasn't unique, given the close proximity of football locker rooms.

Fred Zamberletti, who has worked for the Vikings since they put the sign up in 1961, was the team's trainer back then. Zamberletti recalled a pre-practice when Tarkenton was griping about someone in the front office. It became an extended gripe. Finally Fred said, "Well, Francis, if you feel that way, why don't you go talk to the guy instead of griping about it down here?"

"Just as I said that," Zamberletti said, "I happened to look at Alan, who was standing behind Francis. He made this little smile and winked at me."

All of this noted, they got along. Both left in 1978, though by different doors. Alan recalled that shortly before being let go by the Vikings, he had suggested to Fran that he and his wife join Alan and Diane for dinner at their home. But events overtook the offer, and the dinner never came off.

Tarkenton wasn't alone in finding Page difficult to read at times. Page's teammates, even some of the defensive players, found his attitude a prickly one. "I'll be honest with you," said linebacker Winston. "There were times I thought Alan was a real good guy and times I thought he was a jerk. But I look back, and I think he may have been dealing with some tough issues. We've met several times in recent years, and I've enjoyed being with him."

Tarkenton also made the point that Page's union activities did not speak for all of the Vikings. Some other teammates also thought Page was over-zealous with his attitude toward the mission of the Players Association. But on one thing, all of them could agree: they had a star in their midst.

Do you know how hard it is to sack a quarterback?

Start with this fact: you have probably three seconds, max, in which to do it. Usually, the ball's gone after that, barring some Tarkenton-esque scrambler. You, the rusher, will face at least one blocker who outweighs you substantially, and more likely, two of them—maybe a center turning to help a guard, or a tackle blocking down. Get past them, and the fullback could be waiting for you…lots of blocking options. In Page's case, sometimes two or three blockers would challenge him. The defensive tackle is closest to the quarterback when the ball is snapped, but he also has the most obstacles in his path.

Blocking, the kind you did in high school, was pretty straightforward. You got your face and hands in the rusher's chest—don't hold, keep your feet moving, and give ground slowly. It's a little different today. Pro blockers pull your pads, grab your jersey, and lock your arms. They punch, gouge, choke, and butt. If they happen to go down in the mêlée, they aren't done yet; leg-whips or shin-kicks are not uncommon. Chokeholds or the odd punch to the you-know-where are tolerated, although not encouraged. Biting is a "no." They do these things and more to keep you, the rusher, from getting hold of their passer.

Alan Page had 173 quarterback sacks in 14-plus NFL seasons. He didn't wear as much padding as most defenders. Jim Osborne, a Chicago teammate, said, "Alan wore this little half T-shirt and skimpy shoulder pads under his jersey. Nothing else. He didn't tape his hands or forearms." Page's game was based on running around people, not through them.

Page was physically tough. Add to that his cat-quick speed and intelligence on the field, and you had a truly rare athlete, as his teammates and Coach Grant recall to this day.

Lonnie Warwick, a middle linebacker, grew up in Mt. Hope, West Virginia, in coal-mining country. He still calls it home. Growing up, townsfolk generally agreed the Warwick boy was a ruffian. They just didn't understand what went into being a middle linebacker. "They said I wouldn't amount to much," he recalled. Lonnie played at Tennessee Tech, but the pros didn't call right off, and he was working as a railroad section hand in Arizona when Joe Thomas, a dogged Vikings scout, tracked him down. Lonnie played a solid eight seasons at Minnesota.

"Alan would change his charge sometimes," said Warwick, "but he always made the play. He just had such a good sense for the play. He's the most intelligent football player I ever saw. He's just intelligent, period.

"Alan understood pursuit angles so well," Warwick continued. "A lot of guys, when the ball's snapped, they don't think, they just go. They go to the ball but, usually, they don't get there. Alan would see a play's direction and take the perfect pursuit angle to meet the play. A lot of times, he'd be there waiting for the ball carrier, or he'd take him down from behind. Alan might get knocked down, but he would be up again, just so quick, and be moving on the right angle to the play. He never stayed down."

"[Alan was] very smart," confirmed linebacker Winston. "It was like he knew what was coming. I know Alan studied hard for games because I did, too; playing well has a lot to do with preparation."

"Before one of the Super Bowls," Buddy Ryan said, "A.P. didn't think the offense was working hard enough in practice. He went in the locker room, put on a pair of old black high-tops, and came back and kicked ass on the practice field. Afterward, I asked him why he did it. 'To make them work,' he said.

"He was so quick, mentally and physically," Ryan said. "I used to give him extra stuff to study, knowing we were never going to use it. I did it so he wouldn't get bored."

"People would say Alan guessed a lot of the time," Bud Grant said. "I don't think he guessed. I think he was prepared and could recognize things and adjust on the fly. That was why we gave him freedom to move around if he sensed something."

"There were times," Alan said, "when I would run over and line up outside of 'Moose' [Carl Eller] on the opposite side the formation. I'd see something I thought I could exploit."

Wally Hilgenberg played outside linebacker behind Page. Alan Page, the player, was a marvel to Hilgenberg. "He tended to do a lot of flying around," Wally said. "He was so quick he could be wrong and still make the play."

Chuck Knox, who coached the then–Los Angeles Rams, spoke once of looking at film of Page to prepare for a game with Minnesota, "He made two separate and distinct mistakes on one play and still tackled the ball-carrier for no gain," said Knox.

The Rams were a postseason rival of the Vikings in 1974. The Rams were down close, ready to score and take the lead in the third quarter. On third and inches, within a yard or two of the Vikings' goal line, Page flashed across the line of scrimmage. Flags flew, and Rams guard Tom Mack was called for illegal procedure. The ball went back five yards, and the Rams didn't score.

"Mack hadn't moved yet," Coach Knox snapped, making clear that a memory of nearly 40 years could still rankle. "I don't blame Page," Knox said. "He gambled and won. But the call was bad."

Alan's eyes twinkled when the Mack story was mentioned. "What did I have to lose?" he said. Then he grinned. "But he did move."

Alan Page was not an emotional player. He was physical, immensely gifted, and bright, but not looking to hurt anyone. The ball was snapped, Alan applied himself to that challenge, then moved on to the next play. But every now and then something would set him off. "When that happened," said Hilgenberg, "he was unblockable."

One of those "set offs" came against the Detroit Lions, a team then living that old line about how if it weren't for bad luck, they wouldn't have any luck at all. They were just in the wrong place at the wrong time when Alan Page went off.

Page was penalized for being offside. Then he was penalized again. Offside. He was visibly angry at the first call because he rarely made mistakes. The second call infuriated him. He got in an official's face. Teammates dragged him off, but he was still steaming. He slammed his helmet down with such force that it must have bounced 15 feet in the air. (A week later, study of films by the Vikings and the league revealed Page was not offside—not once, not twice. It was another case of an official being unwilling to believe a defensive tackle could be that quick.) After the flags were picked up, Page—on consecutive plays—stopped two running plays for losses, sacked the quarterback, and then blocked a kick.

"He created havoc," Neill Armstrong said. Neill was Page's defensive coach at Minnesota and his head coach at Chicago. "He would line up a little bit off true on the center or a guard to make the blocking angle harder. He was so dad-gummed quick and relentless. On third downs, we let him call a lot of his own stunts."

"I always liked Alan," Armstrong said. "Anybody could see that he was a great football player, but he's a real gentleman, too." (If that is so, it must take one to know one, because football has not produced a finer gentleman than Armstrong.) Neill recalled, "I liked to walk among the players in the locker room just before we'd take the field. Alan would be leaning forward, looking down, but when I got near to him, he'd always hold up that big old beat-up fist for me to tap. Never looked up, but he knew I was there."

Alan Page played in 218 consecutive games. Besides the 173 sacks, he recovered 23 fumbles, scored three touchdowns, and blocked 28 kicks. He was named to nine Pro Bowl teams, six All-Pro teams, and twice was named NFL Defensive Player of the Year. That's besides the MVP honor in 1971.

"I believe we reach a point in our lives when self isn't as important as it used to be, and the rewards we have piled up for ourselves seem diminished. That's when we can experience the joy of reaching out to others and helping someone else grow. I loved playing football, but football has faded. I used to play behind Alan, and I marveled at what he could do. But I have much more admiration for him today because he is giving hope to young people. Because of him, a lot of young people are able to hope for a real future. I know that my illness is terminal, but that doesn't mean I have to be. I am grateful and blessed. On my birthday, 40 guys I played with and some of my old coaches came to the house for a party. This morning, my grandson, who is four, wanted me to teach him to run the remote on my wheelchair. We had a great time."

—Wally Hilgenberg, Vikings teammate and
ALS victim, (1942–2008)

Runner: The Dog Man of Kenwood

"He's the Dog Man of Kenwood—that's their neighborhood. He carries dog biscuits in a fanny-pack when he runs. Lots of people run with their dogs, and my dad knows a lot of the dogs by name. He gives them biscuits. I don't think Diane wanted a dog. He came to grips with that after a while, and then had this better idea. Now all these dogs are his friends. I think it's inspired." —Georgi Page, daughter

I'm a witness. I was with Diane and Alan one summer evening, riding around Lake Calhoun in south Minneapolis. Calhoun connects to Lake of the Isles and to Lake Harriet to form a lovely chain of lakes within the city. Sometimes the Pages run all three lakes, but they usually stick to Lake of the Isles, as it's the closest to their home. As we drove, Alan noticed two women running with their dogs. He pulled to the curb, rummaged in the console between the front seats, then said, "Be right back." I watched him cross the street with that springy gait of his as the runners and their dogs approached. "It's two of his friends," Diane said. She meant the dogs. Alan spoke to the women, dropped to one knee, spoke to the dogs, and then held out a treat for each. He had a smile when he got back in the car. "That's the first time I've seen that Springer," he said.

"I played football, but I was never a runner," Page said. "Diane and I were in Hawaii for a Super Stars competition, and I got to watching people run on the beach. I kind of thought, *Hmm.* So one morning I tried it. Then I ran a few more mornings. I liked it. I wasn't an instant convert, but I liked it well enough to try it again when we got home."

Alan and Diane out for a chilly run in Lake Forest, Illinois, during their Chicago Bears years.

Alan and the purple car that had Diane's neighbors "hanging out the windows."

Alan delivers his Hall of Fame induction speech (his presenter, Willarene Beasley, is at far right).

Alan waves to the crowd during the inductees' parade at the Hall of Fame Game.

RE-ELECT ALAN PAGE
A JUSTICE FOR ALL

"The decisions made by the Minnesota Supreme Court affect the economic, community and family lives of all Minnesotans. Therefore, I believe a Supreme Court Justice has to understand not only the law, but life as well."

Alan C. Page

The Justice runs again. "I believe a Supreme Court Justice has to understand not only the law, but life as well."

Children Nina (left), Justin, and Kamie help Justice Page adjust his robes for the first time. Georgi (not pictured) was a speaker during the ceremony.

Old teammates reunited: (from left) Jim Marshall, Page, Doug Sutherland, and Carl Eller.

What makes a judge smile? For Justice Page, it's one of the many toy trucks that adorn his chambers in St. Paul, Minnesota.

Diane and Alan with their 1906 Buick, out for an antique car touring ride. Diane seems more the period dresser than Alan.

Diane takes a photo after Alan ran in the New York City Marathon.

Grandpa Alan and grandson Otis enjoy a quiet moment together.

Wearing his old Vikings jersey over a new bow tie, Justice Page addresses cheering fans before a game in the Metrodome.

Diane and Alan with Ethel Kennedy, the wife of Robert Kennedy.

"Whistle while you work!" Justice Page encourages runners in a Twin Cities race by playing his tuba. It's a yearly happening that has grown to become a favorite with runners.

Alan laughed when asked if Diane ran with him. "Not then. Later on she could run me until my lungs bled, and then look back and ask me what's wrong. But not then. She was a smoker, and she couldn't run from our house down to the corner."

"I knew he didn't like my smoking," Diane said, "but Alan is not about changing people. I tried to quit once. I know I was really crabby. I went back to smoking, then a couple months later I said I was going to try again to quit. Alan said, 'No, don't do it.' He didn't want to go through me being crabby again. Once he said that, I quit immediately. It was the most brilliant strategy. I don't know if he even knew he was doing it."

Georgi Page suggested that running might be a form of meditation for her dad, and she may not be far off the mark. Alan admits to liking a lot of things about running. "There's the physical, the psychological, and the emotional [aspects]. There's something about being out in the open air. I'm physically and mentally active when I run. People talk about a runner's high…it's absolutely true. I think your body chemicals change. It's a good feeling. Even on a bad day, a bad run is better than no run at all." He speaks from experience. Alan Page runs when it's nice and when it's not; when it's a scorcher and humid, and when the temperature is below zero and the wind is blowing. "If I didn't run," he said, "I would feel terrible."

Al Harris, a Chicago Bears teammate, vouches for the fact that Page is no fair-weather runner. "I was driving to practice one December morning. It was snowing so bad, I had trouble seeing. I passed this guy who was jogging along the side of the road. I remember he was wearing a stocking cap, and there was a bunch of snow on top of his cap. As I got even with him, I could see he was tall and he was black. Now, there weren't a lot of tall, black joggers in Lake Forest, so I figured it was Alan, running to work. I knew better than to stop and offer him a ride."

Jim McCarthy, a friend since Alan was a rookie lawyer at Lindquist & Vennum, echoes Harris' observation: "I remember a big snowstorm in Minneapolis. You couldn't get around in your car, and the busses were stopped. It was the only time I went to work on cross-country skis—I couldn't have driven. I live in south Minneapolis, not too far from Alan and Diane. As I was skiing, I looked down 22nd Street. I could see Lake of the Isles from where I was. Who did I see running through the snowdrifts but Alan. He ran to work that day. He might have been late, but the rest of the city was shut down."

"I met Alan as a runner at the Eleven O'Clock Club," said Michael Jordan, a longtime Minneapolis friend. "We ran Saturday mornings. I have run with Alan for 20 years or more. My wife knew Diane because they had shared a maternity room when Kamie was born. We ran around Lake Calhoun. I think Alan and I got along because I was one of the few guys who would talk about something besides football. Sometimes we'd go to a track and run half-miles—six of them," Jordan said, wincing at the memory. "Alan caused me all the injuries I have today. I got them chasing him; he is remarkably fast for a big man."

Tim Baylor played defensive back for the Vikings after Alan went to the Bears. Baylor, too, lived in south Minneapolis. After both of them were through with football, every now and then Baylor would see Alan and Diane running at Lake of the Isles. "One day they waved me over. Diane got us introduced, and then Alan asked if I wanted to run with them. I said I did short distances, not long stuff. He grinned and said, 'Come on, run with us, we'll see how it goes.' We don't run together real often, but we still hook up some," Baylor said. "I count Diane and Alan as close friends, and it all got started because they invited me to run with them."

Being the daughter of such a recognizable man also posed some unique challenges. Daughter Nina Page shared her teenage mortification at some of her dad's running attire. "My dad would do some of the most embarrassing things when we were in high school," Nina said. "My parents would run around Lake of the Isles, and my friends would see him wearing a bright pink leotard. He had this skintight pink body suit, like a ballerina. He had shorts, but he wore the shorts *under* the leotard!"

But while others may be watching Alan Page, the man himself stays focused on the community and people around him. "One thing I like about running," Page added, "is that you see so much more on foot than you do in your car. We run through our neighborhood every day and notice changes that we wouldn't see driving."

Diane Page transformed herself from smoker to runner in what seemed like no time. "She just took to it," Alan said. "I think she had been a runner all her life, in her heart—she just didn't know it. But it sure came bursting out."

"Diane became one of the best in the cities at five and 10 kilometers," Michael Jordan said. "She was on the Reebok running team."

"Running—jogging—was just getting started when I took it up," Diane said. "Running became our social life. We loved running and the people we met. We have kept friends from running. I wasn't running long before I learned that I was fast. I liked running slow with the group, but I loved races, too. I had some success, but when I got into my forties, I started experiencing injuries. I had to give up racing. We still run, but it's really slow now."

Alan ran in Grandma's Marathon in 1979, near Duluth, Minnesota, along the windy shore of Lake Superior. The marathon course—26 miles, 385 feet—ended at Grandma's, a bar and deli on the Duluth waterfront. Alan struggled. He wanted to quit. He felt like dying numerous times, but he finished; he finished 1,113th. The crowd at the finish line—and along the way, for that matter—cheered him lustily. At that time he was the only NFL player to have run a marathon.

"It kills him if he can't get up in the morning and run," said Justin Page, Alan's son. "I see some of the guys my dad played football with, and they can barely move. Then I see my dad, who runs every day. He's like the bionic man. For the most part, he's very serious and soft-spoken," Justin said, "but out on a run, he's a lot of fun."

Page's running has brought both good and bad. Probably all good, truth be told, and it just needed some time to be sorted out. It either cost him or contributed to costing him his job with the Minnesota Vikings—opinions vary. I tend to believe the latter because decisions, like cakes, are made up of more than one ingredient. Alan probably weighed a top of 270 pounds early on at Minnesota. "I didn't have to count milkshakes anymore," he said. But big didn't mean good. "I told Roy [Winston] this new guy was too fat," linebacker Lonnie Warwick said. "If he couldn't move, I figured he couldn't play," Warwick reasoned.

Page figured the same thing and came down to about 245 late in his second year. That was his optimum playing weight before he became a runner. He played at between 245 and 250 pounds for the next four or five years, and he was the best defensive player in football. In time, however, as he became a more and more dedicated runner, and the running chewed up body fat, Alan's weight fell. He played the 1977 season at 225 pounds. Before the 1978 season, Coach Bud Grant told him he was concerned about the weight issue. Alan said he would stand or fall at 225.

He fell. The Vikings placed him on waivers six games into the 1978 season. That means they fired him. Any team could claim Page for $100. Grant said the decision was based upon Page's no longer being able to play at the level necessary for a defensive lineman, that Page was no longer strong enough to play his position. He also said the Vikings had extra defensive linemen but needed help on the offensive line. So they cut Page and signed Bob Lingenfelter, a tackle from Nebraska, who, as they say in the trade, "stayed around for a cup of coffee"— meaning he wasn't around long. Lingenfelter finished out the season but was waived the next year. Minnesotans felt like the team had sold a Rembrandt at a garage sale.

Page played football so that it might lead him to things he loved: a good life for his family, the law, the court, the Page Education Foundation, and running. He was a football player by necessity, but a runner by choice. Alan Page has run in seven marathons, including New York City.

"Alan helped me leave the game when it was time. You have to go cold turkey, walk away, and move on with the rest of your life. I won't say it was easy, but I did it. I've always been grateful to him for that, but I'm grateful for a lot of things. People helped me out along the way when I was a kid. I had clothes given to me; they weren't new, but they were better than what I had. There was this guy who stopped me from smoking and going into clubs. I'm sure he saved me a lot of misery. Now, I try to repay in kind; if I know of some kid who needs help, I help."

—Jim Osborne, Chicago Bears teammate

No Freedom, No Football

"I was introduced on a CBS panel show by Brent Musburger. He said, 'We have with us today the commissioner of the National Football League, Pete Rozelle; the distinguished mediator, Bill Ussery; and the alleged bomb-thrower, Ed Garvey.' I'm thinking, my parents, my family...they're hearing this. After the show, I asked Musburger where the hell he got the bomb-thrower label. He said that was a story Pete liked to tell: that Garvey was a bitter man because he graduated from Wisconsin too early to take part in the math department bombing there." —Ed Garvey, former head of the NFL Players Association

With his twinkling eyes, and maybe a green derby and a shillelagh for good measure, Ed Garvey would make a fine Irishman if you were to call central casting. No one reported seeing him in a green derby back in the '70s, however, but the shillelagh was in evidence. Ed Garvey said he and his mates—the players of the National Football League—had to battle for every collective benefit they got.

Garvey was a freshman member of Lindquist & Vennum, a Minneapolis law firm with a background in labor negotiations. In 1970—with the merger of the NFL and the American Football League—John Mackey of the Baltimore Colts, Ken Bowman of the Green Bay Packers, and Pat Richter of the Washington Redskins asked Leonard Lindquist to represent the NFL players.

"Leonard didn't know anything about football," Garvey said. "He'd never been to a game. He asked me what I knew about football. I told him, not much, but I'd love a crack at that job."

116

Compared to the rank and file of the big bruisers he spoke for, Ed Garvey was a little bit of a guy. He was not an ex-jock, he was still wet behind his legal ears, and he wasn't a well-prepared David, considering the Goliath he was up against. That's what he *wasn't*. But he *was* feisty and bright and he had a quick wit. Garvey was a guerilla fighter, he could improvise, and he believed in his product. Garvey says the door to dialogue between labor and management was not open. It wasn't even ajar, for that matter. "Rozelle refused to recognize the union," he said. "We had to file with the National Labor Relations Board to force recognition. Our first meeting was in Minneapolis. That was the first time I met Alan Page. Alan came to most of the meetings because they were held in Minneapolis, and he was there with the Vikings." Plus, he was interested.

"There were some writers who were willing to judge our association on its merits," Garvey said, "but for the most part, the press pummeled us as ingrates who didn't understand football and were trying to destroy the game George Halas had invented." Garvey talks today about the old days with the same prickly humor he had at the time. A lot of the writers probably did reflect the attitudes of the clubs' management; they knew the clubs, not this upstart Garvey.

Garvey recalled a meeting between Tex Schramm, who ran the Dallas Cowboys, and John Niland, the team's player representative to the union. "Schramm told Niland, 'Well, I've met your man Garvey, and he's a racist.' Niland said, 'A racist? His best friends are John Mackey, Kermit Alexander, and Alan Page [all black].' 'You don't understand,' Schramm said to Niland. 'Garvey hates white people.'"

Where was the common ground between Ed Garvey and Alan Page?

"Believing that players had rights, and—as Mackey put it—that this was a continuation of the civil rights movement," said Garvey. "I believe the backbone of the union was made up of men like Mackey and Page and Alexander. The black players knew they had to be better than the white players if they were going to make the team, because there was a quota. They also knew that when their playing days were over, they would not be hired as coaches or front-office people, because those positions were all held by whites. When we approached Rozelle about black former players being hired as coaches, Pete said if they were qualified, they would be hired. We asked him if he meant players like Mackey and Page were not qualified. Pete said that if they were, they would be hired." Garvey said Ernie Wright, a veteran player, told Pete that with his plantation mentality, Ernie could see why there was a problem.

Garvey said Hank Stram, who coached the Kansas City Chiefs to a win over Page's Vikings in Super Bowl IV, was the first coach to have a majority of black players on his team. Garvey claimed that until Stram's bold move, there had been an understood one-third quota of blacks on a team.

One of the more contentious issues between players and club owners was the "neutrality" of Rozelle as commissioner. The league went to pains to point out that Pete was the commissioner of *all* football, and he ruled in the best interests of both sides, players (labor) and the clubs (management). Essentially, this left the commissioner above the wrangling of the two sides, free to decide what was best for all. The owners were for it; players thought it was a crock.

During the strike of '74, player reps met in San Francisco. The issue of Rozelle's neutral stance was discussed. The reps came up with a novel idea: if he's our commissioner, too, they reasoned, and we don't think he represents our side well, why don't we fire him? "Everybody laughed and said let's do it," said Garvey. "So we called a press conference and said the players had decided to terminate Pete Rozelle's contract as commissioner since he did not represent them in a manner they thought was equitable. Schramm and Art Modell said, 'You can't do that—we hired him!' To which, we said, 'Thank you.' I mean, you had to have some fun with this because, man, they played hardball!"

I was on that "hardball" team during the 1974 strike. I spent 1973 and 1974 working in the NFL office in New York as the assistant to the president of the National Football Conference (more title than pay). George Halas was the conference president, but what the title really meant was that I was the commissioner's extension cord to the then 13 NFC teams. I did things he didn't have time to do or didn't want to do. One of the things I did was spend much of the summer of '74 in New

York, at 540 Madison Avenue, then home of the NFL Management Council—the league's first-responders against Garvey and his provocateurs. Most of what I did was dispense fruitless answers to fruitless calls from NFC clubs. For example:

> *Club owner:* What the hell's going on up there?
> *Me:* Pretty quiet.
> *Club owner:* Well, keep us informed!
> *Me:* You bet.

The 1974 Hall of Fame Game in Canton was approaching. Despite the strike, the game would be played with replacement players (or *scabs*, depending on your bias; we in management opted for "replacement players"). I was half of the "on the ground" advance team sent to Canton. My partner was the late, inestimable Val Pinchbeck. Our job was to fend off rumored efforts by the players to stop or greatly embarrass the game. We learned the striking players intended to picket with sympathetic union brothers at their side, among them truckers and autoworkers, harder cases than Pinch or I had expected to go up against. Our response, driven by the full faith and credit of everyone at 410 Park Avenue, the League office, and its outposts except Pete Rozelle (who was neutral, remember?), was saturation bombing.

On game day, the two teams' charter flights arrived at Canton-Akron airport just minutes apart and only a few hours before kickoff. Nervous young players stepped off chartered jets onto chartered busses surrounded by chartered cops. With all our busses, trucks, and escort, we rumbled straight to Fawcett Stadium, site of the Hall of Fame Game. Police cars and motorcycles rode fore and aft while a state police helicopter clattered overhead.

Back at the Hall, a prearranged decoy squad of police cars pulled up to the front gate, lights flashing, and cleared a path as if they were expecting the busses. The picketing players and other unionists surged toward the front gate. But we brought the busses in a back gate. Once inside, we had to roll past angry strikers crowded against the front gate. They wore printed T-shirts: "No Freedom, No Football!"

I had a good look at the angriest of those faces, pressed up tight against an iron fence as we passed. It was Alan. I can still see him, clear as if all this had happened yesterday instead of 30-odd years ago. Seeing Alan there made it more personal for me. I remember feeling like we were overreacting, using a mallet to swat a fly. Later, I watched a little of the game, from up on the press-box roof. Jim Kensil, Pete's No. 2 and a solid guy, clapped me on the shoulder, grinning, and said, "Good job, Willie." I wasn't as excited as Jim was.

The game was dreadful; maybe the strikers won after all.

"Without the anger of the black players entering a system they saw as being racial in the 1960s and '70s, I don't think there would have been any changes in the NFL," Garvey said. "The NFL was used to getting its way. But then along came players like Mackey and Page and Alexander and a few others, and the old stuff wasn't selling anymore."

The players played through 1974 without a contract. During the 1975 training camp, Randy Vataha, the New England player rep, attempted to stir the negotiating pot by calling for teams to strike the final preseason game. Several teams expressed support, but not all. Garvey, counting his forces, saw that he had five teams and one player on strike.

"I called Alan," Garvey said. 'My God, Alan,' I said, 'what are you doing? You can't go out on strike by yourself.'"

Alan said he could.

Garvey encouraged him to get his Vikings teammates to go with him.

"They should make their own decisions," Page said.

"Try to convince them," Garvey said.

"I can't do that," Page said. "It's a decision they have to make for themselves."

It was a decision with consequences: Garvey claimed all but two of the player reps were traded or cut that year. Mackey, a Hall of Fame tight end with the Baltimore Colts and the leader of the player movement, was waived. San Diego eventually picked him up, but Mackey was found to have a knee injury in the club physical. "They asked how I got hurt," Mackey told Ed Garvey. "I told them it was from walking up stairs and sitting down at bargaining tables."

Jim Marshall talked to Page. Jim came away sympathetic with Alan's position, but after a one-day walkout, Page rejoined the club. After meeting with mediator Ussery, the players agreed to play, provided the clubs negotiated in good faith. But Garvey said that as soon as the players returned, the league forgot about good-faith bargaining.

"Alan had this quiet dignity," Garvey said. "I don't think the league knew quite how to deal with him. Over time, until we finally got a contract [1977], I would ask Alan to go out to the other clubs to explain the issues. He didn't need any preparation; he knew the issues. Players reacted when Alan walked into a meeting. That's why I sent him—I knew they would listen to him.

"Alan was quiet, but a strong person. I see a natural confidence in him. Alan always had that, not just as a player, but working with us, too. He has charisma, I guess. An intangible [quality] that says you want to like this person, to trust him.

"You don't often find the quality of an Alan Page in any field—I don't care if it's law or football or in some big corporation. Someone like Alan comes along once in a long while, maybe once in a lifetime. He loves the court. He loves the reading, the writing, the studying and reflecting. He loves being a justice. The Players Association was fortunate to have had him."

Looking back on the strike, Alan Page said, "I think unions suffer because every new generation starts off from step one and not step 10, which is where their predecessors got to. They've got to learn, just like we had to learn, and the generations before us. It's very frustrating, but fascinating, the way it works. It's like telling your kids something—until they experience it themselves, they won't understand."

The players union has always had problems. For one thing, it never generated a lot of sympathy from "real" unions because only pension, medical, moving costs, and the like are bargained collectively. Each player retains the right to bargain his individual salary. Not so with the teamsters or the steamfitters or the guy who tosses your suitcase onto the carousel at the airport. For another, the better conditions become for players, the less important the union seems to them. Today's millionaire players look at collective concerns with indifference. And finally, while the fan is sympathetic to a point, he's not really sympathetic—the fan wants his team to play, not go out on strike.

"Players make huge sums of money now," Alan said. "So do the clubs. Players are somewhat free to move within the system now, and they don't go to camp with a lot of the restrictions we had. We had restrictions on our person. This scraggly old beard of mine is a direct result of the rule that we couldn't have beards. When that rule was lifted, I grew a beard. It probably never would have occurred to me to grow a beard until somebody told me I couldn't. The money, the improved personal freedoms, free agency…they make it hard for the union to keep players interested. But it's the union that got them the money, the improved personal freedoms, and free agency. The union got them to where they are today," Page said. "But that's the struggle with every movement, I suppose."

The union of Page's time—not solely, but to a large degree—was energized and driven to grow by African American players. Salaries were microscopic for all players back then, compared to today's numbers. The difference for black players was knowing they would not move into the post-football commercial world with the same ease and opportunities their white teammates had. So they fought hard, not just for the day, but also for their futures…as limited as many of those futures would be.

"I grew up out in the country, on the Iron Range. We were pretty poor. I went to St. Paul College of Law, a night school. I worked at Sears, typing and filing during the day. I was the only woman in my graduating class from law school—women weren't supposed to go to law school in 1955. A woman couldn't get a job with a law firm; you couldn't even get an interview. I got a state job. If you were ambitious, that was a good place—I met politicians there, but I never practiced law. I met [Minnesota] Governor Rudy Perpich while I worked for the state, and he appointed me first to District Court, then to the Supreme Court. I served for eight years on the Supreme Court. Jack Thoreen was my mentor on the court, he taught me how to be a judge. We'd meet at the end of the day, and he'd ask my opinion on something. He didn't need my opinion, I'm sure he didn't even pay attention to it, but that was how he taught me. I owe him a lot. Jack's 89 now, so I take him around to the state bar meetings."

—Esther Tomljanovich,
former Minnesota Supreme Court justice

Bud

"He has so much common sense. Most of us have common sense the next day. Bud had it before a thing happened."
—Jan Stenerud, former Vikings kicker

Bud Grant and Alan Page both joined the Minnesota Vikings in 1967. Both had much to prove.

Grant, who grew up the son of the fire chief in Superior, Wisconsin, was a celebrated college athlete at the University of Minnesota. He won nine varsity letters in three sports—football, basketball, and baseball. He played pro basketball for the then-Minneapolis (now Los Angeles) Lakers. He played pro football for the Philadelphia Eagles of the NFL and later for the Winnipeg Blue Bombers of the Canadian Football League. He might have made it in pro baseball as a pitcher, had his fastball been better. He was named Minnesota's outstanding athlete of the first half of the 20th century.

Grant was never anything but a player or a head coach: a player at Winnipeg, after jumping from the Philadelphia Eagles to Winnipeg of the Canadian League as a result of a contract dispute. (Grant was the second NFL player to do so; Neill Armstrong was the first.) Bud was named head coach of the Blue Bombers when he was 29 years old. His father died the day he got the job. Harry Grant Sr. was found dead in his easy chair, a cigarette smoldering in his fingers. "Bud" (his father gave Harry Jr. the nickname Buddy Boy) has despised smoking ever since. He coached for 10 years in Canada, his teams winning four CFL titles. Despite one year where the record was 1–14–1, Grant's Blue Bombers went 105–53–2.

Alan Page was from Canton, a lunch-bucket, shot-and-a-beer, Ohio mill town south of Cleveland. He was from a family that, although not wealthy, was solidly middle class on the African American socioeconomic scale of that time. His parents both worked. His mother, Georgiana, attended at the ladies locker room at a country club. Alan's father, Howard Sr., was an entrepreneur, and a swinging one at that— he distributed records for jukeboxes, booked big-name black singers and bands into Canton clubs, and owned a saloon with a gambling parlor in the back room. His friends called him "Baker Boy," a carryover from his youth when he delivered goods from his father's bakery.

Alan started out as a lean, long-legged defensive end at Notre Dame, where he won All-America honors as a senior. "They played a wide tackle six," Vikings scout Jerry Reichow said. "That meant the ends were practically out to the sideline, assigned containment, so nobody knew much about him playing inside." Initially the Vikings also tried Alan at end and suggested gingerly to veteran defensive end Carl "Moose" Eller that they might move him in to tackle to make room for Page. Moose lacked enthusiasm for the switch, so the rookie Page began to work inside. It was where he wanted to be, anyway—closer to the quarterback. Center Mick Tingelhoff said Page took to the position like he was never a rookie.

Grant and Page, new coach and rookie player, were surprisingly similar, had anyone thought to look. Over the years, however, some of those commonalities would chafe, and lead, eventually, to their parting. They both were private, quiet, introspective men, their light sides usually battened down under hatch covers of caution and restraint. If Bud Grant had ever suggested to Jim Finks that they take their wives to dinner, Finks would have fallen out of his chair. Bud coached football. When the work was done, he went home. Alan played football. When the work was done, he went home. "In camp," Grant said, "the players would go out for a beer after meeting. Alan didn't drink, so he didn't go. He might run a little or he'd go to his room."

The private aura of both men was seen by many as aloofness, particularly on Page's part. It wasn't, but both enjoyed the separation privacy afforded them. Both were, and remain, deliberate. If you intend to hurry either man into a decision, pack a lunch; you'll be there for a while.

"When you make a decision," Bud said, "take all the time allotted to you. Gather the information available and study it. Do your sums—the plusses and minuses—think it through, and then make your decision. Once you make it, don't look back."

Justice Page's job is to make decisions based on a deliberate gathering of information; impartial application of the law; and the ability to listen to and *hear* his fellow justices, the supplicants, and himself. His decisions reflect his knowledge of the law, his preparation, and the courage of his convictions. Like Grant, once a decision is made, Page doesn't look back.

If they know they are right, you won't change them. They're both confident, and they don't waste time "what-iffing." If you compete with either one of them, they'll expect to beat you, and probably will. Neither is afraid to take chances or be apart from the mainstream. Their shared bottom line? They're comfortable being themselves.

Alan Page played for the Vikings from 1967 until the midpoint of the 1978 season. Over that span, the Vikings' record was 110–46–4. Their postseason record was 9–9, four Super Bowl losses included. The Vikings played beautifully to reach the ultimate game, but once there they fell not just short, but shockingly short. Page and Grant had a similar reaction to the Super Bowl losses—acceptance—and both were panned for feeling that way.

"You can work like a dog in preparation, seek every bit and scrap of information, every bit of preparation that you can," Grant said. "That's really all you can do. But it doesn't always come out the way you want it to. There are some things you have to accept," Bud said.

Bud used to say Super Bowl games were just like other games. I didn't believe him then and I still don't. Each Super Bowl presents a unique challenge to each team, and the team that deals with the challenge—interprets it, prepares for it, and responds to it on the field—has the better chance. I think the Vikings, under Grant, were ready to play going in. In their first Super Bowl—IV, against the Chiefs—they may have been a little stage-struck, and understandably. In subsequent

Super Bowls, the pressure of earlier losses may have become an increasing burden. But I also don't think they adjusted especially well—whether that meant recognizing a pass defense or seeing a trap or the hundred other things that happen after the ball is snapped. Everybody's going to get hurt; the key is stanching your bleeding and exploiting the other guy's, with coaches and players both adjusting. To draw a parallel with boxing (which Bud is fond of), I never felt like the Vikings had a good "cut man" in their corner at those Super Bowls.

Alan expressed surprise at the way the Vikings were scorned after their Super Bowl losses. Minnesota posted excellent regular-season and playoff records to reach the ultimate game, but once there they fell with a thud. Four thuds. They lost to Kansas City, Miami, Pittsburgh, and Oakland, and each loss was tougher than the one that came before it. "If you do your best—and still don't win—then you did what you could, you drop it, and you move on. We wanted to win those games, too," Page said.

After the fourth Super Bowl loss, Alan wondered out loud how thoughtful people could be so involved in a football game. He said the game's lasting impact was small within the grand scheme of life. He was right, but philosophy wasn't what Vikings fans were looking for after those signal defeats. That said, anyone could have seen the cold fury on Grant's face as he walked to the locker room after losing to Kansas City in Super Bowl IV; frankly, there wasn't much philosophy in it.

Ultimately, Grant and Page were being themselves—factual, in a time when their followers wanted anything but factual. Grant had coached his best, and Page had played his best. If that wasn't enough, so be it.

Although both men were private by nature, Grant recalls many conversations with Page. "I talked a lot with Alan," Grant said. "I think I talked more with Alan than I did with any other player, because he questioned so many things that we did."

"If something didn't make sense to me, I would question it," Page confirmed. "Absolutely. But at the same time, in my view at least, I was pretty good at doing what I was told. I may not like what you would have me do, but if it was the rule and what I had to comply with, I complied. I might try to change it, I might get snarly and sarcastic and all that, but I do what I'm told. The Vikings made the rules. I might have tried to change them, but I still followed them."

Page explained, "A lot of people just don't like the rules, so they don't follow them. I suspect it's easier to have people like that around, people who will break the rule, get a slap on the hand, then go on about their business. Those people don't change. And they'll break the rule again, quietly. But if you get someone who questions a rule, and rocks the boat in the process, eventually, that person has to go. There is a very limited willingness to put up with rocking the boat in substantive ways. It's okay to rock the boat by my simply ignoring what you want me to do, but you're not going to put up with me if I'm actually trying to do something about what you want me to do. And I don't think that is unique to football."

"Alan could talk all day to beat a $50 fine," Bud said. "Flat tire, out of gas, whatever. You get fined if you're late because that's what the rule says. I don't think he was accepting of our talks, but he would do his job. If he told you he wanted to know why a thing was done a certain way, that's true. And if he said he always did his job, I'd say that's true, too. Until the end."

A brilliant player who challenges the rules.

Strike one.

Then Alan Page got seriously into running and, as noted, by the start of the 1978 season, had dropped from the solid 245 pounds the coaches were comfortable with down to the 220s, where Page felt more comfortable and equally strong on the field. If anything, his endurance and quickness had improved—but Grant was concerned, and said so. Page stood firm in his decision to "play thin." Alan saw plusses: he could still do his job on the football field and he felt better. Most of the weight loss was body fat, not muscle, and it didn't happen overnight. But Grant, like most football coaches, held tight to core values. One of those values is that interior defensive linemen—men who get hit from two or three different directions at once—need bulk to avoid being knocked out of a play. With the star of their defensive line at a weight more appropriate for playing safety, there was concern.

When Grant brought it up, and Alan said he would stand or fall at 225, it was more than a clash between coach and player; it was the collision, really, of a new concept of defensive-line play (Page's) and the old-school concept to which Grant held fast.

Strike two.

The Vikings lost two of their first three games in 1978. The fourth game was at Chicago. Alan Page hadn't had a quarterback sack. He was pulled from the game at Chicago in the first half. "The season had been going horribly for me," Alan said. "I was furious at being pulled from the Chicago game. If you're a player and you're worth your salt, you want to be on the field."

Page was back in the game in the second half, but then was pulled again. With Page on the bench, Doug Sutherland, his backup, sprained both ankles on the same play. "That turf at Soldier Field was a nightmare," Sutherland said. "I turned in pursuit. I felt one go. I thought maybe I could still get the guy, but then the other one popped."

"Doug was my backup; I should have gone back in," Alan said. "I didn't see him go down. I was mad as hell. One of the coaches told me to go back in. I said 'Why?'" When he realized Sutherland was hurt, Page started for the field. Grant held out an arm as a stop sign and told him to sit down.

Strike three.

"Bud came into my office on Monday morning and told me to start looking for a trade for Alan. He said Alan was done here," the club's general manager, Mike Lynn, said. "I knew what had happened at Chicago, but I don't think I made much of an effort to trade him. I thought we might work it out. But we didn't. Looking back, it was a sad situation for everyone."

Page made the trip to Seattle the next week but then was placed on waivers, which meant he could be claimed by any NFL team for $100. The Vikings had fired the most celebrated player in the history of the franchise.

Diane Page came home from work that Monday evening to see TV crews and reporters outside their Kenwood home. She couldn't reach Alan, so she called Ed Garvey at the Players Association office in

Washington. Diane described the scene and asked Garvey what he thought.

"He said he didn't think it was a good thing," she said. "I never disliked Bud until he cut Alan. All of a sudden, we didn't know what to expect. The guy who is the light of my life just got fired. We had four kids, we didn't have an income, and we had just failed the bar exam. For a wife and a mother, that is a very small, scary window."

Bobby Bryant, Page's buddy, came by that night with the contents of his locker packed in a box. Doug Sutherland said that when he showed up the next day, lockers had been rearranged. "Usually, if a guy left, they just left the locker empty," he said. "I used to be next to Alan, but when I came in, I was next to Jim [Marshall]. It was like Alan's locker had never been there."

Grant left a phone message, expressing his regret that their years together had to end like this. In newscasts and press conferences, Bud praised Alan's contributions to the team over the years, but said Alan simply couldn't make the plays demanded of him anymore. Alan said he thought he could.

Looking back, Grant reflected on Page. "No one will ever accuse him of not being a smart man," he said. "I don't think Alan particularly enjoyed his time at Notre Dame, but he understood that by playing well there he would be able to move on to the pros. I think he looked at pro football as a means to an end. With the Vikings, I know he wanted to do something in education to help young people. When he entered the Hall of Fame, he used his induction speech to point out the need for us to educate our young. Again, he saw an opportunity and he took it. It was the same thing when he went onto the court; he saw the opportunity to be elected rather than have to wait for a governmental appointment."

Grant continued. "I believe Alan really means it when he says football is behind him. I don't think he ever really liked it, despite his great success."

That last part doesn't fly with Page. "I loved everything about playing football," he said. "I just didn't like a lot of the nonsense around it."

"When we have events involving former players," Grant said, "Alan is there and he does what's expected of him. But then he leaves. He doesn't stay or hang around with his old mates. That's not a criticism; he has the right to his priorities."

Grant chuckled. "We get along," he said. "We see each other occasionally and we're fine, we hug and do all the right things. I saw Diane for the first time in years; it was at the Vikings' office. She came running over and gave me a big hug. How about that? What happened between us was a long time ago. We've moved on." Then Grant chuckled again, adding, "Of course, I'm not sure I'd want to go up before Alan on a speeding ticket!"

Alan says he moved on a long time ago from any issues with Bud Grant: "Life's too short to waste on being aggravated about things that went on in the past. Besides, being released by the Vikings was probably the best thing that could have happened to me. It was clear to me that last year I was with the Vikings that something was broken. Going to Chicago couldn't have been better—it gave me a new lease on life. I probably overstayed my welcome in Minnesota by a number of years. Not with the fans, but with the team. The fans have been great; they don't remember that I left."

What about those three strikes? They were probably all in the mix. Page's outspoken criticism of management as a leader of the NFLPA, if not a cause for dismissal, did nothing to endear him to league and club officials, to say nothing of some of his teammates.

We probably could have seen it coming, actually, two strong men who took poorly to pushing. Two strong men who, if they believed they were right, held to their beliefs. Two strong men.

The bottom line?

"I think Alan Page played for the perfect coach in Bud Grant," said writer Jim Klobuchar. "Grant is the ultimate realist; if something's working, leave it alone. Sometimes that meant leaving Page alone. Alan got considerations other players didn't get. But he played. Oh, did he play! I think Grant knew what he had: a remarkable player and a person who challenged authority. They both had their own ways. Bud came down from Canada, and people thought he was bloodless and cold. He was just being Bud; it worked in Canada, why change it here? Page was being Page. Eventually, they had conflict, but they accomplished a lot, too."

Peter Dickinson lives near Lake Michigan on Chicago's North Shore. He is retired, more or less. Pete's a dab sailor and a keen student of wine vintages. He also volunteers two days a week at Yale Elementary School on Chicago's South Side, where he is the teacher's aide for the third grade. He has been a teacher's aide for 11 years. A Yale man himself (the college, not the elementary school), Pete first heard about the volunteer teaching program at a Yale alumni meeting. The high point of his teaching career? "My teachers have missed a day here and there, and I get to take the class by myself." He has been at Yale Elementary long enough that former students stop by to visit now and then. "I've gotten some hugs," he said. Pete has been approached about leaving the classroom to do administrative work at the school. He doesn't want to. "I like being with the kids," he said.

Chicago

"One of the first days I was in Chicago, I was walking up Michigan Avenue by myself. A bus driver going up the avenue honked and waved at me. I waved back, and he gave me a thumbs up. I thought, I'm going to like this town." —Alan Page

The Chicago Bears were the only team to claim Alan Page. There were several reasons why they should have: "Old home week," for one—the Bears were "Minnesota South." Their general manager, his assistant, the head coach, the defensive coordinator, the ticket manager, and the equipment manager all were ex-Vikings. Plus, according to Jim Finks Jr., it took a bit of trickery to make sure the Bears were successful in landing Page.

"After the Vikings decided Page couldn't stop the rush or rush the passer to their standards, they waived him," Finks said. "Dad [the late Jim Finks, then president and general manager of the Chicago Bears and the man who drafted Alan Page at Minnesota] heard that Al Davis wanted to claim Alan for his Oakland Raiders. Dad called Davis and told him, 'Page has lost it. He's washed up.' So Al didn't claim Page, Dad did."

More germane, however, the Bears needed help almost anywhere you looked, defensive tackle included. The one place they didn't need help was running back, where the amazing Walter Payton was already causing league jaws to drop. But the Bears hadn't done much since 1963, when they beat the Giants for the NFL championship on a bitter cold day at Wrigley Field. They had a fearsome defense then—Doug Atkins, Bill George, Ed O'Bradovich, and that crew. They left Y.A.

Tittle, Frank Gifford, and a lot of other New Yorkers battered and bloody in their wake. George Halas, who was more fearsome than his defense, was coaching then.

Alan Page arrived 15 years later, in 1978. There had been one tentative peek into the postseason under Jack Pardee, but nothing serious. In fact Bud Grant, who so recently had jettisoned Page, liked to remind his Vikings to be patient when they played the Bears. "Sooner or later," Grant would say, "they'll do something wrong and present you with a chance to win." He was usually right.

The last of several retirements by "Papa Bear" Halas finally took. Jim Dooley and Abe Gibron followed Halas with dreary results. When Jim Finks took over running the Bears in 1974, he brought in Jack Pardee, a solemn man, as his head coach. Then he brought in Neill Armstrong, a courtly man, after Pardee jumped ship to go to the Washington Redskins. Both were able coaches, but the end of the rainbow eluded both of those men, as well. However, under Armstrong, the Bears were beginning to growl once more. Faintly, maybe, but still a growl.

Finks had his toolkit out again. As in Minnesota, he focused first on both offensive and defensive lines. He built a young, winning offensive line—Jimbo Covert, Keith Van Horne, Kurt Becker, Tom Thayer, Mark Bortz, and Jay Hilgenberg (nephew of the Vikings' Wally). The defense flowered faster, as it usually does—learning to attack comes more quickly than learning to be efficient while being pounded on.

From the time Alan Page arrived in 1978 until he left after the 1981 season, his mates on the defensive line included Dan Hampton, Mike Hartenstine, Al Harris, Jim Osborne, and Steve McMichael. Otis Wilson was a talented young linebacker, and so was Mike Singletary, who, like Hampton, was a Hall of Famer in waiting. The secondary included two young safeties who hit like the crack of doom, Gary Fencik and Doug Plank. Fencik was a Yale man who looked to be above the mayhem, but wasn't. Plank had long, golden hair, a sunny smile, and the air of an eagle scout. On the field, he was a menace to friend and foe alike.

Bear receivers hated to play against Plank in practice. Page cringed when I mentioned the name. "I can still feel it," Alan whispered after a moment, eyes closed. "I was very fortunate as a player, I didn't have many injuries. But in one of my first games with the Bears—maybe the first one—I was one of several people in on a tackle. We were all kind of rolled up on the ground. The play was over. I was just starting to relax, when here comes Plank. I mean, he was like a missile, head down, using his helmet like a battering ram. That's against the rules now, thank God. Anyway, he dove into the stack, and the top of his helmet hit me in the side, just below my ribs. I thought I was going to die. I had to crawl to get up. When I could breathe and talk, I grabbed his face mask and got up close and said, 'Don't you *ever* do that to me again!'"

Fred Caito, then the Bears trainer, remembered Page. "Jim [Finks] told me Alan would pretty much go his own way, and he did. I just introduced myself and told him to let me know if he needed anything. Alan was the only player I knew who didn't want his ankles taped, and if he needed something taped, he did it himself. We talked many times, but never about football. We talked about our kids."

Linebacker Doug Buffone came into the league in 1966, a year ahead of Page. "[Alan was] my kind of guy," Buffone said. "He came prepared. He knew what the practice week was for. A lot of guys didn't take the practice seriously, and you'd see it in their play on Sunday. This game is about being prepared. I prepared, so I was glad to see Alan come to the Bears. I knew what he was—he was a pro. It figured. You don't get to be as good as he was and not take it seriously."

This about a man who freely admitted he didn't like practice. "I didn't," Alan said. "But that doesn't mean I didn't get my work done. Doug's right; it's about being prepared."

"He was so quick," Buffone remembered, "even when he came to us near the end of his career. Every guy he went up against outweighed him. It didn't matter—he could still go around a blocker and make the play."

Jay Hilgenberg was a rookie free agent center during Page's last season with the Bears. Hilgenberg went on to play in seven Pro Bowls and win All-Pro honors. "I went to a Vikings Super Bowl when I was a sophomore in high school," Jay said. "My uncle Wally played for the Vikings. I went to Wally's room one day. I knocked, but he wasn't there. Alan answered the door. He invited me in, and we talked for a good while. He was very nice.

"When I got to the Bears, I practiced against him every day. He taught me more than anyone about playing center in the NFL. He'd take me aside after practice and teach me how to hand-fight a defensive tackle. He taught me how to slip off the tackle's charge and get to the linebacker. All the while, he'd have me preparing him for the center he'd be up against that week. The thing was his leverage; his hands were so fast that he'd get you moving, and when he did that, it was over."

The biggest contribution Page may have made to the Bears was preparing the "pups," those young defensive linemen. Dan Hampton was one of them. If you are old enough to remember Li'l Abner from the comic strips, you've got the idea: a big, strapping, handsome, Arkansas country boy. Al Harris was another: light-hearted and quick. Mike Hartenstine was quiet, solemn, and stronger than a bear's breath. Steve McMichael was nicknamed "Mongo" after the Alex Karras character in the movie *Blazing Saddles*. They were young defensive linemen, waiting to excel. They did, and Alan Page had a hand in their achievements. "We had A.P., Oz [Jim Osborne], and Tommy Hart to teach us how to play in the NFL," Harris said. "We couldn't have had three better guys. I think Alan, especially, taught me how to study. He studied everything."

Harris and Hampton were first-round draft picks in 1979. "Rookies spent preseason in a basement locker room," Harris said. "When we moved up to the real locker room for the season, I was right next to Alan. The first time in there I must have just stared at him because he finally looked at me and said, 'What do you want, rook?' I said, 'You're Alan Page!' He said he knew who he was. I said, 'You don't understand. When I was back home, I had this electric football game. You were one of the plastic men on my game.' Some of the guys laughed when I said that. Alan said, 'Thanks a lot, rook.' Then he said, 'Listen, if you stick around this game, one day that will happen to you.' And it did! I had a free-agent kid tell me I was on his computer football game."

Dan Hampton broke both legs as a kid when his brother cut the rope he was climbing in a tree. His high school coach had to basically shame him out of the marching band to get him to play football. When he was drafted, he told the media he was part Native American. They loved that. Hamp hastened to add, "My people weren't warriors; I think they wove baskets." Asked to comment on his size (6'6" and 275 pounds as a rookie), Hampton said, "I've always been big. I was big even when I was little."

"Alan couldn't have gone to any other clubs when the Vikings cut him," Hampton said. "There wasn't any other team looking for a 225-pound defensive tackle. But Buddy [Ryan, defensive coordinator who had coached Page at Minnesota] was ahead of the curve when it came to situational use of players. This was evident since the mid-1980s with his 46 Defense [named for Doug Plank, who wore the No. 46 jersey], a devastating pass rush based on having too many rushers for the offense to block.

"Alan helped other people," Hampton continued. "Jim Osborne was getting sluggish at defensive tackle. When they drafted me, Oz saw the handwriting on the wall. He got [together] with Alan, started jogging, and got down to 245 pounds. He improved his quickness and endurance and became three or four clicks better as a player. And a lot of it was due to Alan."

Hampton is a very interesting guy: bright, brash, as comfortable laughing at himself as at others, observant, not at all contrived, and with a syntax all his own.

"I could tell Alan was—I don't want to say 'going through the motions'—but he had bigger fish to fry, and even though he got into the running thing and lost all that weight and Bud felt he'd obviously be better with somebody else in there, Alan still had value as a football player," he said.

"I know certain things he brought to the table and I, as a novice, rookie, green-as-grass kid, watched him. Alan was very courteous, he did not have a condescending attitude because here's a guy who's All-Pro, who's going to be Hall of Fame, and so forth. He could have dismissed all of us with a nod or scoffed at us."

Hampton continued. "At training camp, Mike Hartenstine and I roomed the floor below Alan and Ozzie. We were always playing the radio past lights out, having a few beverages, and generally acting up. Alan would come out and holler, 'Go to bed, rook, time for sleep.' I'd come out and holler, 'Ring the bell, Alan, ring the bell!' You'd hear guys laughing from the other rooms when I said that. What it was, we had this big, heavy blocking sled, and if you got a really good lick on it—hit it just right—you'd compress the springs and get this metal-on-metal sound like a bell ringing. Alan would hit the sled, but it never compressed enough to ring the bell because he was lighter. So, that was me—big, dumb rook, sassin' back at Alan Page."

Hampton's take on the weight issue? "Alan was 225 pounds. Some guys could blow him out of the hole; some guys could stymie him on the line. But a lot of the time, he was pretty damn effective at 225. He was always quick off the ball. He always had this great body lean and leverage, and although he didn't have all the power left, he had a real nice knack for diagnosing plays and putting himself in the way. At the end of the day, that's what it's all about. I'd watch film, and I'm thinking, he's uncanny—no great size, and his speed wasn't what it had been, but he's always around the ball, gettin' in the way. That's the essence of a great defensive player: gettin' in the way."

"Alan wasn't afraid to speak his mind," Jay Hilgenberg said. "I remember he called everybody out before a big game. I mean everybody—players *and* coaches. He told them they'd better be ready. He didn't care; he told you a thing the way he saw it. If people were critical of him for speaking his mind, it usually was the people who didn't want to give their best effort. That's what he gave. He told you what he was thinking; if you didn't buy it, that was okay, but he still told you."

The Bears won in overtime in Detroit in 1980 when David Williams ran back the overtime kickoff 95 yards to score. The players were so excited, they piled on Williams in the end zone, and when Williams got off the bottom of the pile, he had a broken nose. When they got in the locker room, Page's voice cut through all the laughing and shouting. "Feels pretty good, doesn't it?" he shouted. "Well, remember the feeling, remember what it takes to win. You've got to be willing to win! And not just once in a while…every week!"

Al Harris talked about a Monday night game, also at Detroit, in 1981. It was a nightmare game in which Lions quarterback Eric Hipple emerged from obscurity long enough to throw four touchdown passes. "Everything was going just awful for us," Harris said. "But at one point the officials clearly blew a call when we had them stopped on downs. I mean, it was probably the only time we stopped them, but the refs called a penalty that honestly wasn't there. A.P. just went off. He called those officials every name I'd ever heard, and I think he invented some I hadn't heard before. I'm thinking, he's out of here…they'll toss him. They didn't even call a penalty! They just stood around until Alan quit hollering, like kids being scolded. I think he got away with stuff sometimes because of who he was."

The Bears were 28–30 during the three-plus years that Alan Page played there. He enjoyed the experience. He was a leader in tackles and sacks.

"I enjoyed playing with the young defensive linemen," Alan said. "They were good guys who wanted to learn. They obviously had a lot of talent. Having Buddy [Ryan] there made it even more fun.

"We didn't win a lot, but where I net out on this is that it's about performance and performing as well as you can. Sure, you want to win and you're angry and upset when you don't. But as contrary as this may sound to the realities of the world, the won-lost column is not what it's all about in the end. The number of wins or losses might not show the quality of a person. But what you gave of yourself during a game, regardless of whether you won or lost, tells a tremendous amount about the quality of the person. In Chicago, I felt like I was part of a group that gave everything they had. That was enough for me. We didn't win many games, but defensively we were a good team. We just didn't have a lot of offense. Walter [Payton] almost made up for it, but he couldn't carry it all by himself. Darned near—just not quite. What an amazing player he was." (Walter Payton died of cancer in 1999. He was, at that time, the leading rusher in NFL history.)

One of Page's signature skills was the ability to block a kick. He blocked 28 of them. Usually they were field-goal attempts. Again, it was his extraordinarily quick reaction to the snap of the ball that let him succeed. Bears teammate Osborne told a story of one kick that didn't stay blocked.

"We were at Green Bay to open the 1980 season," Osborne said. "We were tied 6–6 with just a few seconds left. The Packers were close to our goal, but we held and forced a field-goal attempt. Alan grabbed me in the huddle and said if I really fired out on the center that he would block the kick. Well, I unloaded on the center and knocked him flat back. I felt Alan go by me as I was going down; I ended up under a lot of people. Then I heard thud-thud. When you hear two thuds like that, real quick, you know it's a block. I couldn't see anything, but man, was I happy. I'm yelling, 'We did it, we did it!' But then I heard the crowd start to cheer—a *big* cheer. They were going nuts. I knew a Packers crowd wasn't cheering us for blocking a field goal. I was trying to get up, trying to see what happened. Alan had blocked the kick, but the ball went straight back to the kicker, [Chester] Marcol. He caught it and took off running. I mean, here's this fat, slow, dumpy guy running for all he's worth. Nobody caught him. I guess our guys couldn't believe what had happened. Marcol scored. Green Bay beat us 12–6."

Steve McMichael was one of a kind. He arrived in Chicago in 1981, cut by the New England Patriots. Teammates generally called him "Mongo," although his side-kick Hampton preferred "Ming the Merciless." McMichael is a Texan and was purely fierce as a player. He hunted rattlesnakes, ran a bar, and wrestled professionally. Anyone with even a lick of sense gave McMichael and Hampton a wide berth.

But McMichael was funny, too. In one game under Mike Ditka, the Bears took a drubbing. Afterward, in a hushed locker room, Ditka shook his head and said several times, "Fellows, I just don't know what to say."

McMichael eventually broke the silence with his hard Texas twang: "Well I do...somebody lock the goddamned door so them sumbitches don't follow us in here and start up again."

McMichael laughed. "I always practiced balls out," he said, "just like a game. That was Alan's last year, when I got to Chicago. He was practicing light. One day he pulled me aside. He pointed down at my knees and said, 'Young man, think of your knees as tires. You're going to put a lot of miles on them in games. Don't put all the wear on them out here in practice. They'll last longer that way.'"

Alan Page's last game as a Bear—last game, period—was on December 20, 1981, at Soldier Field in Chicago. It was a sunny, bitter-cold day. The Bears were 5–10 and limping to the barn. Their opponents, the Denver Broncos, were fighting for a playoff spot. Alan was honored in a pregame ceremony. George Halas, team and league patriarch, commended Page for his football accomplishments and for who he was. It was the 218th game Alan Page had played in; he never missed a game because of injury.

Page was in the Broncos' backfield constantly in that final game. He had three and a half sacks, and the Bears beat the Broncos 35–24, dashing Denver's playoff hopes. After the game, when Page walked out to the parking lot, his teammates were waiting for him. They sang "Auld Lang Syne." Those words are from Scottish literature. The English translation? "The good old times."

"I lost it," Alan said.

Dan Hampton, in summation: "Eighty-two [Alan's Bears jersey number in Chicago] was on his own wavelength. It's almost like [for] a lot of the precepts that make up a pro football player, Alan was 180 degrees opposite of 'em. Well, God bless him. I know one thing—I'll bet he doesn't spend much time goin' down memory lane, does he?"

Not much, Hamp.

Ted Albrecht was a solid offensive tackle whose bad back made him a successful travel agent before his time. Ted played against Page as an opponent and then practiced against him as a teammate. Alan Page, Albrecht recalled, was "savvy and so smart. When he was at Minnesota, they usually came at you straight up, [Page] and Marshall, but sometimes they'd run twists. You knew, sooner or later, that Page was going to be coming out around the corner, right at you. You had to tie yourself to your guard's hip and be patient. Precise. If you weren't, he was by you. He was such a gentleman when he was off the field, but when he went on the field, including the practice field, it was like he turned a switch. He was pretty intense.

"We had two conversations that I remember," Albrecht said. "When he got there, I asked him how his kids were with moving. He told me that if his kids saw that he and Diane were good with it, then they would be. When he retired, I asked him how he felt about leaving football. He said he felt like it was time to walk the other paths of his life."

"If I didn't make my bed, I got lectures about trust and respect and responsibility. I got lectures if I asked for something. I wanted to borrow some money for a bike trip when I was an adult, and I started to get a lecture. I said, 'Forget it—I don't need the money that bad.' Now, I ask for advice. I used to call it lectures. I don't get lectures anymore. I have learned that through patience, perseverance, and smart decisions, I can do anything I want. But if you're not open to learning, nothing comes easily. I think what my dad has been doing all along is putting people in the right place to make good decisions."

—Nina Page, daughter

In Pursuit of Perry Mason

"We didn't hire him because he was a football star. We hired him because he's a good lawyer." —Leonard Lindquist, Lindquist & Vennum

"What did Alan bring to our office? Dedication and discipline. He wanted his efforts to benefit the public. A lot of lawyers are very good at what they do, but they aren't all that concerned with the plight of the people. Alan is. That's important." —Hubert H. "Skip" Humphrey III, former Minnesota attorney general

"When you're a kid, you daydream about what you'd like to be when you grow up," Alan Page said. He smiled. "Aside from the fact that I'm still not really sure what I want to be when I grow up, when I was a kid I thought about being a lawyer. I watched a lot of Perry Mason on television. What he did seemed pretty cool to me. It didn't seem like he had to work very hard, he wore great-looking suits, and he almost always won. Being a lawyer didn't look that difficult. I thought I'd be able to play golf and live a pretty comfortable life."

Alan Page does not play golf. He works long hours, usually seven days a week unless something special keeps him from his legal papers on Sunday. He doesn't always win. He does wear nice suits, set off by lively socks and bow ties. The bold socks and ties make it into the courtroom, too. Susie Collins, a friend of the Pages and a socks and bow-tie scout for Alan, said, "Here's this big, tall, serious-looking

African American guy wearing a long black robe. He needs something to perk it up."

Back in the day when Alan played for the Minnesota Vikings, players routinely found off-season jobs to supplement their income. Alan bounced around. He owned a snack vending business for a while. He sold cars, too—and although sales weren't great, he met a mechanic at the dealership who would become his one-man pit crew for drag racing. "The best part about the vending machine business was that's how I met my wife," he said. But the business advice he received was not always sound, and his earnings showed it.

Forays into the commercial world behind him, Alan decided he would rekindle old dreams set by Perry Mason and go to law school. He entered the William Mitchell College of Law in St. Paul.

"From the time I started until the time I left took about three to four weeks," Page said. "It only took about two days to realize I was in hopelessly over my head. I wasn't ready. I thought law school sounded like a good thing to do, but I didn't have a clue of what would be involved. The rest of those weeks were spent getting separated from law school."

Alan's biggest problem was that he didn't know how to study. "I learned to float by in high school; I learned the tricks," he said. "It wasn't something I'm proud of. Notre Dame was harder because football took a lot of my time, but I got by. I could have done better. I wasn't avoiding learning, I just wasn't struggling to learn; I wasn't excited by it. Learning to learn is like everything else that's worthwhile—you go through a struggle to get it. The love of learning just for the sake of learning didn't captivate me until I was in law school for the second time. My kids are fortunate; they learned how to learn and became excited by it much earlier in life than I did. It's probably like a lot of things—it's easier to do when you're younger."

Page entered the University of Minnesota law school and graduated from it while still a player for the Vikings. Just as he applied discipline to his approach to football, when he went back to law school to stay, he did the same thing. In sports, you hear the term "grinder"—like a hockey player who will go into a crowded corner to dig for the puck, flying elbows and sticks notwithstanding. It's about deciding a hard thing is worth doing. Worth grinding for.

It's about discipline.

"When I dropped out of Mitchell," he said, "it was because I was in so far over my head. I didn't realize everybody else was in the same boat, I thought it was just me. Law school's different from undergraduate. I imagine most graduate schools are. It's much more intense.

"It was, in a way, like the jump from college to pro football. When you come into the pro game, people say everything is speeded up and you have to be there for a while before the game slows down to where you have some confidence and the game seems more manageable. One thing that helped me in school was being involved with the NFL Players Association as a player. I worked with a lot of lawyers and I was comfortable around them.

"I had some dawning when I went back to law school," Page said. "I developed a real sense of who I was and how important it was for me to prepare for the future. I had a family; I wasn't going to play football forever."

He took light class loads during the season, then picked up the pace during winter and spring quarters. Bud Grant let him skip training camp one year. "I knew he'd be in shape and ready to play," Grant said. "Alan asked me the next year if he could skip camp again, but I said no. I had enough players mad at me as it was."

"Law school actually made it easier to continue playing football," Page said. "It gave me something to think about at practice." And you could find people who would agree with Page's next statement: "I was never real good with the concept of practice. Practice was boring for the most part. There's not much new that goes on, especially after you've been a part of the team for a long time. You know the routine. I wasn't real good with repetition, and that's what practice is about. I knew I needed to do it, and thinking about law school gave me something to break the tedium."

Alan actually began his successful run at law school in the summer of 1975, when he took two classes at the University of Texas. He enrolled at Minnesota that fall and finished in the spring of 1978. While

Page prepared for the bar exam that summer, the football-driven atten-tion given to his weight loss proved a distraction. Page's numbers were still good as the 1978 season began, but neither man could resolve the playing-weight conflict. The chemistry between coach and player was failing. For years, Grant had accepted Alan's recalcitrant approach as coin for his immense talent. That approach probably became more bur-densome when Grant feared his star was falling where it counted, on the playing field.

Just after learning he had failed his first attempt at the bar exam, Alan was informed he'd been fired (or "waived," in NFL parlance) from the Vikings.

He didn't stay failed or fired, of course: he played three and a half more years for the Chicago Bears and passed the bar exam on his sec-ond try. He was hired in 1979 by Lindquist & Vennum, a Minneapolis law firm known for its work in labor issues. Page worked part time while his career with the Bears wound down. L&V knew Alan from his days as a player union leader, when he had been a burr under the NFL saddle as a leader of the NFLPA. Alan challenged the NFL's views on bedrock issues like player movement (free agency), salary structures, and revenue sharing.

The league didn't see a problem in these areas. There was no free-agency issue. Salary structure then meant reluctant accommodation to the few best players and thin soup for the rest. Revenue sharing did not exist in Page's time. African American players were at the forefront of union activities because their jobs seemed to be harder won and harder held.

Whatever sigh of relief the NFL Management Council—the league's labor relations representative—may have felt at Page's retirement as a player evaporated when he showed up as counsel for Lindquist & Vennum, representing the NFLPA in non-injury arbitrations.

Alan actually wanted to stay in Chicago after he finished playing—and he had opportunities. But he didn't. He explained: "I wanted to take a job that was offered to me in Chicago in the worst way. Diane said, 'Fine, but I'm going back to Minnesota.' Of course, the kids said they were going, too."

Jim McCarthy, another newcomer to Lindquist & Vennum, had the cubicle next to Page. Jim remembered seeing Alan around law school at the University of Minnesota. "During football season, he'd be limping on Mondays and Tuesdays," McCarthy said. "After we started working together, we'd go to lunch together most days. We had a real meal—meatloaf, mashed potatoes, stuff like that. And always, a piece of apple pie. It wasn't long before I started putting on weight. I'd look at Alan, and he never changed. That's when I remembered he ran five or six miles every morning. Not some mornings—every morning."

Alan worked in the area he was familiar with from his days in the player union—labor relations. Gene Keating, a Lindquist & Vennum partner, and "a few others" taught young Page to be a lawyer. "Gene was a good teacher," Alan said. "The things he talked about were the same ones I had heard in football—hard work, discipline, perseverance."

One thing Keating, et al., didn't teach Page was confidence. "I don't know if confidence is something born in you or a gift you acquire, probably from your parents," Alan said. "I know my parents supported me in a positive way. They let me know that they believed in me, and that they expected me to be somebody. I don't know if it was from them or not, but I have always felt confident that I could do whatever task was set for me."

As a fledgling lawyer, Alan represented a railroad carrier in a case against Pillsbury, a legendary name in Minnesota commerce. It was his first appearance at court. Pillsbury's legal team was quick to point out to the court that Alan had made his name as a football star. Alan ignored the jab and went about his business.

"Alan has encountered that situation many times in his career," said McCarthy. "He is there as an accomplished lawyer, but he's also Alan Page, well known in the community, and a former football star. How does all that balance? In that Pillsbury case, Alan did what he has always done—his job. His presentation was solid," said McCarthy.

"There have always been people who wondered if I was really a lawyer or just a football player playing lawyer," Page said. He was a lawyer. He argued his client's motion well. After the hearing against the Pillsbury attorneys, they asked Page for autographs for their sons. He obliged.

Alan was proving an asset at Lindquist & Vennum, but he wouldn't be staying long.

"Many lawyers get into a private firm, serve private clients, and make their careers there," said McCarthy. "Some take a broader look. I think Alan understood that if he was going to make a greater contribution to the community, he was going to have to broaden the base of his experience." Almost certainly, there is more money in the private sector. Better perks, too. Why not stay? "Underneath everything else," McCarthy said, "I think Alan is driven by his caring for people. He cares about his family, his community, and his country. He's involved in so many ways, but, in the end, he always comes back to caring for people. That allows him to keep a singular focus. His success as an athlete, the prominence of his position on the court, and his popularity here in Minnesota has never really turned him aside from those goals. I think they are what make him a good judge."

There was also a less altruistic side to this. Besides Jim McCarthy's true view of his friend, there was Alan's realization that he did not enjoy one of private law's most important chores—drumming up new business. "I'm not a salesman, and I'm a poor businessman," Page said. "Ask the car dealer I worked for. Those things don't fit me. I love the law and I loved my work, but I spent more time worrying about billing the hours than doing the work and doing it well."

Skip Humphrey had a solution.

Hubert "Skip" Humphrey III, the son of Minnesota's beloved "Happy Warrior," Hubert H. Humphrey II, served as Minnesota's attorney general when Page was at Lindquist & Vennum.

"Leonard Lindquist called me one day," Skip said. "He told me he had an opportunity I should consider." The opportunity was Alan Page.

"I wasn't directly involved with Alan's work before he came to our office," Humphrey said. "I didn't know him well as a lawyer. Of course, I knew who he had been as a football player, and I knew he was a friend of my dad's. Alan and the other Vikings defensive linemen had campaigned for Dad, and he and Alan had become friends. I knew that Alan had a positive reputation as a lawyer. I set up a meeting with him and asked about his interests."

"I told Skip I loved the work I was doing," said Page, "but I wanted to be a full-time worker in the law without having to go out and, in a sense, be a rainmaker for a law firm."

"I talked to people I knew about Alan," said Humphrey. "With Leonard Lindquist's comments, that made a pretty positive read. We have a review process in the AG office, and Alan came through with flying colors. So I appointed him."

"It was a great place to work and to learn," Alan said. "The focus of the job was on representing clients. There was no political agenda other than representing the people of the state of Minnesota. I thrived."

As a football player, Alan Page loved the game, but not the "stuff" that surrounded it. He made the same discovery in the law. He loved the law; he just didn't care for the ancillary stuff—the cocktail parties and other recruiting efforts.

Alan was a staff lawyer with the attorney general's office. He worked in employment litigation. Actually, his role in the AG's office was the reverse of his frequent role at Lindquist & Vennum, where he had represented the employee side of labor issues. Now he represented state agencies in employment litigation. He also worked in worker's compensation and OSHA cases.

He had found a law niche that suited him—pure casework. But he knew it wouldn't be permanent. The idea was already forming for the last move Alan Page would make within the legal system.

Looking back on Alan's years in the attorney general's office, Skip Humphrey said, "One thing I liked was that he always wanted to hear both sides of an issue. He tried to see if there was a way of resolving problems before getting into court. That's the way I think law should be practiced. When Alan worked for us, his capacity to be a good advocate for the government was always there, but he also tried to seek a reasonable solution."

If it's possible to play defensive tackle in the NFL quietly—and it probably isn't—then Alan did it. Quiet, but relentless. Tireless. Intelligent. He lawyered the same way in the private sector and in the attorney general's office. Most of Alan Page's accomplishments, in sports and the law, have had more to do with preparation, effort, and discipline than with fanfare.

"I'm proud of the work I do," Alan said. "I'm proud of the effort that goes into producing the result. This applies everywhere—the results are the same whether you're cooking a chicken at home or making a tackle on the football field or pursuing the truth in law. Like someone said, it's the journey, not the destination. Sometimes the destination is a bit of a disappointment. But the effort—the journey—is what's there for us."

Alan Page has measured his legal career and life in general against sport. "There's something about winning that, at some level, you can feel good about because you know you were responsible for it, at least in part," he said. "But at another level, it's pretty empty, pretty hollow, because when you're done, you think, what was that all about? What do I have to show for it? But at the same time, losing, painful as it can be, sometimes is more fulfilling than winning because you have to deal with that pain and, hopefully, grow from it. I suppose that's why it's what goes into the journey that is important."

"*I try to be a good listener. I think people want to be heard, so I listen. I want to find out about them. I'd rather listen to one person for 20 minutes than listen to 20 people for one minute; I think it does more. I also believe strongly in child protection. I still travel to speak on our need to improve justice for children.*"

—Kathleen Blatz, retired Minnesota
Supreme Court justice

The Page Education Foundation

"Ultimately, I have learned life is about what you create. I am motivated to work hard." —Vang Tou Xiong, Page Education Foundation scholar

The Page Education Foundation (PEF) marked its 20th anniversary in 2008. By then, it had raised more than $10 million and assisted some 3,000 students of color from Minnesota. (Today the number of students assisted exceeds 4,000.) PEF supports students at public and private universities, colleges, and technical schools in Minnesota.

The year PEF was founded, 1988, was the year Alan Page went into the Pro Football Hall of Fame. Induction into the Hall provides every inductee with a platform from which he may express himself. Most confine their remarks to football or family and the great honor afforded them. But there is no formula.

Alan set the stage for his remarks by choosing as his presenter not a coach nor an old teammate or a family member, but a schoolteacher. And to increase that departure from form, it was a female schoolteacher, one Alan didn't even know particularly well, and who was completely unheard of to those at the induction ceremony on that steamy summer day in Canton, Ohio.

To begin, Page thanked the Hall of Fame's directors for their recognition of his football achievements. Then he got down to his real message: the need to educate our children. He shined his spotlight brightest on our impoverished, ignored, imperiled children of color. And he was heard. Heard first on that sweltering afternoon in Canton, and heard since, as his remarks resonated down the years.

"I wasn't trying to ruffle anybody's feathers," Alan said. "I've heard that some people were taken aback by my speech. I wanted to show appreciation for my football career being honored—that felt good. But in reality, I tend to live more in the here and the now than I do in the past. It struck me that I could talk, too, about the importance of motivating our children in their educational pursuits."

The Page Education Foundation is the vehicle by which Page pursues this dream.

The first Page scholars were chosen in the 1989–1990 school year. There were 10 of them. There were no scholars and no money in 1988, the winter before Alan's Hall of Fame induction. But there was a meeting on a frosty Sunday afternoon in south Minneapolis at the home of Steve and Karen Boros. Steve Boros was a neonatologist and Alan's closest friend. Karen Boros was a college journalism teacher. Mike Jordan was also there. Jordan is a wry jack-of-all-trades—lawyer, teacher, and a member of city government. All were friends of Alan Page, although "friends" probably isn't a strong enough term. "Soul buddies," maybe. "Steven and Alan loved the fact that they brought out the wackiest humor in each other," Karen Boros said. "One would call the other at night and maybe say two words—just nutty stuff—then hang up. Then they'd both roar with laughter." Diane Page was present, as well. While Alan was PEF's namesake and point man, Diane was its energy core—urging, envisioning, pleading, and pounding the pavement, especially in the frazzling formative years. The group's shared interests were education and young people.

"We all wanted to do something about educating the young," said Karen Boros. "We just didn't know exactly what. That Sunday meeting was all business—no snacks, no coffee, no water, we wanted to get something done."

The group arrived at a set of parameters, Alan explained. "We wanted to encourage young people of color in Minnesota to see education as the way to improve the quality of their lives, and we wanted them to see it as something they could achieve. I grew up in Canton, an industrial city. For a young black man growing up in Canton in the '60s, there weren't a lot of options. Education was my way to avoid working in a steel mill.

"We wanted to reach the mid-level student," Alan said. "The A students would have opportunities without our help. We were more interested in the kid in the middle of the pack who was more apt to get forgotten. We accepted the fact that college isn't the answer for everyone, so we broadened our concept to include any postsecondary students who wanted to go to tech schools, vocational schools, nursing schools, whatever.

"We didn't want a foundation that said they had to go to school; we wanted the students to realize that furthering their education was a goal that was within reach. A lot of kids lose hope. They accept what they think is fact—that they won't be able to break out of the way of life they've always seen. We want them to know they can."

Talk about a group that felt good about their mission statement! Alan and Diane could not wait to tell their kids. They outlined the plan and waited for a flood of approval...or at least shared excitement.

Diane Page recalled one reaction: "When we told our daughter Georgi, she just sat there for a moment. Then she kind of scratched her eyebrow and said it seemed like something was missing. We were shocked; we thought we'd covered everything. Georgi mentioned mentoring, but she said she wasn't sure what that would involve."

Because she wasn't sure, Georgi and her friend Matt went to the library to learn about mentoring. Driving home, they were brainstorming, bouncing ideas off each other. They decided it would be great if Page scholars would help other, younger kids from their neighborhoods to learn about the importance of education, just as they had. That way, the program would have continuity. They said the little kids would look up to the Page scholars. Eventually, "little kids" meant students between kindergarten and eighth grade.

"We thought the money was the important thing," Diane said. "Our kids said the scholars, the recipients, had to contribute, too, in order to make it work. Our kids saw the need, right away, for the Page scholars not just to receive a grant, but also to help grow the pool of potential scholars. The young scholars were the ones the younger kids back in the neighborhoods would listen to."

"Georgi and Matt's suggestion, that the scholars go back and connect with the little kids, has been the key to our program," Diane said. In a nutshell, Page scholars must agree to "give back" at least 50 hours during the school year by returning to their communities to tutor and mentor children in kindergarten through eighth grade. Failing that, with help, they mentor kids in the community where they are furthering their own education. Many Page scholars give back more than the required 50 hours. In fact, in 2008 Page scholars gave back nearly 200,000 hours. They spark an interest in education in the little kids; they keep the wheel turning.

Jim Klobuchar had this observation: "It's almost an ethic in Minnesota, the thinking that 'I can help.' I don't think it was an accident that Alan ended up here. Think what the Page Foundation would be like if he was playing today. He'd be making millions and millions of dollars. I don't know his salary, but at his high water mark it probably was less than $200,000 a year. He would have been able to take the Foundation national. Of course, maybe he did it just the way he wanted to do it, which would be Alan."

Mona Harristhal worked for PEF for 19 years. She resigned recently, but she still mentors a young woman who is a Page scholar. Like they say in football, Mona has a "high motor." A chemistry major in college, Mona decided, after joining the work force, that she was a people person, not a researcher. She joined the Peace Corps and ended up in Micronesia as an advisor to government and small businesses, and an English teacher on the side. Mona still returns to visit her adopted Micronesian family, but when she was in the Peace Corps dengue fever sent her home to Minneapolis just as PEF was getting off the ground. Mona's sister was in market research and had worked with Diane Page. Mona needed some spending money; Diane needed someone to work part time for PEF.

"I told Diane that if they ever hired somebody full-time, I hoped she would consider me," Mona said. "Diane said that would be at least a couple years away. Six months later I was working full-time for PEF."

Diane and PEF's board of directors had to intervene on that one. Alan's strong vision was that all PEF work would be voluntary and that every penny of every dollar raised would go to the scholars. Alan had been paying Mona $8 an hour, out of his own pocket. "We had to make him see we needed full-time employees if we were ever going to grow the Foundation," Diane said. "He agreed, grudgingly."

Mona wasn't a money person. "I'd say, 'We need more money,'" Diane said. "Mona would say, 'Oh, don't worry, the money will come,' and somehow it did. We couldn't have made it without Mona; she took concepts and made them into structures, well-run structures—and all the while, she treated the Page scholars like they were her own nieces and nephews. Even though she's retired, I know she still stays in touch with a lot of them."

Mona smiled, adding, "Once we got a kid in the program, I kept my hooks in them."

PEF started out with free space in the basement of an auto parts warehouse. Mona's phone line went through the company switchboard. "They'd say, 'Bumper to Bumper,' and someone who wanted me might hang up," she said. "When I answered and said it was the Foundation, some guy who wanted a generator would hang up. But somehow it worked."

The "somehow" was a tall, stern, young lawyer.

"Alan is a quiet man, but he is a fire-breathing dragon when it comes to protecting our young people's right to seek education," Mona said.

"Alan set us on the path," she said. "There are so many things in starting up and running an organization that can sidetrack you, but Alan kept pulling us back to what was important. He helped me a lot, because I can become pretty scattered. We would like to be everything to all kids, but we can't. Alan can boil down the issues; he's so good at staying on point. And he was available. We talked back and forth by phone, but if an important issue came up, Alan was there."

The Foundation contacts schools across the state. Schools are notified that scholarships are available. Applicants must each write an essay stating future plans and hopes and provide letters of recommendation, family income information, and a school transcript of grades. A lot of

PEF's growth has been by word of mouth. "Kids in the program tell their friends, and they tell younger siblings," said Mona. "They tell them this is something they should be involved in. That's a lot of how it took off."

"Alan's favorite word is *prepare*," Mona Harristhal said. "Prepare for the next step. That's the word we want our scholars bringing to the little kids when they come back in the community as mentors."

There's groundwork to be done when a Page scholar goes to school away from Minneapolis. While many PEF scholars are from the Twin Cities, they're apt to show up on campuses anywhere in the state. When they do, PEF establishes an adult contact to mentor the Page scholar. "We don't want to just send a scholarship check to the college," Mona said. "We want people who are qualified to serve as mentors, to know there's a Page scholar at their school, and to be there for them."

There are more female Page scholars than male. Concerned about that, the Foundation started a recruitment program for African American males. It's working, Harristhal said.

A young man named Joe was in the PEF program, but then dropped out. "He called me one day," Mona said. "He told me he wanted to go back to school. I just hollered. I said, 'God, Joe, that is so exciting!' He said, 'Wow! Nobody's been so excited to hear from me, ever.' Joe graduated from college in 2007 with a degree in accounting," Mona said. "He struggled to stay in school. We understand those things; our kids can't always do it in one chunk."

Mona told of one of their young women who attended the University of Minnesota despite those around her telling her she might shoot for a community college, at best. But she went to the university. She got her bachelor's. Then she got her master's. Then she got her doctorate. Now she's in Connecticut, running an educational program.

Alan's concern about not squandering money on paid employees seems still to be in play. This is a tight ship. When Harristhal was director, her full-time fellow staffers were Carolyn Jones, director of development, and Patrice Howard, a former Page scholar and the student support officer. With Harristhal's retirement, Jones added another hat, and the staff shrank to two full-timers, herself and Howard. The staff says its success is due in great part to the involvement of volunteers like Mike Jordan and Karen Boros. And the Pages, of course; although Alan, as a judge, can't participate in fund-raising, his wife is under no such restrictions.

"Diane volunteers all the time," Mona Harristhal said. Alan participates in PEF functions and goes out to schools to encourage students to pursue their educations.

Not surprisingly, Alan tends to talk about preparation. "He tells them there is help through the Page Foundation," Harristhal said. "He's supporting what our scholars say when they go out to mentor the little kids: 'Prepare yourself for your life.' Alan is all about preparation."

The justice still visits schools, still encourages young school children, and urges them to see their studies for the precious tool that they are. Nothing angers him more than the mistreatment of children or their being denied a better future.

"I'm very proud of the Foundation," Diane Page said. "I'll be out, and a young person will come up to me and say, 'Hey, I'm a former Page scholar.' We go to awards ceremonies or orientations and meet these incredible young people, and learn what they're up to. It's wonderful, but it's like having a fifth child. The fund-raising is an ongoing challenge; we need to raise a million dollars a year. It's hard because Alan can't be involved in fund-raising while he's on the court, and he would be our best fund-raiser."

Diane worries about the future. "We're not getting any younger." The Pages are in their mid-sixties. Alan is eligible to retire from the court in 2010, but he has chosen to run again.

"We don't see ourselves as retired," Diane said. Surely, the Page Education Foundation would not welcome their stepping down—and that concerns them.

"Every year, it's like, okay, we've got to raise another million," Diane said. "After 20 years, I am sort of weary. Alan is pretty removed from the day-to-day issues, so if somebody's going to leave, finding the right replacement, personnel issues—it's a lot. It's that fifth child of ours who's never going to graduate or find a job. It's one of the biggest accomplishments in our lives, but I worry…will it go on? I think it's probably going to be okay. It seems like we've always had guardian angels looking after the Page Foundation—always. We believe it will go on, but we haven't figured out a long-term strategy."

"I'm proud of the Foundation in the sense that we've created the opportunity for some really good things to be done," Alan Page said. This is pure Page—making the profound sound simple. He doesn't talk about the things he and Diane have accomplished; he talks about creating an opportunity for the young people of Minnesota to better themselves. The accomplishments are made by the Page scholars.

Derek Francis, a Page scholar, went to Longfellow Elementary School in Minneapolis. Now he mentors "little kids" at Longfellow. He takes his charges to Augsburg College, where he studies communications and journalism. Derek wants to become a broadcast journalist.

"I want to give those kids a sense of hope," Derek said. "I want them to have a picture of what college looks like. They do not understand what college is, and I want to show them." Derek said the kids ask a lot of questions. "The Page Foundation has given me so much more than a scholarship," he said. "They have shaped who I am and who I hope to become."

On April 29, 2010, Justice Page addressed the Chamber of Commerce in Cannon Falls, Minnesota, about 30 miles southeast of the Twin Cities. His topic was judicial independence, but in light of the addition of a brand-new member of the town's Chamber, he also touched on the Page Education Foundation and its purpose, noting that not talking about PEF "would be a wasted opportunity, with a shining example of what we're all about in the audience."

Gail Rosenblum of the Minneapolis *Star Tribune* reported on this special day. The new Chamber member/"shining example" was Johny Sanchez, owner of Sol de Mexico, one of the town's most popular new restaurants. Sanchez is also a Page Scholar, having attended Riverland Community College aided by a two-year grant from PEF.

Sanchez said PEF gave him a gift that made him believe anything was possible. Like all Page Scholars, Sanchez mentored younger people—in his case, Hispanic middle school and high school students—reminding them about the importance of sticking with education. "The Page

Foundation really helped me," Sanchez said. "A lot of Hispanic people don't go to college. They don't think they can make it."

If Alan has concerns for PEF's future, he keeps them to himself. But he believes creating it when the opportunity was there was the right thing to do.

So how do you meet the unknowns of the Foundation's future?

"Prepare," Alan Page said.

"Alan spoke at his Uncle Floyd's church in 1989. I thought it was a very important day for our family. I was nervous doing it, but during the benediction, I took a deep breath, stood up, and interrupted the minister. I said, 'Sir, I hate to interrupt you, but I want this congregation to know that besides Alan, all of Floyd Umbles' family is here today, and will they all stand up.' Afterward, my brothers said they could have killed me for doing that, but I think it's important to show that we are family. I'll always feel that way. So now it doesn't bother me so much to get up in front of people and say what I think needs saying. That's important, too."

—Gwen Singleterry, Alan's cousin

Hail and Farewell

"After the induction ceremony, we had a family gathering back at the hotel. There was a Whitney Houston song ['The Greatest Love of All'] that was popular then, about believing that the children are our future. We had a boom box, and someone played that song. When my dad heard it, he started to cry. It was the first time I had ever seen him cry—you know, a good, full-hearted cry. It was like the Rock of Gibraltar was crumbling." —Nina Page, daughter

Alan Page was inducted into the Pro Football Hall of Fame in 1988, his second year of eligibility. To be selected in one's second year of eligibility is rare.

Alan wasn't surprised he was passed over in 1987, his rookie year of eligibility, nor that he was honored a year later. But that's Alan—he doesn't blink much. If you were able to look inside his head, you might have seen that he believed his accomplishments as a player merited first-year selection. He also believed that questioning rules and authority and speaking your piece—when your piece might not be popular with management or your fellow players, or both—could kink the thinking of some selectors.

Don Pierson, whose retirement diminished the *Chicago Tribune's* pro football coverage, was a Hall of Fame selector. Each of the cities in the NFL is represented by a voter. There usually are several other at-large voters, so the number is in the mid-30s. The majority of voters are print journalists, although more and more are from the electronic side of the aisle.

"I like it better than the way baseball selects their Hall," Pierson said. "The baseball votes are sent in. For HOF, we get together, face-to-face, for the last rounds of balloting." Pierson laughed. "It can get pretty exciting. Baseball has statistics for everything, but football doesn't, not for everybody. You know how many passes a guy caught, or how many yards a back ran for, but it's harder to point to a lineman's stats. You have to sell him on some values that aren't recorded, aren't down in black and white. If a candidate is from your city, you don't just present him, you want to sell him to the others. And there's horse-trading that goes on."

Early balloting begins in the fall. Cuts are made as the votes continue. The final 15 candidates, as Pierson said, "get into the room." Not in the flesh, but their names are there. More pare-down votes follow, not face-to-face, but ever more difficult. The face-to-face voting takes place the day before the Super Bowl in the site city and usually lasts between three and six hours. The number of candidates reduces as "in the room" voting takes place. A candidate must receive at least 10 percent of the vote to continue.

Alan Page's Class of '88 eventually was whittled down to four: Fred Biletnikoff, Mike Ditka, Jack Ham, and Alan Page.

Biletnikoff, a spindly receiver for the Oakland Raiders, was not especially fast, but he was a genius at finding holes in defenses and making the critical catch. So critical and so frequently, in fact, that he prompted a rule change in the league. Biletnikoff would coat his hands and forearms with a sticky substance not unlike pine tar. It was hard for a ball to escape his grasp, actually. Terry Bradshaw, a rival quarterback, once complained to officials that Biletnikoff's glop was making the ball stick to his hand as he attempted to pass.

Ditka, along with John Mackey and Jackie Smith, created the modern tight-end position. Bear, Eagle, and Cowboy, but ever a Bear at heart, "Iron Mike" was a ferocious blocker, but he also had surprising speed and soft hands. And he was next to impossible to bring down after he caught the ball. Ditka despised losing; he once chased his older brother Ashley home and beat the tar out of him for dropping a crucial fly ball in a grade-school baseball game.

Jack Ham, a linebacker for the Steelers, looked well suited to wearing a tux and welcoming diners to a high-end restaurant. He looked even better suited to wearing Steelers black and gold. He was agile, athletic, intelligent, swift, and tireless—in other words, another one of those honor graduates of Penn State's "Linebacker U."

Biletnikoff was presented by Raiders owner Al Davis; Ditka by Bears teammate Ed O'Bradovich; Ham by Joe Paterno, his college coach; and Page by Willarene Beasley, a black woman who was principal at North High School in Minneapolis. Willarene was not the first female presenter: Marie Lombardi, Vince's widow, had presented Packers Forrest Gregg and Jim Taylor before her.

Alan's class was inducted on Saturday, July 30, 1988. It was vintage Canton summer weather: sweltering. "We was happy, but we was all sweating," said Gwen Singleterry, Alan's cousin. Page was the first Canton native to be inducted and is the only inductee who helped build the Hall of Fame. "I had a summer job sweeping raw concrete floors," Alan said. "We did some work at the Hall site. I swept a lot of floors."

Did he dream of someday being enshrined in the Hall when he was part of a construction crew that built it?

Alan laughed. "It would make for a good story, wouldn't it? And it is interesting to look back," he said. "The importance of football to Canton had the community excited, but when you're younger, you don't think that much about that. You're thinking about your broom and sweeping a section of floor, which, in the end, you will have to sweep again, almost before you get done with the first sweep. So I didn't think a lot about the historic part of it."

When asked what he remembers most about induction day, Page paused in reflection, then laughed. "The heat and the hard hats," he said. "This probably sounds crazy, but I couldn't get over those hard hats. A lot of the fans wore them, and you have to remember, all four of us inductees were from the northern Ohio–western Pennsylvania area. The hats were hysterical; they had beer cans attached to them and tubes coming down from the cans so the wearer could drink beer while he was wearing the hat. That was a classic football crowd—they were loud and they were having fun. I thought they were great."

Although he admits to being nervous, Alan tried to keep the day normal. "Diane and I went for a run early in the morning," he said. "I had prepared my speech and I thought it was okay, but writing it and then giving it in that setting are two different things."

Willarene Beasley met Alan when he was one of a group of volunteers who met with students at her high school to encourage them to further their educations. The two were not longtime friends, but when Page decided he wanted his induction remarks to address the importance of education, "I thought of Willarene, and I knew she was the person I wanted to present me." The guys in the hard hats with the beers attached were less certain.

"I sat there listening to her comments, listening to her talk about me," Alan said. "She talked about things I had done. I remember thinking that maybe some of those things really were important."

"Willarene was great," Diane said. "She didn't talk about Alan the football player so much as she told the people in the audience what Alan had done for his community and, especially, for the young people."

As Beasley concluded her remarks, Alan was thinking about family, "about Diane and our kids, my parents, my brother and sisters. Everyone was there except my mom. I thought about my mom a lot that weekend, but I always think about her; she is a very strong presence in my life. I wished she could have been there; she would have been proud. But then, I know she was."

"I'm sure she was," Diane added. "I believe Alan's mother has been at his side since he was a boy, and that she has guided him."

Page was the final inductee to speak. "The sweat was running down my face," he said. "When I stood at the podium and looked down at my notes, my sweat was puddling on the paper, making the type hard to read. When he started to talk about the need to educate our young people, a guy hollered, 'Lighten up, Page!'"

Alan laughed. "I don't blame him; it was hot and we'd been there quite a while. But really, the crowd was receptive. I know they heard me."

Page's path back to Canton was not the smoothest, but he is typically philosophical about this, too. "My time in football wasn't about getting to the Hall of Fame," Alan said. "If I made it, fine, if I never made it, that would have been fine, too. The thing that was important to me as a player, all those years, was to perform as well as I could. The thing that drove me was the fear of not playing up to my ability."

When he first saw the Hall of Fame's bust of himself, he said it was "kind of scary. Definitely humbling. A little strange. It's a hard feeling to describe. You know that thing, that image of you, is going to be there long after you're gone. But when I think about my being on the court, that gives me pretty much the same feeling. Our work impacts laws that will be influencing people's lives long after we're gone," he said.

Diane Page shared memories of the weekend: "All of the people we met were nice, but Joe Paterno stood out. He was such a gentleman. He looked after Willarene. He knew she was in an environment she wasn't used to, so he made sure she was always part of the group."

A picture of distinguished guests behind the speaker's lectern registered a delightful range of reactions as Beasley addressed the crowd. Skepticism and surprise stood shoulder to shoulder. The late Pete Rozelle looked baffled. Only Paterno, with a wide smile, looked like he understood—and liked what he heard.

One of the hurdles the Pages faced in returning to Canton was that memory of Howard Sr., Twila, and Roy being arrested for an alleged disturbance in a Canton café. The enshrinement weekend was Alan's first visit to Canton since that incident.

Twenty years and more later, the bust of Alan Page stands in the Hall, flanked on the right by classmate Biletnikoff, who revealed much of himself in his acceptance speech when he spoke to his former wife, who was in attendance. He spoke of his regret and apologized for having treated her poorly. To Page's left? Defensive back Mel Blount of the Steelers, Class of '89.

The words of Alan's acceptance speech still echo in the Hall today. In part, he said:

> I don't know when children stop dreaming. But I do know when hope starts leaking away, because I've seen it happen. Over the years, I have spent a lot of time talking with school children of all ages. And I have seen the cloud of resignation

move across their eyes as they travel through school without making any real progress. They know they are slipping through the net into the huge underclass that our society seems willing to tolerate.

At first the kids try to conceal their fear with defiance. Then, for many, the defiance turns to disregard for our society and its rules. It's then that we have lost them—maybe forever. But we can make a difference if we go back into the schools and find the shy ones and the stragglers, the square pegs and the hard cases, before they've given up on the system…and before the system has given up on them. Then we say to those children: "You are important to our world and to our future. We want you to be successful and have the things you want from life."

I've learned from school, from football, and from the law that even the biggest, scariest problems can be broken down to their fundamentals. And if all of us cannot be superstars, we can remember to repeat the simple fundamentals of taking responsibility for ourselves and for the children of this country. We must educate our children. And if we do, I believe that will be enough.

Alan Page's induction remarks remain one of the most-requested of any Hall of Fame inductee's.

A friend of Larry Smith's said, "You just never know when to keep your hand down." Larry volunteers. He is president of a senior center. He organizes the annual pancake breakfast (a big deal) in Deerfield, Illinois, a suburb north of Chicago. He serves on the Deerfield Safety Council, is an usher at his church, delivers meals to the homebound, and works with teens through a high school program. "You meet a lot of nice people when you get out," Smith said.

Popsy

"I can't tell my mom because she can't keep a secret. She just can't. You can tell her, and it's gone. My dad? You tell him a secret, and it dies with him. That information is gone, into the vault of no return." —Nina Page

The Page kids are all athletic. All have run at least one marathon. Nina did a triathlon several years ago in Chicago with her dad there to cheer her on. Kamie, rangy, with square shoulders and a great smile, is the best athlete. She played soccer and basketball and ran track in high school, and played soccer in college. The kids have grown up competing, whether in the classroom or in games played at the kitchen table. They have Alan's (and Diane's) curiosity and need for knowledge, and a commitment to do the best they can. Alan sends frequent emails to his kids, often signing them "Popsy." He admits to being "button-busting" proud of them.

Nina Page works as a paralegal in Minneapolis. She's single. She seems her father's opposite—lively, outgoing, and spontaneous. Her comments are quick and occasionally over the top. And funny. She is quick to laugh.

Nina taught English for a year on Miyako, an island south of Okinawa. She was the tallest woman on the island. Before Miyako, by her own admission, she had "a little too much fun" her first three years at the University of Wisconsin. "My parents said enough is enough and cut me off. I worked three jobs to get back in school and finish," she said. "Then I went to Japan. After I came back, my dad helped me get a job in Washington in the Clinton administration. I was there for two years, but I found politics was wearing me down. That's why I went to Chicago before coming home."

Nina began by describing her dad as "direct—he keeps it simple. You get no details—at least not many. He lets his actions speak for him. He's a man of few words. He's not gregarious; he's not the life of the party. People mistake that for his being standoffish or angry. That isn't true. If my dad wants to achieve something, and it takes A, B, and C to achieve it, he will do A, B, C, and D.

"If there's something he wants to do, and he believes it's right, he's going to do it," Nina continued. "It doesn't matter what people tell him he can or cannot do. He doesn't rock the boat; he just does it. He does what he thinks is right. I don't think he ever doubts himself. My dad's a good jurist for the same reasons he's a good parent—he listens to all the information. He doesn't see creed or color. He makes his decision on information alone. It was the same thing growing up—we could make all the excuses in the world for what we had done, but he went by the facts and did what he believed needed doing."

Nina noted that her dad "has a terrible memory for things he doesn't care about. When he goes to the grocery store, we have to send him with a list. He doesn't sweat the small things, he really doesn't."

Alan Page also has a sense of humor, even if it is at times lost on Nina—or her friends. "He'll tell a joke—he thinks it's hilarious, and it's awful. I'll say, 'Are you kidding me? That's funny?' And he'll just laugh harder.

"He knocked one of my high school friends into Lake of the Isles. My parents were running with friends, and they took up the whole path. My friend went by, running the other direction. A lot of my friends were kind of afraid of my dad back then. So anyway, my dad just bumped my friend with his shoulder—right into the lake! I asked my dad about it later and he said, 'Well, he shouldn't have run so close to the water.'"

Another time, Nina recalled, "I was babysitting near the home of some friends of my folks. It was the night of the last episode of *M*A*S*H* on television, and the friends were having a party. I went there to get a ride home after baby-sitting. I walk in, and there's my dad, dressed like Klinger. He was in drag! He was wearing a dress, and I think he was wearing a woman's hat."

Nina went right from her burst of laughter to a warm look at her father and her family: "I admire his integrity, it's bigger than words can describe. He always does his best, and he asks our best of us. As long as we do our best, he's proud.

"Our family is extremely competitive—we are high achievers," Nina said. "Scrabble at our house is not pretty. My mom says she doesn't see why we play because all we do is fight. We talk over each other. We hear each other, but we just all talk at the same time. My dad will hang back and listen, then he'll come out with a few zingers." (Georgi confirmed the competitive tone of these games, saying, "I called my dad six months after one game. I had wanted this word, and he said there wasn't such a word. I called to tell him I'd seen the word in the *Times*. I was right.")

Nina continued. "He works out every single day, no matter how hot or how cold. Every single day. He's running, or he's at the gym. One day it was 20 degrees below zero. I emailed home and asked: who worked out? He emailed back: me.

"It was sort of surreal when my dad went into the NFL Hall of Fame. There was a luncheon for him at this country club where his mother worked when he was a kid. It's like one day you can't go in the front door of the country club because of the color of your skin, and then you're being honored there."

Alan Page was always ready to help his kids, even from a great distance. Nina said that when she was in Chicago, "I had to fix something in my apartment, a faucet, I think. I didn't know how to do it, so I went to this huge fix-it store and got my dad on my cell phone. He actually walked me around the store long-distance, telling me what I needed and where to find it. And I fixed that faucet by myself."

Nina summed her dad up by saying, "My dad could exist with nothing but the clothes on his back, Diane, us kids, and a car. That would make him the happiest person on Earth. He competes against himself. He inspires himself to do better. His heroes are Lincoln, Martin Luther King, Gandhi, and the Dalai Lama. Great people look up to great people."

Georgi Page is remindful of her father. She lives in Harlem, not far from City College of New York. She's single and a website producer. I won't say she and her father are contrarians, but I won't say they aren't, either. Both thrive on debunking.

A sampler:

> *Author:* Have you ever heard your father play the tuba?
> *GP:* Yes.
> *Author:* Is he any good?
> *GP:* Not really, but I don't think that's the point.

Georgi is named for Alan's mother. She describes her dad as being "dignified, wise, extremely moral, and lighthearted—with a great, dry sense of humor. He's more buttoned-up away from home. At home he's in grungy sweats and joking around. My dad's very creative in his way. He's an original thinker. He's not afraid to break a barrier or do something quirky.

"His mother was—and is—a [source of] strength to him," Georgi said. "I think my dad has a strong sense of her watching over him. In some way that I don't understand, I think he draws an incredible amount of strength from his mother, a strength that has helped him get over obstacles. Diane's a very big asset for him, too—they make each other better. Now that we're adults, we consult with him; we value his opinions. He keeps us grounded; he's our bedrock.

"My dad is patient. He can understand people and empathize with them, but there's a point beyond which he doesn't tolerate or have time for. He can be very clear on what he's going to spend his time on, and he can be very frugal with his energies.

"He was fair with me growing up, as far as boyfriends went. He didn't impose his opinions on mine. He gave me enough room to make my own choices.

"My attitude about being his daughter has changed over the years," Georgi said. "When I was little, it was something to brag about. Then I didn't want people to know he was my dad; I wanted them to know me on my own. But now I think it's a great thing, and it has opened doors for me."

Georgi said her father's eating habits have gotten healthier over the years: "He eats beans now, and he's added salad. He's never really liked vegetables, but he's branching out. I think, at heart, he'd like some nice pork spareribs with sauce on them."

Georgi described her idea of a great time with her dad: "When he visits New York, we go for a run, we have a meal in a great restaurant, and we talk about world events and share our opinions."

Finally, Georgi said, "What I admire most about my father is his public persona. He's very democratic. There's no person he's going to privilege more than another. He's going to greet President Clinton the same way he's going to greet someone who stops him on the street and asks him for an autograph."

Justin Page is tall and lanky. He shows faint speech and balance symptoms of the cerebral palsy he suffered at birth, when he was deprived of oxygen for a time. Justin says he's got his father's sweet tooth, but, fortunately, his mother's lean build. He also has her engaging smile and manner.

Like his father, Justin Page is a lawyer. Now he teaches law, too. How is it to be a lawyer in a town where his dad is a prominent jurist? "I love it," Justin said. "We talk about things. I might run something by him; not because he's a judge, but because he's been in the legal profession. He has a lot of wisdom to offer." Justin went on, "My dad is a stickler for getting a thing right. If I give him something I've done to look over or edit, his red pen is all over it. He's very precise and meticulous. I think Kamie inherited more of that from him than I did. I'm more like my mom: 'Sounds fine to me.'"

Justin also shares his father's passion for education. "I believe in trying to insure that other kids have the opportunity for an education. I'm on the board of the Page Foundation, so I am aware of problems facing the young people in our community."

Justin's passion for football, however, only took him so far. He laughed about it, saying, "Look at me, I'm tall and skinny. I thought it would be neat to play football, but I couldn't bulk up. I was just as happy playing soccer and running cross-country in high school. In college, I learned the law can be a rough experience for anybody. It's a tremendous amount of work. I look at my dad: he played pro football, raised a family, and went to law school. I barely got through law school with no other responsibilities. What he did still boggles my mind."

Justin describes his dad as being "very studious, smart, soft-spoken. But when we're out on a run, he can get crazy and be a lot of fun. It kills him if he can't get up in the morning and run. He'll run when it's 20 below. He's kind and loving. He's always there for you. You can always rely on him. Always. How many people can say that about their dad?"

He added, "I don't think you could grow up in our house and be indifferent to the world and its problems."

When asked about his parents as parents, Justin said, "It's great to have parents who have been together as long as they have, and in such a loving way. I have friends who have issues with their parents. I have to just sit and listen when they talk, because it's not a problem I have."

Being Alan Page's son "doesn't strike me as hard," Justin said. "People say, 'Oh, what's it like?' I always tell them he's my dad and I never had another—no one to compare him to. But it's been great. I love him, and I love the fact that he's my dad."

The Khamsin is a feisty wind on the Sahara desert.

"Naming me Khamsin was my dad's idea," said Khamsin "Kamie" Page.

Kamie teaches second grade at the Blake School in Hopkins, Minnesota. Her husband, Ben Friesen, teaches middle school earth science in the same community. Kamie is the youngest of the Page kids. She was a good athlete as a youngster and remains a good athlete today—backyard volleyball games at Kamie and Ben's house are not for the faint of heart.

"My parents were very supportive when I was growing up," Kamie said. "'You don't have to do this,' they'd say, 'but if you do, you have to do your best.' If I failed, I had to take ownership of that, too."

Kamie said her dad is even-keeled, "even when I don't want him to be. I'll call and ask for advice, and he'll say, 'What do you want to hear? Here's what I think.'"

She continued, noting, "He's a tech freak. It's a family joke that when he goes to Costco he's going to come back with something he knows nothing about."

Kamie also said her dad is usually nearby and ready to help out. "We were putting a new sidewalk behind our house," Kamie said. "I was in the middle of sledge-hammering out the old concrete. My dad showed up—didn't call, just showed up. He asked if he could have a few whacks with the sledge. He stayed all afternoon. When we were done, my mom showed up with lemonade and sweet corn. Sometimes my parents will come to our parties. My mom will buzz around and meet everybody. My dad will just kind of sit back and watch, but they're both having a blast. They're very young at heart.

"My dad likes to kid me about the early years," she said. "I became so passionate about soccer, but back when I first started playing, Dad says I just liked to sit on the field and pick flowers. A ball could go right by me, and I'd be oblivious to it."

Kamie was recruited to play soccer at Notre Dame, her father's alma mater, but she transferred to Northwestern after a year. You get the sense that neither father nor daughter was completely happy at Notre Dame as a student. Both are independent people today and were in their years in South Bend. Both felt isolated there. Alan stayed, Kamie didn't. "I just didn't fit," she said. When she transferred to Northwestern? "It felt right, right away."

This is an independent lady.

Like her siblings, Kamie loves seeing the "goofball side" of her dad. "He can be quirky. He has no sense of rhythm, but he will dance. My mom and I were watching an NCAA basketball tournament game once and just biting our nails because it was so exciting. And here's my dad, off in the corner, dancing by himself—just goofy. My mom is like, 'Kamie, who is this man I married?' But he's the rudder on our boat."

Kamie's husband, Ben, added, "If he's the rudder, it's beneath the surface, because he doesn't make waves." He went on to say, "One of my favorite memories of Alan is sitting there when Kamie graduated from Northwestern. I was watching Alan watch Kamie graduate; it was a moment I will always remember."

Ben followed an unusual routine in asking Alan and Diane for their permission to marry Kamie. He arrived at his prospective in-laws' house carrying a suitcase. It was a custom he had learned in Ghana while traveling after college. Only Diane and Alan were at home—Kamie had been sent to her apartment. Justin tried to drop by, but was quickly shooed away by his mother.

Ben's suitcase contained a running shoe, a can of chicken noodle soup, and Kamie's favorite stuffed animal. Ben explained that the items represented his relationship with Kamie. They also represented his love for her. The Ghanaian custom was to illustrate that he would care for Kamie and provide for her—clothing, food, and special needs.

"I walked in with the suitcase," Ben said. "Diane said, 'Ben, what's the suitcase for?' I sat them down and opened the suitcase and started explaining the items. All the while, the phone's ringing because Kamie doesn't know where I am. Diane and Alan knew why I was there. They were both laughing, but Diane was crying, too, and Alan was wiping away tears. I asked for their permission to marry Kamie. Diane jumped up with both arms in the air and just hollered as loud as she could."

Today, Alan and Diane are not only parents, but grandparents. Alan was baby-sitting grandsons Otis (Kamie's son) and Theo (Justin's son), both under one, when I called to check a point. The point was being cleared until Alan said, "Hold it." When he came back he explained: "Otis was starting to eat out of the dog's dish." The dog, Riley, is known as "Grand Dog."

Football teams coached by Ara Parseghian won 170 games, lost 58, and tied six. They won two national championships. His Notre Dame teams posted a 95–17–4 record. Parseghian is in the College Football Hall of Fame.

Ara is on the far side of 85 now. He still has the dark, flashing eyes and that close-cut, curly gray hair. Ara and his wife, Katie, have enjoyed the best of times and the worst of times. Three of their grandchildren— Michael, Marcia, and Christa Parseghian—died of Niemann-Pick disease type C. This is a genetic disease found in children. It can cause fatal damage to the nervous system. Ara's sister Karan has multiple sclerosis. Ara has fought both of these killers with the same resolve he brought to coaching. The Ara Parseghian Medical Research Foundation is seeking a cure for Niemann-Pick. Ara has generated nationwide support for the foundation.

"The only thing we can do for our grandchildren is to work as hard as we can to see that other kids are spared. You're going to have challenges in your life, and to go on, you're going to have to face them. That's what we are trying to do," Parseghian said.

The Court

"People were amazed; they thought it was a very brassy thing to do. For someone who was a lawyer in the attorney general's office to come in and challenge the governor and the state Supreme Court and say, 'I want to be on the ballot,' took a lot of moxie. He set himself a tough row to hoe. There were plenty of people who didn't believe he belonged there. He proved them wrong, though, and emerged as a very strong voice on the court; strong enough that people who had been skeptics originally were glad to see him there." —Peter Knapp, law professor and student of the system

He decided to sue the governor. Skip Humphrey, his old boss, laughed. "Isn't that just typical of Alan Page?" he said. "That he would take on a situation where most people would say, 'Well, that's impossible—how's he going to do that?'"

Bud Grant, his old coach, wasn't surprised. "Alan always recognized opportunity," Grant said. "He's done that all his life. In high school, he saw that playing football would be his ticket to a college education. At Notre Dame, he saw that pro football could lead him to the future he wanted." A Grant coaching trademark was to remind his Minnesota Vikings teams that there would be opportunities for them to turn games around, opportunities to win. There might not be many of them, so the trick was to keep a sharp eye out. "Alan had a gift for recognizing those opportunities," Grant said, "and he didn't stop recognizing them just because he stopped playing football. I think it followed that when he came to the point in his career when he wanted to be on the court—and he saw a way to do it without waiting out the usual method—he went for it."

Alan Page's legal career began in 1979, in the private sector, with Lindquist & Vennum, a Minneapolis firm known for its labor work. He had an office with a view of the Metrodome, where the Vikings play football today. In Page's day, they were at Metropolitan Stadium in Bloomington.

He left the private sector after six years to take a job as an assistant to Minnesota Attorney General Hubert H. "Skip" Humphrey III, where his eventual emphasis came to be on representing state agencies in litigation. He loved the fact that being on the AG's staff meant he had just one job, the law. As former boss Humphrey explained, "Alan didn't have to be a rain-maker anymore." That's another term for drumming up business, a vital part of every private law practice. Alan liked everything about the attorney general's office, including the fact that it brought him in contact with one of his special interests, the state's educational system. The improvement of that system for all children in Minnesota had been a long-held goal of his. He got his start by visiting elementary school classrooms and talking with kids. He loved that, too.

That's pure Page. As a football player, he loved the game, loved to play, and wished people would leave him the hell alone and let him play. In Alan's words, he "wouldn't give you two cents" for the rest of it. He lawyered the same way. He loved the work—just don't come at him with politics and posturing and pleading for business.

Page joined the attorney general's office as a special assistant but was promoted to assistant attorney general. "Alan became an important member of our staff," said Humphrey. "His visibility because of his football career benefited him, but at the same time, people expected the same level of accomplishment and determination in the courtroom that they saw in him as an athlete. They got it. I think our office gave Alan a great opportunity to display his abilities as a lawyer, whether in the courtroom or resolving labor disputes." Indeed, Page had high-court experience before be was elected to serve there. He'd represented the state in arguing 10 employment-discrimination and workers' comp cases. His record was 10–0.

It was a good fit, because the focus was on representing clients. There was no political objective, no agenda other than representing the people of the state and giving them his best. Page thrived there.

"I was a damn good lawyer," Page told the *St. Paul Pioneer Press*. "I know it's not my place to talk about myself, but I think I was a good lawyer."

However, you can thrive in one job, yet crave another, and Alan Page, to his depths, believed his greatest contribution to Minnesota and its people would be as a jurist, although he had a devil of a time proving that. His several efforts to be appointed to a Minnesota district court were unsuccessful. Privately, his goal was to sit on the Minnesota Supreme Court. "I thought the appellate court's work best fit my skills and interests," Alan said. But he found a dead-end there. He filed for election to a seat on the high court in 1990, but a resignation removed the election from the ballot before Alan was even aware of a vacancy. He planned to file again in 1992, but the judge he would have filed against, Lawrence Yetka, applied for a term extension. Governor Arne Carlson granted the extension, again removing an election from the ballot.

"I had worked 14 years as a lawyer and I had a wide background of work. I knew some people questioned my qualifications to be on the court, but I felt good about them. I believed I had something to contribute," Page said.

Justice Yetka would retire in 18 months, when Page's 1992 filing was thwarted. Terms are six years. Justice Yetka sought a term extension, seemingly to improve his pension status. He already was assured a pension, but this would be a way to better it.

"I thought it was a fair question, to allow the people of Minnesota a choice between the incumbent and a candidate who would serve out the full term," Page said. That question, however, looked fated to go unanswered. A frustrated Alan Page and his attorney, Tom Kayser, thought Carlson's grant of a term extension to Yetka was wrong. Still, challenging the governor of Minnesota seemed a daunting path for an assistant attorney general, even when the assistant attorney general had been one of the state's preeminent athletes, and the governor was a sports fan to the degree that his formal portrait, hanging in the state capitol, has him wearing a maroon and gold University of Minnesota letterman's jacket.

Tom Kayser was an athlete, too; he played Division III basketball and baseball at Lawrence College. He first met Alan while Alan was going to law school and playing football at the same time.

"Alan was a good lawyer and is a good jurist for the same reasons he was a good football player," Kayser said. "He prepares thoroughly and he is very focused. This is somebody who gets right on to whatever it is he's doing and comes to a conclusion. He doesn't let a lot of extraneous stuff get in the way. He loves being a judge," Kayser said, "and he works hard at it."

In 1992 getting the chance to be a judge was the issue.

Kayser smiled, and then repeated a good line believed to have originated with the late Jim Finks, a creator of all sorts of good lines, who ran the Vikings during Page's glory years. The line was Jim's description of Alan: "If Alan Page says he will play five more years of football at the highest level, he will do it. If Alan Page says he will run a marathon, he will do it. If Alan Page says he will become a member of the Minnesota Supreme Court, he will do it. And he will do it quietly and without a lot of fanfare and chest-thumping. He just does it."

Page and Kayser did their due diligence. Their decision to challenge wasn't a first, but most people assumed an extension such as the one proposed for Yetka was the governor's prerogative. Such acts weren't often challenged. "It was our opinion that what the governor did was wrong, and that his action contravened Minnesota law," Kayser said.

"Ultimately, we had to bring suit against the governor and the secretary of state, challenging to have the election put on the ballot," Page said. The sitting court disqualified itself from hearing the suit, and a panel of independent justices was appointed, retired Court of Appeals Judge Daniel Foley presiding. The suit attracted wide attention. The limited spectator space in the courtroom was filled well before proceedings began. The "substitute" court ruled in favor of restoring the election that the governor had attempted to drop. Justice Yetka decided not to seek reelection, and Alan Page—who rarely took a seat on the bench during a 15-year pro playing career—was free to run for a seat on the most prominent bench in Minnesota.

If he won, not only would he be the first African American named to the Minnesota Supreme Court, he would be the first African American ever to hold a statewide office.

Retired justice Kathleen Blatz said, "I don't think Alan's route to the court had been taken previously. But I will say this: I believe Alan would have come to the court on his own merits; I believe he would have been appointed in time. I know he wanted to be on the court, he was qualified, and then this whole kind of quirky route presented itself—like the stars were in line."

"Alan is shy," said Diane Page. "The idea of running for office was a daunting one for him, but you should have seen him campaign. He was tireless. I don't think there was a town in the state that he didn't visit. Alan is very goal-oriented and focused, and he took nothing for granted. I know it wasn't easy for him, but he did it."

The candidate stumped Minnesota from the dairy lands of the south to the scrub pine towns along the Canadian border; from the Wisconsin border on the east to the Dakotas on the west. He shook hands, stopped in stores, and visited with people on the street. He made speeches. He signed autographs and had his picture taken with countless beaming citizens. He went on radio and television and did print interviews. He visited schools. He chewed his way resolutely through service club lunches and dinners. He ran in the morning when his schedule permitted. He asked people about their concerns for the state, for the court, and for the future. He listened when they responded. His campaign slogan was "Alan Page, A Justice for All."

His qualifications were questioned by the campaign of his opponent, Kevin Johnson. "They said the only thing I'd ever done was play football. They identified me as a big, dumb jock," Page said. "What they didn't say, but what was out there for implication, was that I was a big, dumb, black jock. From my standpoint, the 14 years of experience I'd had was the best kind—private practice, public sector, and the attorney general's office. I had litigated from the time a client came in the door up to the end stage. I knew I had the right experience."

Diane Page heard the allegations that her husband's qualification for high office was his having been a star athlete. "I'm sitting there thinking, *Alan isn't qualified?*" she said. "His life experience, his educational background, his work in the law—how could anybody say that? That was just...oh, that was very upsetting."

In his campaign, Kevin Johnson said that he didn't believe anyone would take Page seriously if it weren't for his fame as a football player. The state's lawyers agreed, giving Johnson an edge in a straw poll.

Nick Coleman, writing in the *St. Paul Pioneer Press*, cautioned: "When lawyers endorse somebody, the public is wise to vote for the other guy."

Minnesotans did. They listened to Page, not his detractors, and chose justice for all. Alan Page won the election, overwhelming Johnson by an almost two-to-one margin, and on January 4, 1993, was sworn in as a member of the Minnesota Supreme Court.

Was he nervous, approaching the highest bench in the state? Honest answer, now. "No, I was confident, going onto the court," Alan said.

That's bedrock Page. He has always been confident. He didn't know much about football, but he never doubted that he could play. Coming out of high school, he thought he could play in college football. Coming out of college, he thought he could go pro. And once he took it seriously, he thought he could be a lawyer. Perhaps tuba-playing is his only side with room for doubt.

Justice Page smiled above a lively orange-and-purple bow tie as he reflected on his first day at court. "Usually, a new justice has an acclimation period—a few days, at least, to watch and listen, to get used to things before they are assigned a case. I got a case my first day." His eyes brightened; for a tough guy, Alan Page has soft, expressive eyes. "I don't think that was an accident," Alan said. "I wanted to go home and celebrate that first night, but I had too much reading to do."

He's still reading. The seven justices receive about 900 appeal requests each year. They accept a much smaller number, closer to 100, but they still run full schedules. Justice Page puts in full days and brings work home at night. Most judges take time off during the summer recess; Alan doesn't. "It's a good quiet time to catch up," he said. He crams the occasional recreational reading into his schedule—*Shadow Divers* was a favorite—but most of his reading is trial reviews, opinions of fellow justices, other opinions, and research.

His Honor's chambers are not overly large but comfortable and attractive. He sits in front of a fine view of the capitol grounds, and his office is brightened by a collection of antique toy trucks as well as signs, pictures, and other memorabilia from a time when much of white America displayed its disdain for black America more openly than it does today. Nothing in his chambers says football. Page showed off his space late on a weekend afternoon once he found a janitor—he'd left his keys at home. There is a stand-up desk—sort of a large lectern—near his conventional desk. He often writes standing at the lectern. His opinions take form on legal tablets and in his cramped, careful hand. "I'm blessed," he said. "Laurel [Bulen, his assistant] is able to decipher my writing." Laurel gets both longhand drafts on yellow tablet paper and edited typescripts. Alan works on a computer, as well. In fact, he takes a treasured 30 minutes early every morning to scan newspapers, foreign and domestic, online. Don't those huge hands and gnarled fingers have trouble with a keyboard? "Spell check does help," he said.

Does a justice do all of his own work?

Page smiled. "We're like ducks. We look serene, sitting on the pond, while our law clerks are down below the surface, pedaling as fast as they can."

Why does a law clerk clerk? He could go into a firm and make a lot more money, couldn't he?

"Probably," Page said, "but a clerk can learn more and experience more in a year here than some lawyers will in a career." In looking for a good clerk, Justice Page said he wants "more than grades and law review. I look at their life experiences and their curiosity involving the law. Clerks change every year or two, and that benefits both sides; they've figured out how to do things, so it's time for them to move on. New clerks come in and have to learn from us, so that keeps us fresh, too." What doesn't he want in a clerk? "One who tells me what he thinks I want to hear. What I do want is a clerk who gives it to me straight, whether I want to hear it or not."

Why wasn't Justice Page a clerk? "I wouldn't have had the patience for it," he said.

Page doesn't think of the long hours he puts in as work. "The majority of people don't really like their jobs, which makes me very fortunate," he said. "I don't really think of what I do as a job; I love the work. I am excited every day in my job. When I put on the robe and walk into the courtroom, I'm just as pumped as I was running onto the football field. I enjoy what we do, knowing at the same time that what we do is a very serious business. We examine laws and their application; by doing so, we will impact the lives of people for so long as there is a state of Minnesota."

Alan Page is a literal man who still works at softening his edges.

"When I was in law school, some people could write chapters," he said. "I would write X, Y, Z. What else was there? In terms of expanding my horizons, I struggled. I would take things literally. I'd read a passage. It said what it said. People would ask what the 'real' meaning was. To me, what it said was the real meaning. We'd sit in classes in college and have these grandiose discussions and none of it made sense to me. I'm thinking to myself, *You're the only one too dumb to get it.* I didn't find *The Canterbury Tales* very interesting. It didn't make a lot of sense to me and, as far as interpreting the meaning, I'm afraid I took the words on the page for what they were. My tendency, all along, has been to take things literally and not extrapolate beyond what's there.

"I've gotten better. I think I read the lines and between the lines now. But my writing, I hope, is still very literal. I want to be clear about what I say. I don't want the reader to have to guess, to fill in blanks. I don't want there to be any doubts. What intrigues me, being an appellate judge, is reading opinions that can go five different ways and having to work through them and figure out precisely what they're saying. I think, for this particular line of work you have to be able to write clearly so the reader doesn't have to try to figure out what it is you're saying. I try to be the best writer I can be. It's something I've worked hard on from day one." Alan grinned. "But that Chaucer teacher at Notre Dame probably would look at my writing today and say, 'Man...he still doesn't get it.'"

"Alan is an excellent writer," said retired justice Blatz. "His opinions are tight and well-written. I didn't always agree with him, but I admired his writing; I knew he had done draft after draft until he got it right. Lawyers can get in a lot of legal trouble when they say too much. Alan has avoided that. I always enjoyed editing the opinions of my fellow justices, but editing Alan was hard—there just wasn't much to put a blue pencil through. He'd already done it."

"I understand the need for people to see beyond boundaries," Alan said, "but when you are writing something that directly impacts people and their lives, then I think there is no room for that kind of writing."

Peter Knapp of the William Mitchell Law School faculty is an avid student of the court. He talked about Justice Page. "There is a lean quality to his writing," Knapp said, "and very little in it that is sentimental. Justice Page is unflinchingly principled. He is very careful on procedural issues. He has, through his opinions, sent out a message to other lawyers: follow the law, even if the result is not popular."

"Alan uses logic to assist him in his decision-making," said Diane Page. "Once he has arrived at a decision, he can be tough-minded and unbending."

Fellow justice Paul Anderson said, "I try to get Alan early, before he takes a position on an issue. I don't want to poke a stick into that beehive unless I have to, because he can come back at you with ferocity."

In her work as a market research analyst, Diane Page conducts focus groups to assess new products.

"Diane works on the fly," Alan said. "She's very creative. Ideas spin off of her like sparks. She will occasionally ask a question within the family, trying to get some creative feedback on an idea. I am not allowed to be part of those discussions because what's being discussed isn't concrete."

Justice Page applies his logic to all cases, great and small.

"When you become a judge," he said, "your concept of being a lawyer changes. Lawyers are advocates. The last thing we should be is an advocate."

Justice Blatz was asked what it takes to be a justice. "Intellectual curiosity, open-mindedness—a desire to get it right as opposed to a desire to be right. You have to want to serve the law. Our decisions are supposed to be difficult; if they weren't, you'd only need one justice. We need seven, because we come from differing perspectives on issues. We need to meet and work through our differences."

"We are not reviewing guilt or innocence," said Page. "We are reviewing whether legal procedures were followed correctly, whether the law was interpreted and applied properly and, in essence, whether the trial was fair."

Justices follow a trail, and frequently a trail not easily followed.

In the case of Dennis Darol Linehan, the trail seemed glaringly apparent. A lifetime offender, Linehan began a career of sexual crimes in his teens after he himself had been physically and sexually abused as a child. At 15, Linehan pulled down a four-year-old girl's shorts and was sent to reform school. At 19, he had intercourse with a 13-year-old girl. He was a window-peeper. In 1963 he and a friend beat and raped a girl. At 24, Linehan kidnapped a young woman and killed her while attempting to sexually assault her. He admitted to perpetrating two other sexual assaults before the killing. He pleaded to kidnapping rather than murder, and was sentenced to a maximum of 40 years in prison. Linehan escaped prison in 1975 and assaulted a 12-year-old girl in a ditch alongside a Michigan road. He did five years in Michigan before being remanded to Minnesota.

Dreadful.

Now, follow the trail of legalities.

Linehan's prison term was to end in 1992, but shortly before that happened, the state of Minnesota moved to further hold him under the state's Psychopathic Personality Commitment Act (PPC). A district court ordered Linehan to an indefinite commitment on the PPC basis, although review examination did not meet all criteria. The Supreme Court, in 1993, held for the district court, and then reversed itself, saying the state had failed to substantiate the appellant's "lack of power to control his sexual impulses."

Linehan was free? Not really. Upon release he was paroled to a special residence on the grounds at Stillwater prison, there to remain under "intensive supervised release." He later was removed to a facility at Moose Lake, Minnesota.

Not long after the reversal in Linehan's favor, Minnesota's legislature enacted the Sexually Dangerous Persons Act (SDP). Ramsey County district court held that Linehan, under the terms of SDP, had had his three strikes and was out. Linehan appealed, citing due process. The case went back to the Supreme Court, where a court majority—to say nothing of a majority of Minnesotans—supported the lower court. The court held that Linehan's constitutional rights had not been violated and that the district court had not erred in evaluating the evidence. Both high and low courts agreed that Linehan's past had taken away his future. Linehan was not on supervised parole any longer...he was back in the general population at Stillwater, regardless of where he slept. SDP, the state said, permitted it to detain Linehan based upon a projection of future wrongdoing.

Two justices dissented.

Esther Tomljanovich, retired now, lives well east of St. Paul in a lovely, remote, wooded area. She enjoys tending her gardens. Esther is a small woman, but don't be fooled: she is from Minnesota's Iron Range, and she is Iron Range tough.

Justice Tomljanovich wrote the dissenting opinion, *In re Linehan*. Speaking of her opinion years later, she reduced pages of legal dissent to a few words: "I believe our laws are designed to punish people for what they have done, not for what we think they might do."

Justice Page joined Tomljanovich.

Writing in dissent, Justice Page said there was no question in his mind that Linehan was an extremely dangerous person, and that he had been tried, convicted, and punished under Minnesota criminal law. "Some might argue," Page wrote, "myself included, that the sentence he received was not severe enough. Certainly, if constitutional limits did not exist, I would have no qualms about Linehan remaining in preventive detention for the rest of his life.

"But such limits do exist," Page noted, "and we must respect those limitations, even if it means the Dennis Linehans of the world must be set free after completing their criminal sentence." Page, in summation, wrote that he must dissent because, in his opinion, the SDP act went well beyond the limits imposed by the constitution, permitting unrestrained preventive detention based solely upon an individual's "dangerousness."

Through application of the SDP act, Page wrote, the court had concluded that the only real measure for commitment was dangerousness. In essence, he said, the court had concluded that there are no constitutional limits on the state's use of preventive detention.

"I think that's a slippery slope," Alan said, looking back on his opinion. In that opinion, he wrote, "Today, the target is people who are sexually dangerous. Which class of people who are different from us, and who we do not like, will it be tomorrow?"

Page, along with co-dissenter Tomljanovich, received public criticism for his position in the Linehan matter. Why dissent? Nothing changed. Linehan is at Stillwater and surely there to stay. Dissenting had nothing to do with sympathy for Linehan. It had everything to do with respect for the law. Remember, as Page said, "We are reviewing whether legal procedures were followed correctly, and whether the law was interpreted and applied properly."

Peter Knapp was a lawyer on the state attorney general's staff while Alan Page was there. He is a longtime and learned student of the Minnesota Supreme Court. Lawyer Knapp offered his insights on Justice Page. "He calls it like he sees it. He's very consistent. One of the focuses in his writing, in both majority and dissenting opinions, has been the fairness of the process and his concern for the rights of the individual. He has no patience for lawyers who do not fulfill their ethical responsibilities to the court and to their clients.

"As a fairly new member of the court, Justice Page took a stand in a case regarding the financing of Minnesota's school system," Knapp said. "The majority of the court upheld a lower court ruling that the system was a proper one. Justice Page dissented, saying we cannot have a system that says to some Minnesotans, 'You are entitled to hope, at most, for an adequate education,' while others receive educations that are more than adequate. That is something we have come to expect from Justice Page. He has been a persistent and strong voice in reminding the court—in reminding us all—that the law must take an even-handed approach to all people. It struck me that Justice Page's dissent in this case was formed by his view of kids and his love for them."

"He's very down to earth," Knapp said. "He's one of the best listeners I know. A kind of quiet thoughtfulness seems to loom over him."

It is nearly dark on a November afternoon, and Alan Page, senior justice on the highest court in his state, sits on the couch in his office. There's only his desk lamp on, so the light is minimal. It is hard to see the black robe hanging on the coat rack near the door leading to the courtroom. His old uniform bore the number 88—at least in Minnesota. There's no number on this one, but it's still his uniform.

The justice is wearing soft trousers and dark, soft shoes that look more like running shoes than judging shoes. His white shirt seems to glow in the gloom beneath his dark face. It's too dim to identify the color of the habitual bow tie.

He talked about his job and the people he works with.

"We hear a lot of cases where kids suffer," Page said. He measured the words out slowly. He didn't expand on that remark, but his tone said he didn't have to; it measured the pain such cases bring.

"We're four months into the court calendar, so I've probably got eight cases I'm responsible for," Page said. "Plus, I have to be familiar with 48 other cases assigned to my colleagues." You can hear traffic noises, but they are faint. "It doesn't ever really leave you," he said. "I can go home at night and have dinner, but the cases are still there, in the back of my mind. Sometimes I wake up at night with one. Some of the best thinking I do is when I'm running in the morning. An answer can come in so sharp and clear. The problem is, I can't write it down while I'm running. I really have to focus on the thought, because it can go away just as quickly as it came."

I asked if being a judge was like playing football.

"Sure," Justice Page said. "We're a team, and the same things are important—focus, preparation, compromise. Our court has managed not to make differences personal. It's like fighting. Why make it personal when there are other things you can do? If nothing else, you can articulate your position. Sometimes there are issues you really feel strongly about. You think, what are those people—the other justices—thinking? And yet, if you make it personal, the whole process breaks down. And if you internalize emotions, you go home and feel lousy. If you get them out, you come back the next day, and it's a whole new day."

Retired court member Blatz spoke of the closeness of justices working together. "When you are on the court, you read each other's work constantly. You don't just write your own cases; every workup on a case is shared among all of us, and we comment on every case. It's not my line," Blatz said, "but I have heard it said that a weak system focuses on its strong points while a strong system focuses on its weak points. I think Alan works to improve his weak points and the weak points in our system. His voice needs to be heard."

"You have to learn how to compromise and how to work together," Page said. This from a man noted for his stubbornness. He grinned in the dim light. "You compromise to the extent possible, then if there's no further compromise, you do what you have to do. Maybe the court isn't the ultimate example of a team, but it's right up there. That sense of team is in every decision we make," Page said. "Even when we disagree and it seems like the team is at war with itself, we still have to do our job, and do it in a manner that is constructive, not destructive."

When asked to describe himself on the bench, Page responded, "I'm not the one to categorize myself. I think I bring common sense to what I do as a judge and don't bring any ideology or agenda other than trying to ensure that what we do is done at the highest caliber. Each one of us must be scrupulous in his impartiality; we must try to insure that we treat everybody who comes before us the same."

It's past dark, so we shut it down for the day. It's time for the justice to go home for supper.

On another day—a bright and bitter December day—a mean-spirited wind scours the faces of pedestrians seeking entrance to the Minnesota Capitol Building, especially the faces of out-of-towners who don't know which door to use. But inside, it's warm in the ornate and distinguished old court chamber. Supreme Court sessions are heard in this courtroom periodically instead of across the street at the courts building. A late arrival finds a seat. He faces the six justices present that day.

Attorneys presenting stand at lecterns facing the court. Spectators sit behind them. An interesting discovery: one can measure degrees of nervousness without seeing a person's face. Watching learned counsel's hands and fingers, hidden behind their backs from the justices, but not from the audience, is all the evidence you need. The lawyer holding forth has fingers like nesting snakes. The court can't see them, but I can. The lawyer makes up for nervous fingers with a kind of snippy, combative tone.

Justice Page is the tallest by far of his peers, but that's hard to determine because he is slumped in his chair, one elbow on the counter top, a hand supporting his chin. He looks sort of piled into his chair. But his eyes are alert.

Surprising, at least to this first-time observer of a Supreme Court hearing, the lawyer addressing the court is wearing a rumpled jacket, his pants are baggy, and his shoes could stand a shine. I assumed people got spiffed up to speak before a Supreme Court. Although rumpled and, to my ear at least, irksome in tone and manner, the lawyer does seem well-prepared.

The bench I'm sitting on is incredibly uncomfortable, and if I'm hearing correctly, this appeal has to do with someone who took a truck, not their own, from Minnesota to Wisconsin, removed the seat from the truck, and then, I believe, abandoned it. Either that, or the truck seat was removed in Minnesota and taken to Wisconsin. It seemed to be a jurisdictional thing, among other concerns.

Four young women are sitting across the aisle from me. Their indifference seems profound. Two young men sit beyond them, pecking occasionally at notebooks with ballpoint pens; I put them down as reporters.

A fresco remindful of Moses looks down on all of this from high above the justices. During the presentation by counsel representing the state—nicely dressed, by the way, in a black suit with skirt and tall, shined winter boots—I can see the front of the badly dressed lawyer.

His front is as rumpled as his back, and he has sharp features and a pointy nose. I'm not surprised. I think counsel on both sides are starting to sound venal.

Justice Page refers to some papers and asks a question. His voice is so low and polite that I can't hear what he's saying. A yellow-and-red bow tie spices up his black robes. During rebuttal, the defense attorney's fingers still fidget, although he seems to be gaining steam. He's practically lecturing one of the justices now, baggy pants notwithstanding.

I don't know how the truck-seat case came out, but now a presentation begins on a trial concerning child neglect and abuse. There is talk of a baby having bright red buttocks from being hit, allegedly, by her father. The father was put out of the house by court order, but he doesn't stay away. He has a history of violence, and the child's mother has a history of letting him off the hook. The women across from me have gone from looking indifferent to looking sort of doleful. They're part of this case. The father is identified by his initials, not his name; the mother, too. The mother, despite aid and direction by county social workers, still exhibits improper parental care. There are two children—the oldest is 19 months, the youngest nine months. The father, we are told, grabbed the older child so hard his knuckles turned white. The lawyers talk as they flip pages, looking for supportive notes. It almost seems like the court is leading counsel through its own points, and they're moving at a brisk pace.

Ode to neglect and blame. It would be bad enough to hear about adults damaging each other, let alone children. I realize the mother is one of the women sitting across from me. She's heavy, her chin is down on her chest, and she seems drawn in upon herself. I'm guessing she doesn't make a lot of connection between this courtroom and her real life. This appeal spoke to vacating parental rights and putting babies into foster homes. It spoke about families failing.

In my notes from that morning, I wrote, "This is about angry adults, scared babies, and sadness. It's about wanting the law to pick up after the failing of their responsibilities."

When the session was over, the rival attorneys in the truck-seat case stood behind me chatting. He: "I hear you're off to Hawaii on vacation."

She: "We are." He: "Well, safe trip." The women across from me sit, looking like they are awaiting further instruction.

I went out to the capitol lobby. A bunch of school kids on a field trip were out there with me, noisy and excited, their chaperones hustling to keep up. Just then Justice Page came out of the courtroom. He had taken off his robe and was wearing a long, dark overcoat, stocking cap, and mittens.

Now, these kids weren't alive when Alan Page played football. Most of their parents weren't alive then, either. But they started hollering, "Alan Page, Alan Page, Alan Page!"

The justice removed his mittens to sign a few autographs. The good, soft smile never left his face while he signed.

Betty Weinberger has a Georgia drawl you could knock off with a stick—even though she has lived up north most of her life.

Betty has her own college counseling service and has volunteered for 11 years in helping disadvantaged children—especially those who are gifted musically—to get into college. She works with students at Chicago's Merit School of Music. "I spend time at the school with the students, but I spend a lot of time on the phone," Betty said. "I've gotten to know a lot of people in college scholarship offices." Betty loves her work with students, but the really fun part of her week is playing ukulele with the Hummers and Strummers, a band of lively seniors who entertain at retirement homes. "It's so much fun," she said. "You can just tell that the people are happy to see us. At one of the homes, this sweet little lady always says to me, 'Now, how long before you all come back?'"

Sure, I Know Alan Page

"Describe Alan? Smart, committed, a hard worker, gentle. Gentle, but passionate for justice. None of us are perfect, and the systems we devise are imperfect, as well. But with those disclaimers, I think Alan truly believes in our justice system and believes in it to the hilt." —Kathleen Blatz, Minnesota Supreme Court, retired

A lot of people know of Alan Page, but few know him. I think it's about his "circle," and actually, Alan probably doesn't know he has one.

Here's my take on it: if he's comfortable with you, enjoys you, *trusts* you, then you're in the circle, and there you will remain, because Alan is one loyal dude. You get into the circle by being you, and by not wondering if you're in the circle or not. If you think you can see the circle, and want in because the man is some *total* Minnesota icon and you'd like to be in the team picture with him for whatever self-benefiting purpose…well, if that's the case, then I don't like your chances.

I asked people who know Alan Page to describe him to me. Not all of the respondents lobbed marshmallows back to me. Roy Winston, a Vikings teammate said, "I'll tell you the truth: Alan could be a real jerk when he wanted to." Page himself, referring to his playing days in Minnesota, admitted, "I know I got snarly." Some teammates in Minnesota and at Notre Dame found him standoffish. His Chicago teammates didn't, but Page had mellowed by the time he got to Chicago.

Some of Alan's old Notre Dame mates don't understand why he has not maintained ties with them and his old coaches, as they themselves have. Part of that's about being Alan. He doesn't maintain close ties with his brothers and sisters. He loves them, they're important to him, he would be there for them, but they are not in his Here and Now. I also believe that being at Notre Dame was hard for Page. He was black and shy. He wasn't Catholic, and he was poor. He was one of a handful of African Americans attending Notre Dame in the early 1960s. When he was a senior, he was the only African American on the team. Some people reached out to him, but reaching back was hard for Alan—and it still is, much of the time. I don't think the Notre Dame of his student years was a warm place for him. It has warmed for him in retrospect; he has been back numerous times and has been honored for his after-football achievements.

By the time he got to the Vikings, Alan had grown a protective shell. And he had some money. Not much by today's ridiculous standards, but some.

A number of his old Vikings teammates ignored the opportunity to talk about him. Chief among the ignorers was Fran Tarkenton, still elusive after all these years. A few non-playing Vikings passed up the chance, too. Fred Zamberletti, trainer for the ages, said he didn't really care for Alan. That same Fred wrote a note when Page was cut by the Vikings, saying he had enjoyed their time together and would miss seeing Alan's kids in the locker room on Saturday mornings. Times change. We do, too.

Despite Alan's unhappy departure from the team, the Pages are quick to say that the Vikings organization has come to be a staunch supporter of the Page Education Foundation, formed after Alan's playing days. Vikings fans still love him, including ones who weren't even around for his glory days. "It's like I was never away," Alan said of his relationship with the fans. He was, however, waived—a decision that was refuted over the next three years by Page's play in Chicago. He still may be a skeleton in some Vikings closets.

Mike Lynn, the Vikings' general manager when Page was waived, described the move as an "unfortunate incident. Looking back, we probably didn't handle it very well."

Former teammates are heard from in this chapter, but this isn't only about football any more than Alan Page is only about football. For that matter, the comments of many former players are illuminative of more than banging their helmets against one another.

Where to begin but with the lady of his life, whose brief assessment seems spot-on. Diane Page is a story in her own right. She once was the only woman registered to run in a men's cross-country meet. The meet director was upset. "He wanted me to run in the Powder Puff Derby," Diane said. "First prize there was a cake pan." She ran in the men's event. Diane went into the marketing-consulting business for herself in 1974—Leapfrog Associates. She's still at it.

"Alan doesn't resist change, he resists being changed."
    —*Diane Page*

Kamie Page Friesen is tall, pretty, broad-shouldered, and the owner of a great smile. I have the impression she could either charm me or knock me on my kiester, whichever seemed to her more appropriate. Kamie laughs a lot. She's the baby of the family and proudly presented "Popsy" and Diane with their first grandchild, Otis, in 2008. While Kamie's older siblings speak of their dad's stern streak when it came to parenting, she giggles and admits she didn't pay a lot of attention to it.

"My dad officiated at our wedding. He sought input from us, [asked] what was important to us, and then made sure that our vows were along the same lines. He kind of spun everything together and really made it a call to do something: don't just be passive. He made a lot of environmental references: do something for the planet."
    —*Kamie Page Friesen*

You probably don't know Jim Marshall, and that's too bad; Jim's every bit as unique as Alan, just sketched in bolder hues. A former teammate and a special friend to Page, Marshall would have made a great buccaneer...or a pioneer...or the guy leading a charge from the trenches at the Argonne. Besides all that, he's observant. Alan presided at Jim's wedding, too.

"Alan questioned things. That can be an asset, you know, and I think it was for him. He and Bud had their differences, but that's what happens

when strong wills meet. They're a lot alike, Alan and Bud. They're deliberate, they believe in themselves and if they believe they're right, you're
not going to move them. I would say what happened between them is
history. Alan is too logical to hold on to bad feelings, and I'd say the
same of Bud. Besides, neither one of them spends much time looking in
the rearview mirror."

—*Jim Marshall*

"When you're an educator, it's kind of like being a farmer: it's a lot of
work. The student is the crop. The student works, the educator works,
too, helping him grow. You start with potential and see it through.
Gosh, we're proud of Justice Alan Page—not just as a great athlete, but
as a fine student, too. He always used the brains God gave him. He's a
great role model for minority kids, and his message to them is that if
God gave you talents, use them; don't feel sorry for yourself. Alan is a
beacon to young people of color; he is what they can be. Besides all that,
he's a nice guy."

—*Rev. Theodore M. Hesburgh, Notre Dame president emeritus
and Renaissance man*

"We liked to go to the country club where our mother worked to look at
all the fancy cars. We both liked cars, even then. Alan loved trucks, too.
I remember being in a store in Cleveland when we were kids. Alan
wanted this toy truck. Mother said no. Alan started hollering, and pretty
soon he was down on the floor, just pitching a big, loud fuss. He's got a
lot of toy trucks now, but he didn't get that one. He was different. He
wasn't so much rough and tumble as a kid, but he was tough-minded.
He did his own thing and he didn't look for a lot of help from the rest of
us. Alan performed the service when Rosalind and I were married. He
had to get special permission from the state of Virginia to do it. It meant
a lot to me, having my brother marry us."

—*Howard "Roy" Page Jr.*

"He was always having little accidents, then saying, like, 'Oh, why is this
happening to me? Why? Why?' Of course, nothing really wrong was

happening to him. Alan was quiet, but he had a temper and he was stubborn. Our mother taught Alan, taught all of us, to be true to ourselves. I think we have been. When Alan went into the Hall of Fame, I thought back to when he was a kid, and then through all those years of football. He worked hard to get back to Canton. I was so proud of him. I was there when he was sworn in as a judge, too. I was just as proud then."

—*Marvel Page Jackson*

"ACP [Alan] and I get along because we are both painfully independent. We're both willing to bear the pain. I think Alan is more measured in his independence than I am, and he's a moderating influence on me. He's a more deliberative guy than I am."

—*Michael Jordan, friend, runner, teacher, fierce "un-bureaucrat,"*
and PEF pioneer

"I think of Tootie [Alan] as a quiet little kid who was pretty much of a loner. He liked playing by himself. He liked learning to play the tuba when he was young because he could do it by himself. He is an honorable man. I don't think he feels worthy of all the attention he got because he was a football player. I think football was a job for Alan. I don't know how much he liked it, but it was a means to an end, and he made the most of it."

—*Twila Page*

Alan Page played for a lot of coaches. When I asked him who his favorite was, he said Buddy Ryan. Ryan wouldn't have been my choice; I was thinking of Jack Patera when I asked the question. Jack was a big, handsome guy with a killer smile that was equal parts charm and "watch it, pal." Patera related well to the players. But when I mentioned Patera's name, Alan paused and made his polite smile, the one that says, "Thanks, but you don't really know what you're talking about, here."

I worked with Ryan. I'd describe him as salty. Tough. A survivor. He beat combat in Korea and cancer in Chicago. He escaped the Vikings before Grant fired him. Neill Armstrong took him to Chicago on his staff, and when George Halas fired Neill, Ryan was asked to stay on because the defensive players wrote a letter to Halas asking him to retain Ryan.

"It wasn't anything against Neill, but it was apparent that Neill would be leaving," said Gary Fencik, a Bears teammate of Page's. "All of us defensive players felt Buddy had started something special. We wanted him to be able to keep us moving."

When the Bears were rolling in the '80s, and Ryan came up with the 46 Defense, it was as monumental to the game as it was devastating to the offensive teams facing it. Ryan overloaded a great defensive line with two linebackers, Otis Wilson and Wilber Marshall, both fast and fierce, rushing shoulder to shoulder alongside a terrifying front four. Offenses couldn't block them all. Quarterbacks were savaged. Archie Manning, the father of Peyton and Eli, and himself a quarterback of repute, took a fearful pounding from that 46. Ryan wasn't the easiest guy to like. He encouraged his defensive players to adopt a team-within-a-team attitude, generally at the expense of the offense. Once, when on the Houston staff, he got in a scuffle with an offensive coach on the sideline during a game. He was a head coach twice. His twin sons, Rex and Rob, are fine coaches in the league today. After football, Buddy raised horses in Kentucky. He now spends most of his time with his wife, Joan, who is ill. This is a gentler side of Buddy Ryan than most of us had seen before.

Ryan was Page's favorite, he said, because "he just asked one thing of you: can you play? He didn't care about the rest of it."

"It's easy to coach a guy like Alan, provided ego doesn't get in the way. His never did. After he retired as a player, I had him over to Philadelphia; I was coaching the Eagles. We had dinner before a game, then he spoke to my team. He did a hell of a job. I hope he learned something from me, because I sure learned a lot from him."

—*Buddy Ryan*

"He created havoc. He just exploded off the ball. Often as not, we'd let him call his own stunt [charge], because he had such a great feel for what was happening. He penetrated so quickly and he had those quick hands. Fred Cox tried three 'live' field goals—max protection—in practice one day at Minnesota. Alan blocked all three kicks. Now, that just isn't supposed to happen. For a defensive tackle to make the plays he made was unheard of. He was unique, an exception to every rule. More important, he was and is a true gentleman."

—Neill Armstrong, Vikings/Bears coach

I identify Nina Page as the family character. She's bright and quick and funny. She taught school on a remote island south of Okinawa. She was the tallest woman on the island. Nina has had a variety of jobs, but what she'd really like is to be a dog trainer. She's outspoken. She likes to poke fun at her father, but she lets you know she's very glad that he's her father.

"My dad is a gentle person—that's why kids like him. I was teaching in Japan when he was elected to the court. I voted by absentee ballot. When I learned he had won, I told him we always knew he was a good judge and now all of Minnesota would know it. Some people have said my dad had it easy. How? Losing your mother when you're a kid isn't easy. Excelling in a sport you don't really and truly love isn't easy. But he knew that if he didn't play football, he never would have been in position to provide a good life for us. When my dad decided he wanted to be a judge, he went out and did it. People said he was a football player, not a judge. But the politicians couldn't beat him. How do you beat my dad? He went out into every corner of the state and showed people who he was. He's a good dad and a good man."

—Nina Page

"It was those hands; they were so quick. If you were trying to block him, and he got his hands on you, it was all over."

—Jay Hilgenberg, Chicago teammate

"Quick. Way, way quick. You couldn't ever sit back on your heels, or he would be around you before you could blink."

—Ted Albrecht, Chicago teammate

Justin Page, Alan and Diane's son, is a tall, handsome, pleasant, and polite young man. And, like his dad, he's a lawyer. He and his wife, Christine, have an infant son, Theo—Alan and Diane's second grandchild.

"I can always rely on my dad for advice. I might not want to hear it, but it's probably what I need to hear."
—*Justin Page*

"I'm not surprised at what Alan has done with his life. I think his expectations of himself were always high. I know my expectations for him were, and he didn't disappoint me."
—*Ara Parseghian, Notre Dame coach*

"Alan was lanky and very fast, and not just [fast for] a defensive lineman; he was fast for any position. He was a great young man, never a problem, and a good student. Both of those boys [Alan and Howard Jr.] were well-mannered and polite."
—*John McVay, high school coach*

I have talked to Georgi Page, but I haven't met her. I think she's a lot like her dad. Her answers were as measured and deliberate as fudge hardening.
  "He's not a devil's advocate, he is very fair. He respects other people's points of view. He's humble; it's almost a Zen-like attitude. I think he believes this is just how his life has unfolded. I don't know if he will be remembered as an important person. Maybe. Who knows? I don't think it matters to him. It doesn't to me. I know who he is."
—*Georgi Page*

"I liked Alan; he was friendly. He wasn't rude, like a lot of players could be. I think some people were afraid of him because he was so direct. That's not always comfortable. But he was available, and he was truthful. Long after he played, he yelled at me once from across the street in downtown St. Paul. He was wearing a dark overcoat and that little stocking cap and he had his great smile. He waved, and hollered, 'Hi, Ralphie!' How many players would do that? I asked him a question once, I don't remember what it was, but it must have been a pretty good one. He paused and thought about it, and then he said, 'You know, you can ask the damnedest questions.' I felt really good about that."
—*Ralph Reeve, an all-pro reporter*

"[Alan Page is] a quiet guy with a bow tie who seems shy but is very confident, very solid, and very engaging. You get 30 seconds into a conversation with Alan and you realize he is a man of few words, and comfortable being so. You know he's cordial, but you will know from his responses that he is different. His answers don't just pop out quick, but are thought-provoking. And he will influence your thinking."
    —*Tim Baylor, fellow runner, former player, friend*

"The year he was named MVP, he played with ferocity. No one could stop him, and I don't think a lot of people wanted to try. He won a car for being named MVP—a Dodge, I think. He needed company for a trip to Minneapolis, so I rode with him. Even then, it wasn't much of a chance to talk, all superficial stuff. He liked to drive fast, and I admit, I was a little scared. I don't think he was very happy that year, despite his success on the field."
    —*Michael Umbles, cousin*

I'll be damned mad if Sid Hartman dies before this book comes out. I also would be shocked. I think Sid's past 90—he'll deny it, but that's what I think. As I write this, he still has a column in the *Minneapolis Star Tribune*, and Lord knows how many radio shows. His only concession to the years is that he doesn't go to road games anymore. His writing remains unadorned and still wanders off in directions to discourage the most assiduous grammarian, but it's full of newsy tidbits, and everybody reads him. Like a lot of legends, people have forgotten with the passage of time what a huge pain Sid could be in his salad days. Now they say, "Isn't he something?" and marvel at his longevity. George Halas reached the same age-conquers-all stage in life. People said Halas was a sweet old guy. Sweet? Sweet, like a cavalry charge! But Sid? Hey, he's Sid, and that's a good thing.

    "Mister Page...we had our moments, but we get along pretty well now. At least I think we do. I think the thing with the Vikings...I mean, Bud put up with a lot from Alan. Alan questioned everything. Then, when he lost all that weight and his play started to tail off, that was it. But he went down to Chicago with Finks and Neill and Ryan and all those Viking

people, and he played pretty damned well. So you never know. Then he came back to Minnesota, and he certainly has carved a high mark here."
—*Sid Hartman, essentially mythical Minnesotan*

A voice of reason, crying out in the wilderness of letters to the editor during the furor over the Vikings waiving Page:

"I grant that if Alan Page had lost 40 pounds of bone, muscle, and gristle, he would not be effective, but from his appearance, he has lost only fat. The notion that heavier players are better players dies hard. If anyone had suggested that the trainers hang 40 pounds of leg and belt weights on Page, Bud Grant would have vaporized them on the spot with The Steely Stare. Fat weight only results in slower and less enduring performance. I think Page was just smarter than the rest of the league and recognized that he could extend his career by taking up running and reducing his weight to a willowy 225 pounds, thereby postponing the natural erosion of his talents."
—*F. Douglas Whiting, MD*

"I asked him to take part in a run for [special-needs] kids. He said he would try to make it, but not to count on him. When it came time for the run, he wasn't there. We started out, and I was toward the back of the pack, running and talking with some people. I had pretty much given up on him showing up. Then I heard excited voices around me. I looked back, and there was Alan, running full out to catch up. He fell in alongside me and nodded, but he didn't say much of anything."
—*Jim Klobuchar, writer*

Bobby Bryant was one of Alan Page's closest friend as a football player. They roomed together at the East-West Shrine Game as collegians, and later as Minnesota Vikings. Bryant was a rail-thin white defensive back from South Carolina, and Page was a bulky black defensive lineman from northern Ohio.

"The first thing I think of is how articulate Alan is. Here's this great big guy, and so well-spoken. And a gentle voice, too, unless he was out on the field. I grew up with black children in our neighborhood, but there were no blacks on our team at South Carolina. Alan and I roomed together before every game; that's a lot of time spent talking. We definitely got to know each other. I believe we have something near to love for one another."

—*Bobby Bryant*

"He's the same guy now that he was as a player: very determined and disciplined. I think his views and perceptions have never changed. That's what's outstanding about him."

—*Carl Eller, Vikings teammate and Hall of Famer*

"His bid for the court was not the route usually taken. People thought he was relying on his football stardom. I've heard the same complaint in my own life: 'You're Hubert's son.' I say go for it. My dad was especially fond of the Vikings front four (Page, Eller, Marshall, and Gary Larsen); he thought they were men who were aware of the people."

—*Hubert H. "Skip" Humphrey, III*

Dan Hampton is another fellow you'd enjoy. His play as a defensive end and tackle for the Chicago Bears put him in the Hall of Fame, which is fine, but that's not the interesting stuff. Hamp played saxophone, not football, in high school in Cabot, Arkansas, until the football coach dragged him out of band practice and chased him onto the football field.

"Lou Holtz [Hampton's coach at Arkansas] used to say a team was like water in a bucket. You put your hand in, you displace some of the water, and you become part of that bucket. But when you're hurt, and take your hand out, you're not part of it anymore. It's like the water closes up, and you were never there. Then others close ranks, and the bucket stays full. What I'm tryin' to say is that when we left Halas Hall after practice, we young guys were still a team mentally, still in the bucket. Alan was able to disconnect and take his hand out of the bucket—and that is in no way to disparage him. When he was at Halas Hall, he was a football player, part of the team. But when he walked out that door, he was Alan Page, and all of the things he was away from football—like a future Supreme Court justice. I think I knew that about Alan back then. A lot of the guys may not have, but I did, I knew he was special."

—*Dan Hampton, Chicago teammate, protégé, and Hall of Famer*

"He didn't read the sports pages, he read the other parts of the paper. He was always about you bettering yourself. He challenged me to go back and get my college degree. I did."

—*Al Harris, Chicago teammate*

"My dad was a coalminer in West Virginia, and I was kind of a rowdy young buck. I remember hearin' Dad tell a friend of his he'd be surprised if I made it to 21. So the Vikings were the best thing that could have happened to me. I didn't know Alan well at first, but we got to where we'd sit down of an evening at training camp and talk. He's one of the greatest players I ever saw. It was hard, finally getting out of football. It's like the people you could really trust in life were the ones you met playin'. Alan was one of them."

—*Lonnie Warwick, Vikings teammate*

"Alan is soft-spoken and articulate. Knowing he had been a great football player, you might expect a more aggressive personality, but Alan is the opposite. However, I do know he is very determined at pursuing what he believes to be right. His interest has a wide range. He cares about kids—all kids. He has a mobility of energy."

—*Rev. Edward "Monk" Malloy, Notre Dame president emeritus*

"I'll tell you the truth: Alan could be a real jerk when he wanted to be—sour. But other times, he was fine. He had some tough years, but he got through them. Bud kept me around for a year as a backup when my time was winding down. That was fine for me, but I don't think Alan could have done that. He had to play. And he was one amazing player."

—*Roy Winston, Vikings teammate*

"What do I think of when I think of Alan? Professional. I was in pro ball, but I didn't know what being a pro meant. Alan taught a lot of us young players how to be professionals."

—*Matt Suhey, Chicago teammate*

"He doesn't see the same limits to life that so many others take for granted."

—*Kevin Lamb, reporter*

Ed Garvey is a lawyer in Madison, Wisconsin. He has twinkling eyes and, although the years have banged on him some, he remains feisty. Ed preceded the late Gene Upshaw as director of the players union. People say Upshaw led the players to financial success and freedom. That's true, but Garvey was the guy who fought his way ashore under heavy fire and established the beachhead for Upshaw to move forward from.

"I see President Obama walk to a podium to give a speech. There is naturalness to his confidence. Alan always carried that natural confidence in him, as a player, and as a leader of the players union, and now in his career. Several people in my life have had that 'something'—when they walked into a room, people knew something special was happening. John Mackey [player and unionist] had it. So did Bobby Kennedy and Alan Page. They all had this charisma, an intangible that said you wanted to like them and you wanted to trust them."

—*Ed Garvey, lawyer, unionist, and tireless tilter at NFL windmills*

"In 1974 we were fighting for the players to have more freedom in determining their future. Our motto was 'No Freedom, No Football.' During the really rough days, Alan Page was a pillar for a lot of us to lean on. You could look across the room at a meeting and see Alan. You knew that if he was there, everybody would be with you. That's the kind of leader Alan was. We didn't win that fight in 1974, but it was the start of the freedom players enjoy today."

—*the late Gene Upshaw, former player, Hall of Famer, director of the NFL Players Association*

"I was amazed when I got to know Alan. For a person as successful as he was in football, and at the position he played in football, he was marked by quietness and thoughtfulness. He was a gentleman. Those were qualities I would not have typically ascribed to being the best defensive lineman in pro football."

—*Jim McCarthy, lawyer and friend*

"I think Alan is caring and involved, but not entangled. He is a realist; he realizes you can't help every kid. I have this saying that sometimes a thing worth doing is worth overdoing. I can go over the line. Alan has pulled me back from that line many a time."

—*Mona Harristhal, former director of the Page Education Foundation*

"We played next to each other. Alan got me into running. We became close while he was here. What a great feeling it is as players to really rely on each other. When he left, for me, there was a void."

—*Jim Osborne, Chicago teammate*

"We had hearty laughs together, good times. We often would see the humor in a situation and roar with laughter. We shared hard times, too—the deaths of friends. When I left the court, I felt like I was leaving a good friend. We live just a few blocks apart. Some mornings, we'll see each other; he runs and I walk or ride my bike. We'll wave and yell at each other. We meet for lunch now and then. I had to break our last lunch date. I hated that; I hated missing being with Alan. This is a good reminder to get another lunch set up."

—*Kathleen Blatz, Minnesota Supreme Court, retired*

"I knew him from growing up in Canton. He didn't have much money. When he came to South Bend for a visit, I took him out for pizza. He was as serious about football as he was about studying. Preparation— Alan was all about preparation. He didn't play hunches, he prepared."

—*Norm Nicola, Notre Dame teammate*

"Alan and my husband Steve ran together for 10 years. They just clicked as friends. They must have run a thousand miles together, and I think they laughed all the way. They loved to get each other's goat. They both liked to analyze things. Neither one of them went along with the crowd. My husband was an internationally known physician, and Alan was a famous athlete and a prominent jurist, but they weren't self-important. When Steve died, I looked out the window and there was Alan, standing in the driveway. I think he just knew he was supposed to be there. He was devastated."

—*Karen Boros, friend and PEF pioneer*

"I'm not surprised that he's a good judge. I'm sure that's about preparation, too."

—*Doug Buffone, Chicago teammate*

"My father said your word ought to mean something. Alan's does. What makes his educational foundation so wonderful is the scholars don't just get money—they have to mentor others, younger kids. That's how it spreads. I think Alan has just kept growing as a person. All of us have to reach out and do more, like Alan is doing. And there's a lot more to do."

—*Willarene Beasley, retired educator, friend, Hall of Fame presenter*

"When I first knew Alan, we went together to a swearing-in ceremony. We got there just before it started, so we were standing in the back of the room. People were turning around, smiling, and I thought, *Isn't this nice?* and I'm smiling right back at them just as hard as I could. Then I realized they were smiling at this tall guy standing right behind me."

—*Esther Tomljanovich, Minnesota Supreme Court, retired*

"He's a genuinely nice person who is not overwhelmed by his celebrity. I think he's proud of what he did as a football player, but he has now moved on to something else. And there's going to come a time when he will move on from being a justice. Then, the fact that he was a justice will have been an interesting time in his life, one that he's proud of, but he will have moved on to something else. I think that is what defines Alan, and I think that's the kind of person he is. A lot of people still think of him first as a football player and a black guy, and don't look beyond that. They miss the boat in understanding him. They don't see the whole man: the bright, analytical, thoughtful person."

—*Tom Kayser, attorney and friend*

"Proud, relentless, intelligent, consistent. He refuses to do anything halfway."

—*Frank Gilliam, Vikings scouting director*

"A lot of what he did as a player had to do with physics. He weighed 225 pounds when I knew him, and a lot of the guys he played against weighed 300 or better. Leverage…we talked a lot about leverage. The best way I can describe it is how you get your hands on a blocker, where you place them, and how quick you are able to get them there. The lighter guy can beat the bigger guy if he beats him to the punch. Alan almost always did. He has a great laugh, too. We lockered next to each other. That was fun."

—*Doug Sutherland, Vikings teammate*

"Bit of a loner…worked hard…quiet, studious…goal-oriented…dealt with the media well. It had to be a tough thing then for a young black man at Notre Dame. His social life was pretty much nil."

—*Roger Valdiserri, longtime Notre Dame sports information director*

"Introspective and thoughtful. When you think about it, the fact that he has dedicated his life to the Page Education Foundation expresses Alan as well as anything. He has presented young people with the opportunity for equalization within the social order. I was his accountant and agent in Minnesota, [and then again] when he went to Chicago. When the Bears claimed him on waivers, we flew to Chicago, and Alan stayed

in my apartment in the Loop. I remember it was Yom Kippur. He gave me his jersey from his last game as a Bear. Do I still have it? Hell, yes, I still have it."
        —*Dick Lurie, friend*

"Alan marched to his own drum. We weren't especially close, but we got along fine. We became better friends after we played. He really was amazing. I mean I'd see him do things and ask myself, *Did I really see that?* I played linebacker behind him, so I saw him up close. He was so quick. He could do something fundamentally wrong, and I'd think, *Oh, no...,* but he'd recover and make the play. He was extremely competitive, but he really didn't seem that emotionally involved. Every once in a while, though, something would set him off, and he would go into a frenzy. When that happened, he was unblockable."
        —*the late Wally Hilgenberg, Vikings teammate*

"Steadfast. That's how I remember him."
        —*Kevin Hardy, Notre Dame teammate*

"He's so strong as a person. He has a very dry humor and so many sides. Alan once told me, 'I don't care so much about what you think, as what you do.' He's a runner, a great father, and a champion of social justice. Our paths are different, but many of our interests are the same."
        —*Jack Reuler, friend and operator of the Mixed Blood Theatre*

"I'd like to have a conversation with Alan. Playing together was kind of like going to war; you formed a bond, and it lasted. Alan was friendly, but we didn't see a lot of him away from football. I'd like to see him again."
        —*Tom Rhoads, Notre Dame teammate*

"It was easy for me to hit it off with Alan. [He was] tranquil, yet thoughtful. I worked on two of his election campaigns. I'm more into tennis and basketball, but I have run with Alan and Diane. During his campaigns we had some great times, just sitting around talking after

dinner. I loved our time together. When my first wife died, the Pages were there for me."
—*Lee Sheehy, friend*

"I'm sure, in his heart, he wants to do whatever he can to encourage the kids who really need someone to push them, to be behind them; to let them know that there are people out there who care about them. Who would have thought that Alan's spot in life would have made him so caring of other people?"
—*Gwen Singleterry, cousin*

"It would have been easy to let his successes go to his head and have an inflated view of himself, but Alan has kept his career and his life in perspective. I believe he's to be admired for that."
—*Paul Anderson, associate justice, Minnesota Supreme Court*

"I've known Alan Page for more than 40 years. I think he's comfortable in his own skin. A lot of us aren't. He's not afraid to look in the mirror, neither absorbed nor put off by what he sees there. He leaves the issue of his celebrity to others. I have heard it said that he hates being black. I don't believe that. I think he hates attempts to slot him, and would, regardless of color or all the other mean options. I think he takes great pride in his race, its history, and its accomplishments. His home is a Hall of Fame of black courage and perseverance. His eyes are very expressive. His voice is light and pleasant. He is comfortable in silence.

"He has walked lightly, especially for someone his size, and for someone who has carved his mark so high. There are no excesses to him, no baggage, unless you count family and the law. He has walked the remarkable glens and dales of his life, leaving hardly a twig bent or a leaf bruised...unless you count football, where a lot of grass was bruised. But even in the havoc of games, he was within the controls he set. And as he has crested each rise and moved on toward new horizons, it has been with scarcely a look back.

"Justice Page. Alan Page. Tootie. Pops."
—*Author*

"When I was seven, I would stand up in front of my second-grade class and say I wanted to be a lawyer. Today I am a lawyer. It's so important for kids, regardless of their circumstance or environment, to realize that there are people who will help them pursue their dreams and goals. The Page Education Foundation did that for me. Justice Page was my mentor when I was in PEF. He helped me realize my goals. Then I mentored others. My greatest memory is of being sworn in as a lawyer by Justice Page."

—DeGalyn Wade Sanders, lawyer and PEF scholar

All Rise

"If you want to change the world, change yourself."
—Morgan Freeman

By degree.

There is a story of an old man who walked a beach at dawn and noticed a young man picking up starfish off the sand and flinging them into the sea. The old man asked the youth why he was doing this. The young man said the starfish would die if they were left stranded on the beach in the sunlight. The old man pointed out that the beach went on for miles and there must be thousands of starfish with the same problem. He asked the youth how his effort could make any difference. The young man looked at the starfish in his hand and then threw it into the safety of the water. "It made a difference to that one," he said.

Alan Page has been asked how his efforts can seriously impact the "big picture" of educating our young people, especially those without the means or the direction to obtain an education. The need, like the starfish on the beach, seems endless. "One child at a time," is how he answers the question.

We are all "All-Risers"—that is to say, we have it in us. Maybe we just need to spend more time looking out, seeing others and their needs, than we do looking in, seeing only ourselves. Here are a few "All-Risers" I know.

Take T. Med, for example. You've heard of people who would *give* you the shirt off their back? Tony Medlin would gladly *take* your coat…gently used, of course. Tony knows Matt Suhey, who managed to give a year-long hug to one of the slipperiest characters you could ever meet.

My sister Mimi doesn't know T. Med or Matt, but she knows Melissa and a lot of other people who need a friend, and that's enough to make an All-Riser out of Mim.

Andre Cowling and Mike Koldyke are also All-Risers. They love to help kids and want to see their minds and their lives reach their capabilities. Both do much more than wanting, however, which goes back to Joe Kapp, that old roughneck who played quarterback. Joe didn't play pretty, but he won. "Hell, everybody *wants* to win," Joe growled. "Wanting's nothing! Who's *willing* to do what it takes to win?" Andre and Mike are.

I never met Ray Harris, but I wish I had. What a full life he lived. Ray was an All-Riser.

Paul Binder and his remarkable wife, Joyce, spent a year and a half making almost daily visits to an old lady who was near the end of her days. They went because no one else would. And that's just one of their many adventures.

Jackie Raino held onto Olga, even when the holding was hard. And when she could hold her no longer, Jackie made sure a world that had not done much right by Olga would at least give her a proper place of rest.

Ever say "good morning" to someone you pass on the street? If you say it with a little conviction, and maybe even smile, it's amazing how often that person will smile in return. How about slowing down in your lane to let someone out of a side street? Hold a door open? Thank the kid who refills your water glass in the restaurant? Wait your turn? Share—not just what you have, but who you are?

Well, now...how about opening the shutter a little wider? Ever do anything for someone that takes you out of the house on a crummy night, or when there's a game on you really wanted to watch? Support a worthy cause—with money and more? Volunteer at a homeless shelter, and even smile at the person you're spooning up the soup for? Cheerfully?

When I started this book I thought it would be nice to introduce Alan Page and his life by the term afforded judges when they enter the courtroom: "All Rise." It is a call for respect. But Alan wanted the title to reflect on others, not just him. And he wants to leave all of us with the question, what would happen if all of us would rise? What if all of us ignored the reasons why we couldn't or shouldn't, and went out and made a difference in the lives of others? And in our own lives—the two work together, actually. I suppose it's easier for Alan Page in a way...he's a celebrity, and when he speaks, people listen. When he leads, people follow. Most of us aren't celebrities. Our audiences are a lot smaller than Justice Page's. Indeed, the only audience many of us have, for sure, is ourselves.

All Rise.

Ray Harris liked bow ties, dancing, and fly-fishing. He also liked to befriend those less fortunate than himself, and did so for 30 years. That included the two years he lived with a brain tumor. The tumor finally got him, but that's okay because Ray left few, if any, of his life's stones unturned.

Ray visited the homebound elderly. Jacqueline Witz said he made her feel important. He took on the tough cases, too, the ones easiest to ignore. He would drive to visit his people weekly and stay for hours, sharing his love for classical music and literature. He took buses and trains when he couldn't drive any longer, and then when he could no longer travel on his own, family or friends would drive him and help him up the steps. Ray's sister Mary said he didn't want just to volunteer in an office, but "he wanted to be sort of a continuing presence on the outside for people who could no longer get there."

All Rise.

Here's a bet I'll win, if we make it: you won't find a nicer person than my sister Mim. She loves to garden, admire birds, and visit the "elderly." Mim's 82. She also has become good friends with a young woman named Melissa, who is 32, blind, has diabetes, and has lost part of one leg. Melissa's father looked after her until he died. Mim and Melissa are close now, but they weren't always. Melissa wouldn't talk much when Mim first went to visit her. After a couple of false starts, Mim decided to tell Melissa about herself. So she did. "Then I said she had to tell me her story," Mim said. With coaxing, Melissa did. Now they talk about all sorts of stuff. They are good friends, and they both look forward to seeing each other.

All Rise.

What do the "Golden Apple" awards, the Academy for Urban School Leadership (which could use a peppier name), and the Albuquerque Isotopes (very peppy name) have in common?

Mike Koldyke is what. Actually, Pat and Mike Koldyke. The Koldykes were watching the Academy Awards show in 1985 when Pat said, "There should be an awards program like that for teachers." Mike agreed. Both Koldykes have always placed a priority on education. Now most of us, when we come up with a nice idea like that, turn it this way and that in our mind's eye—admiring the sparkle, feeling good about having thought of it—and then forget about it.

Most of us aren't Michael J. Koldyke.

Mike was on the board of a Chicago educational television station when Pat got her inspiration. He got the station to say it would televise a teacher awards event, providing he could get one started. Then he prevailed on a university president he knew and won sabbatical funding for these as-yet-undiscovered award winners. So armed, Koldyke started ringing all the support doorbells he knew of, and he knew a lot of them.

In 2010 the 25th Golden Apple Awards attracted 542 nominees—teachers from grades four through eight throughout the Chicago area. There are 10 winners each year. Those few who receive a Golden Apple—presented to them by one of their own students—are judged the most remarkable of the most remarkable. They get nice gifts: a golden apple, a funded one-semester sabbatical at Northwestern University, $3,000, and a new computer. More important, they get to demonstrate their love for their work and their students, and to reopen the eyes of the hundreds attending the annual Golden Apple gala, and a television audience, to the truth that nothing is as vital to our future as the education of our young people.

In 2002 Koldyke had an idea to augment the force of teachers in Chicago's inner-city elementary schools. "I had been in some of the schools," he said. "When you see the conditions a lot of kids face, it's hard to walk away and forget about them." Mike wondered if there were not talented people out there who would make good teachers, people who would like to leave whatever they were doing for something more fulfilling, but didn't really know how to do that. Mike got the endorsement of Mayor Daley and the Chicago school board to start AUSL, the Academy for Urban School Leadership. Entrants have to be college graduates. Half the AUSL student body usually consists of people who made a mid-career change, deciding they wanted to find more stimulation in their work. Others are recent college graduates. AUSL teachers now staff two elementary schools in Chicago.

Mike Koldyke has a shock of white hair, a grin wider than a car salesman's, and a laugh to rattle doorknobs. He loves to sing and act. And talk. He went to a lunch in New York where he met a woman who started the Principal for a Day program in New York City. Mike asked if she would transplant the concept in Chicago. She did. It's a program where community and business leaders and other high-profile types run a school for a day. They love it, so do the kids, and the schools love the attention and support it brings to them and to their needs.

The Koldykes have a ranch in New Mexico. One day Mike was riding through Albuquerque with his friend, Duffy Swan. Mike is a keen baseball fan. He asked Swan about the local minor league team, the Dukes. "Oh, they got sold to Portland," his friend said.

"I thought that was terrible," Koldyke said. "I mean, how could we not have a baseball team?" He answered his own question by making some calls. Branch Rickey III, who ran the Pacific Coast League, was sympathetic, but not encouraging. But then more calls led Koldyke to Ken Young, who was in Florida, and who had the right credentials for starting up and running a franchise. "I got back to Rickey and told him I had Ken Young," Koldyke said. "I didn't actually have him, but I figured I could get him. Rickey said, 'Ken Young…really.' Then he said, 'Hmm.'" Then followed conversations with Tacoma and Calgary, cities with minor league teams that might be available to move to New Mexico, but to entice any team meant Albuquerque would have to build a better ballpark. More calls and more scrounging for support by Mike and others.

The Albuquerque City Council approved a better ballpark, and Calgary agreed to move. There wasn't much local money left to buy the team, so Mike partnered with a friend to buy the team. "Part of the deal," Koldyke said, "was that we had to run the team in Calgary for a year while our new field was being built. We had 21 snow-outs."

What to call the new team in Albuquerque? A fan vote was held. The old team had been called the Dukes. Koldyke assumed the new team would have the same name. Not so. By a two-to-one margin, the new name was the Isotopes. How come? Homer Simpson of *The Simpsons* was, at the time, involved in an episode where a baseball team, the Isotopes, was fighting being moved out of town. So Albuquerque Isotopes it was. The 2009 Isos set a season attendance record: 602,129. Koldyke has a team cap and wears it with flash. He's still involved, although to a lesser degree, and sees a game when he can. However, I suspect the fun for Mike is in the doing—putting skin on dreams.

I saw him on an elementary schoolyard on Chicago's South Side, surrounded by laughing, noisy African American kids. He had his arms around the shoulders of two of the kids. Mike Koldyke's laugh soared above theirs. His smile told me why he was there, and why he loves dream-chasing.

All Rise.

Paul Binder has no sense of taste or smell, and his hearing is gone in one ear—motorcycle accident. "People ask me why I don't just buy hamburger instead of a good steak," he said. "I do it because I can remember what a good steak tasted like."

When he was in Vietnam, Binder was an assistant to Chaplain Tom Eagan. Chaplain Tom heard about an artillery crew that was lost in a hot area. He told Binder, then a corporal, to grab a jeep, and they'd go look for those lost artillery boys.

"This wasn't some *M*A*S*H* episode, and I wasn't Hawkeye," Binder said. "You didn't just grab a jeep. But I grabbed a jeep. It wasn't our jeep, but he was a major...what was I gonna do? I told him we should catch a ride on a chopper, but he said, 'Oh, no—we'll drive, we'll be fine.'"

They drove, they found the artillery crew, and they called in an evac helicopter. Then they drove back to their unit, arriving shortly before two MPs busted Binder for theft of a jeep. He was reduced to private E-2—the bottom rung on the Army's social ladder—and deprived of pay and allowances for three months. Within days of this chastening, the then clean-sleeved private Binder had to stand formation with the rest of the company while Chaplain Eagan was awarded the Bronze Star for gallantry displayed in rescuing the artillery crew. "I couldn't help it," Binder said. "I fell down on the ground, laughing." (Father Tom did offer to lend Binder money during his impoverishment.)

Binder's wife, Joyce, is some lady. She not only puts up with most of her husband's adventures, she's usually part of them. Joyce has walked downstairs many a morning to find a street type or two snoring fragrantly on the front-room floor. She just makes more coffee. Binder seems attracted to people in need. When his mother, who had been isolated from the family for years, became ill, Paul told Joyce he had to do something. "She told me to do what needed doing," Binder recalled. So he moved home to take care of his mother. He was there much of the time for her last two years.

The Binders visited Opal, a lady who lived on their street, because she had no one else. There was a granddaughter, but she wasn't involved. Opal went into a nursing home when she was 97. The home was about 20 miles from where the Binders live. They visited Opal weekdays for more than a year, until her death.

"It really wasn't a bad drive," Binder said.

All Rise.

Tony Medlin's one-time boss, Gary Haeger, started the project, but T. Med has been running it for years—the Chicago Bears Coat Drive. Gently used coats, caps, gloves, mittens, and so forth are collected and distributed through the Salvation Army to needy people in the Chicago area. The Bears designate a home game at mid-season, promote the drive, and the fans bring coats and other winter gear. For people who can't make it to the game, Tony has found other drop-off resources. The program is more than 20 years old. "We average about 10,000 coats a year, although we received 27,000 a few years ago," Tony said.

T. Med is the Chicago Bears' equipment manager. He is much shorter than the large fellows he equips, but they all look up to him. He runs a no-nonsense locker room. A rookie came in one day eating a sandwich. Tony promptly took the rook's arm, turned him around, and marched the young man out the door. No food in the locker room. Tony used to coach a women's amateur basketball team in his spare time, but he's throttled back some; now he coaches his daughter Brandy's after-school team. Tony and his wife, Chandra, "adopt" a family each year to spend Thanksgiving and Christmas at the Medlins' home.

All Rise.

Like Alan Page, Walter Payton was a famous football player. When Alan played out the end of his career with the Chicago Bears, Payton was reaching full stride in his historic run with the same team. He was a running back—one of the best ever.

Payton's best Bears friend was his fullback and lead blocker, Matt Suhey. Walter grew up in Columbia, Mississippi. He said he got good at football from playing tag as a kid; he hated being "it." Matt grew up in State College, Pennsylvania. Matt was of the fourth generation of Suheys to play for Penn State. Now Matt's son, Joey, and a cousin are on the team.

They were not a matched set, Payton and Suhey. Getting Payton to be serious was like trying to pin a hair ribbon on a bolt of lightning. Getting Suhey to be a prankster was almost as difficult. But they fit. After football, Walter got into this and that—restaurants, clubs, and so on. His name remained prominent. Matt became a trader and worked his way to anonymous success in the market, much as he had on the football field.

Then Walter got sick. He would still come around; I remember getting one of those bear hugs of his—those hugs used to take your breath away. But no more. He didn't look right. No one knew what was wrong, or wouldn't say. Finally, Walter did. He said he had liver cancer, a rare form. His look, not his words, spoke of the gravity of his illness. There was a press conference, because he wanted to get all of the public speaking behind him. He was a shadow of his once super self. A reporter asked him if he was afraid. "Hell, yeah, I'm afraid!" he snapped. "Wouldn't you be?" But then he softened and thanked people for their support and friendship.

We didn't see him after that. He was at home, or in the hospital, but he was gone from our view.

But not from Matt Suhey's.

Matt pretty much carved a year out of his life and gave it to Walter. The only people who knew about it were the Paytons and Matt's wife, Donna. Matt ran a lot of his business from his cell phone and his hip pocket because his focus was on the Paytons—Walter; his wife, Connie; and their children, Jarrett and Brittney. Suhey lived about 30 miles from Payton, but he was there most days, and always when he was needed. I know some of it's about being a teammate—the going-through-combat-together thing—but it's more than that. I doubt Walter would have had the discipline to do for Matt what Matt did for him. I'm sure Matt knew that. I'm also sure it didn't matter to him. He did what he knew needed doing, to the end and beyond.

I asked Matt what they talked about. He shrugged. "I don't know...everything. Just stuff. And some of the time we didn't talk. Maybe we'd sit and watch a game on television, or just be quiet." He laughed. "Quiet was hard for Walter. When I'd leave at night, he'd be sitting at the window as I drove out. We'd give each other the finger."

Walter Payton died on November 1, 1999. He was 45 years old. After his death, Matt spent months straightening out Payton's affairs. Suhey remains a factor in the lives of the Paytons. Back when Jarrett was recruited to play college football at the University of Miami, Matt Suhey made the school visit with him.

All Rise.

She was a grandmother, although she didn't look like one, young and slender and pretty. Her one concession to looking like a grandma was looking worried. Her granddaughter—I'd guess her age to be 10—had her head down, bulldogging. She was trying for defiant, but looked closer to scared. Both of them were standing outside of an elementary school, on the sidewalk, in the shadow of an extremely large—6'8", maybe 300 pounds—black man. He was using his principal's voice, which was deep as a well. He didn't sound angry, just in charge. Way, way in charge.

"Her actions," the large man said to the grandmother, "were not appropriate for our school."

The grandmother nodded, her mouth set so tight it could have been drawn by an auditor's pencil.

"She can come back," the man said, "but today I want her to go home and think about what happened this morning. If she decides she can return to school and show appropriate behavior, she will be welcome. But I want her to arrive at that decision by herself."

"Can she come back this afternoon?" the grandmother asked hopefully.

The tall man shook his head, slowly and definitely. Every word, every motion left zero room for debate. "No. I want her to realize that we are serious about this."

Later, inside the Harvard School for Excellence on Chicago's South Side, Andre Cowling leaned back in his principal's chair, racked a spit-shined, size 14½ black dress shoe against an open desk drawer, and thought some before he spoke.

"That girl and her grandmother—the ones I was talking to when you came up—the girl got into it with another student this morning. It was bad. She has been upset ever since her father died. I am sorry he died, but she still has to come into our school with respect for her teachers and the other students."

Cowling spoke again. "Two boys came to school one morning, both of them riled up. Everything about them said anger. I told them they weren't going to their classrooms like that. I told them to go into my office and we'd talk. At first they didn't want to talk, but eventually they told me their friend had been killed in a shooting...just a boy, walking down the street, when some gang members drove by. They shot him dead. No reason, just dead. Those boys were just full of anger at losing their friend. I got my arms around the two of them and talked about their loss. At first, they just stood there stiff, like sticks, but then they started hugging me, crying. I cried, too." Cowling grinned. "Between the three of us, my shirt got soaked," he said.

Andre Cowling is from Suffolk, Virginia, one of seven children. His father was an oysterer. Andre was a captain in the Army in George H.W.'s Iraq war. He was in combat, in an armored unit. "You learned real quick to sit on your flak vest against explosions from under your vehicle," he said. After he left the Army he worked in the food industry—first for Frito-Lay, then Mars candy. "I'm still a Snickers man," Andre said, smiling, "but I always wanted to be a school teacher. My mother kept a drawing I made in grade school. There was a school in the picture and a parking lot in front of the school. I even drew in a sign in the parking lot for the principal's car." Cowling smiled again. "I've got that parking spot now," he said.

Cowling had an undergraduate degree from Norfolk State when he was a production manager at Mars. He had a good future with the company, but something nagged at him, telling him the candy business wasn't enough.

"When I told my mother I wanted to leave Mars and be a teacher," he said, "she wasn't surprised; she'd known all along." His boss at Mars was disappointed. He asked Andre if he was sure—Andre was leaving a $135,000-a-year job. He said he was sure. His boss said he would see what he could do to help. Mars ended up paying for his books and half of his tuition at National Louis University, a Chicago school emphasizing education.

Cowling worked a night job while he attended school. He was having breakfast one morning after work when he saw a little neighborhood paper. He noticed an ad for AULS, Mike Koldyke's "come as you are" teachers college. Andre threw the paper in his car.

"I was washing my car a couple days after that," he said. "I always use newspaper to clean the windshield, so I grabbed that little paper. When I got done with the window, about all that was left of the paper was the AULS ad. I decided the little ad was trying to tell me something." Cowling called AULS. "I knew it was for me as soon as I called the number," he said.

After AULS, he was fast-tracked for five years in the Chicago system before being named principal at Harvard. "The year before we came in," he said, "Harvard ranked 3,090th out of 3,095 elementary schools in Illinois. It was a mess. The first day I went there, the kids were out of control, running the halls as they pleased, cursing teachers. Their parents were out of control, too." The former armored captain put the hammer down. "We had to change the culture of the school," Cowling said. "We had to fix it up so it didn't look like a battle had been fought there. We needed a better atmosphere for the kids." Cowling took over with a staff made up mostly of AULS graduates. "Most of the teachers who had been here quit," he said.

"We had to foster a safe environment for the kids," he said. "We told ourselves we would have to set the table first; the food would come later. My brothers and sisters couldn't believe I gave up Mars for this."

No one runs the halls at Harvard today. The school is neat and clean and so are the students. About the only sounds you'll hear as you walk a hall come from the music room or a basketball game in gym class. They're still kids, full of energy, but they are directed, and the direction seems to be working. Cowling and his staff have introduced the students to discipline. They seem to like it.

"The Gangster Disciples used to sell drugs right outside our school," Cowling said. "The police got them off our block. We had a problem with a convenience store across the street, because the kids would stop there for treats before coming to school and they'd end up being late. I talked to the man who owned the store and asked him not to sell to our students after 9:00 AM. He said he didn't see how he could do that. I said maybe I should call our alderman and see what he thought. The next day there was a sign in the store window: 'No sales to Harvard School students after 8:30 AM.'"

The school's ranking is up. So is attendance. Neighbors are aware of the change in Harvard and its students, and most are supportive. There's never enough time or money, but good things are happening at Harvard. Andre Cowling was enjoying spring when I visited with him, but really looking forward to summer. His mom was making the trip out to Chicago to see Harvard School and the principal's parking spot. *All Rise.*

Jackie Raino's friend Olga died. Olga was an Aleut Indian. She didn't know her parents; her mother died when she was a baby, and her father abandoned her. She was taken into a home where the man abused her sexually as a young girl. She left the Aleutians when she was 20 and hitched a ride on a semi, all the way to Chicago.

Jackie and Olga met in Uptown, a tread-lightly neighborhood on Chicago's North Side. Jackie was a volunteer at her church's mission there. Olga was applying for a food basket. That was about 30 years ago. There were bumps along the way. "Olga was depressed, so she'd drink," Jackie said. "Then she'd drink because she was depressed. There was a 72-hour detox program. Olga would go to detox, then she'd come out, then she'd drink, then she'd go back to detox. It was her pattern through the years."

What made them friends? "We got to know each other. There was something in her that drew me," Jackie said. "She had this almost child-like quality of acceptance. And she was loyal. I think we became friends because I was around. If you're around for a while, if you connect with the people who come into the shelter and if you look them in the eye and talk to them...and listen...they begin to trust you."

Jackie became Olga's advocate. "She led a rough life," Jackie said. "The men she was with over the years abused her. She had so many broken bones, sprains, cuts, and bruises. Eventually, all that abuse took its toll. I'd go to the hospital with her to see that she got the care she had coming. There's a lot about being poor that's hard; one thing that's hard is that you don't always get the attention you should get. That's why I went with her."

Jackie helped get Olga into a nursing home, but Olga would find a way out and go back to the old life, usually with the help of a man. Jackie didn't see Olga or hear from her for a three- or four-week period several years ago. Then Olga's latest boyfriend called Jackie to say Olga had died. The circumstances were murky; poor people can get overlooked in death, too. However, with the help of Sister Mary Kay, a nun friend from Uptown, and the police, Jackie located Olga in the Cook County Morgue.

"I had a real strong feeling about her having a proper burial," Jackie said. "I knew that unclaimed bodies, once a certain number have accumulated, are buried in a common grave—a potter's field. I didn't want that for her. Olga had been kicked around all of her life; it was important that she die with some dignity."

Because of procedural delays, Olga was in the morgue for nearly three months. By that time, another volunteer friend had made contact with an Aleut Indian agency and obtained a $2,000 tribal burial grant. Cook County contributed $250. An undertaker offered a reduced fee and burial arrangement, and a priest was found to officiate. A burial plot was obtained at the Maryhill Cemetery outside Chicago.

Jackie brought roses to the burial. "The coffin was made out of cardboard, but it really was very nice," she said. The undertaker brought flowers, too. The service was attended by five Native Americans, Sister Mary Kay, a nurse who knew Olga, Jackie, and Jackie's husband, Nick.

Jackie doesn't go down to Uptown much anymore—once a month, maybe. "I do stuff with some of the seniors," she said. Why did she go there for all those years?

"They're really great people," Jackie said. "And they could be any one of us. Once you get by the way they might look, their clothes, or maybe the way they smell, they have beautiful hearts."

All Rise.

Oscar Wilde said the cynic knows the price of everything and the value of nothing. Today it seems easier to take a shot at something or someone than it does to say or do something positive. To be an All-Riser.

Is Alan Page telling us to change? To rise? I don't think so; it's not like him to tell anyone what to do. But I think he is showing us what we can do.

Epilogue

Incumbent Norm Coleman and challenger Al Franken ended up in what amounted to a flat-footed tie in the 2008 Minnesota senatorial race.

Coleman was a one-term Republican who won the seat in 2002 after then-incumbent Paul Wellstone died in a small plane crash while campaigning. Resolution of the 2008 race looked weighty from the start. When the polls closed, Coleman was believed to hold a 215-vote lead out of some 3 million ballots cast. But by morning, the State Canvassing Board declared Franken—author and television personality—to be the winner by 225 votes.

Claims, counter-claims, media scrutiny, mountains of paperwork, and contention clogged the outcome. Progress, if any, dragged.

After recounts and the canvassing board's sign-off, the contested election went to the Minnesota Supreme Court for resolution. The Court's duty was to appoint an impartial, three-judge panel to hear evidence by both parties and rule on the election result's validity. Selection of that panel would, under other circumstances, fall to Eric Magnuson, the Minnesota court's chief justice. Magnuson, however, recused himself from that duty and passed it on to the court's senior justice, Alan Page. Magnuson gave no public explanation for his action (nor was he required to), but the fact that he served as a member of the state canvassing board that found for Franken was generally recognized as the reason. Magnuson's action left Justice Page charged with developing a bullet-proof panel of judges, a panel that would not be distracted nor deterred by the jousting of the two camps, the press, and the public. Page was plowing rare ground in Minnesota: this would be the second state-wide challenge in Minnesota history.

It was a big job—especially for a justice who already devoted evenings and a lot of weekends to keeping up with his benchwork. Justice Page met his challenge. The panel he appointed represented three recent state administrations in an even-handed recognition of all three major political parties. Elizabeth Hayden, a district judge seated during the administration of Democratic governor Rudy Perpich; Kurt Marben, from the Independent administration of Jesse Ventura; and Denise Reilly, from the administration of Republican Governor Arne Carlson.

The proceedings before the Page-appointed panel lasted nearly six months. Lawyers for Franken and Coleman were heard. Eventually, the panel found nothing to support Coleman's charge of an inaccurate vote count. After first suggesting further appeal, Coleman conceded, and Franken was seated as Minnesota's new senator and sworn in on July 7, 2009—more than six months after his term officially began.

Justice Page's attention to the selection of the three-judge panel, the media attention (which was considerable), and the historic trial's lengthy birthing and resolution came at a personal cost. Due to Franken-Coleman, Page fell behind in his regular judicial chores and had to scramble to catch up months after Senator Franken was in Washington. Drawing the added assignment of inventing and overseeing the election trial was just that: an added assignment. The usual case flow kept coming at court, the cases assigned to Alan and all the others assigned to his fellow justices, and every case required reading and a response.

Asked how her husband had responded to the weight of his added assignment, Diane Page smiled and said, "Oh, he was a little grumpy at first."

Now he's just busy.

"I'm swamped," said the Justice.

Any chance for a vacation soon?

"No chance," came the forceful reply.

Probably just as well…he's always been a worker.